CICS: A HOW-TO FOR COBOL PROGRAMMERS

Computer Books from QED

Systems Development

The Complete Guide to Software Testing
Developing Client/Server Applications
Quality Assurance for Information Systems
Total Quality Management in Information Services
User-Interface Screen Design
On Time, Within Budget: Software Project
 Management Practices and Techniques
Managing Software Projects: Selecting and Using
 PC-Based Project Management Systems
From Mainframe to Workstations: Offloading
 Application Development
A Structured Approach to Systems Testing
Rapid Application Prototyping: The Storyboard
 Approach to User Requirements Analysis
Software Engineering with Formal Metrics

Information Engineering/CASE

Practical Model Management Using CASE Tools
Building the Data Warehouse
Information Systems Architecture:
 Development in the 90's
Enterprise Architecture Planning: Developing a
 Blueprint for Data, Applications, and Technology
Data Architecture: The Information Paradigm

IBM Systems Software

REXX in the TSO Environment
REXX Tools and Techniques
The MVS Primer
Cross System Product Application Development
TSO/E CLISTS: The Complete Tutorial and
 Reference Guide
MVS/JCL: Mastering Job Control Language
MVS/VSAM for the Application Programmer
Introduction to Cross System Product
CICS: A How-To for COBOL Programmers
CICS: A Guide to Performance Tuning
CICS Application and System Programming:
 Tools and Techniques
CICS: A Guide to Application Debugging

OS/2

OS/2 2.0 Workplace Shell: The User's
 Guide and Tutorial
OS/2 Presentation Manager Programming for
 COBOL Programmers
Micro Focus COBOL Workbench for the
 Application Developer

AS/400

AS/400: A Practical Guide for Programming
 and Operations
AS/400 Architecture and Applications:
 The Database Machine

VSE

VSE/SP and VSE/ESA: A Guide to Performance
 Tuning
VSE JCL and Subroutines for Application
 Programmers
DOS/VSE: CICS Systems Programming
DOS/VSE: An Introduction to the Operating System

UNIX

UNIX C Shell Desk Reference
The UNIX Industry: Evolution, Concepts,
 Architecture, Applications, and Standards

Management and Business Skills

The Disaster Recovery Plan
Controlling the Future: Managing
 Technology-Driven Change
How to Automate Your Computer Center
Mind Your Business: Managing the Impact of
 End-User Computing
Understanding Data Pattern Processing: The
 Key to Competitive Advantage

VAX/VMS

Rdb/VMS: Developing the Data Warehouse
Network Programming Under DECNet
 Phase IV and V
VAX/VMS: Mastering DCL Commands and
 Utilities

Database

Client/Server and Distributed Database Design
Third-Wave Processing: Database Machines and
 Decision Support Systems
Database Management Systems: Understanding
 and Applying Database Technology

Database — DB2

QMF: How to Use Query Management Facility
 with DB2 and SQL/DS
SQL for DB2 and SQL/DS Application Developers
DB2: the Complete Guide to Implementation
 and Use
Embedded SQL for DB2: Application Design and
 Development
DB2: Maximizing Performance in Online
 Production Systems

Database — ORACLE

ORACLE: Building High Performance
 Online Systems
How To Use ORACLE SQL*Plus

---

*QED books are available at special quantity discounts for educational uses, premiums, and sales promotions.
Special books, book excerpts, and instructive materials can be created to meet specific needs.*

This is Only a Partial Listing. For Additional Information or a Free Catalog contact
QED Publishing Group • P. O. Box 812070 • Wellesley, MA 02181-0013
Telephone: 800-343-4848 or 617-237-5656 or fax 617-235-0826

CICS: A How-To for COBOL Programmers

David Shelby Kirk

QED Publishing Group
Boston • London • Toronto

© 1993 QED Information Sciences, Inc.
P.O. Box 812070
Wellesley, MA 02181-0013

QED Publishing Group is a division of QED Information Sciences, Inc.

Library of Congress Catalog Number: 92-20022
International Standard Book Number: 0-89435-428-0

Printed in the United States of America
    95 10 9 8 7 6 5 4

Library of Congress Cataloging-In-Publication Data

Kirk, David Shelby.
    CICS—a how-to for COBOL programmers / David Shelby Kirk.
        p. cm.
    Includes index.
    ISBN 0-471-58021-X :
    1. COBOL (Computer program language) 2. CICS (Computer system)
I. Title.
QA76.73.C25K535   1992
005.4'3—dc20

                                                    92-20022
                                                    CIP

DEDICATION

This book is dedicated to my father. He gave me much of what I value in life.

Contents

List of Figures

Acknowledgments

SOFTWARE ACKNOWLEDGMENT

This book focuses on one of IBM's premier software products, CICS. Specific IBM products referenced in this book include the following:

- MVS/ESA operating system

- CICS/VS Release 1.7

- CICS/MVS Release 2.1

- CICS/ESA Release 3.2

- CICS/VSE Release 2.1

- OS/VS (and DOS/VS) COBOL Release 2.4 (referenced as VS/COBOL)

- VS COBOL II Release 3.2 (referenced as COBOL II)

- SAA AD/Cycle COBOL/370 (referenced as COBOL/370)

- SAA AD/Cycle Cooperative Development Environment/370 (referenced as CODE/370)

- Language Environment/370 (referenced as LE/370)

Although programs were not explicitly tested with VSE/ESA, IBM documentation (as I understand it) indicates that the programming environment is equivalent (at least to the extent represented in this book).

While the programs were not tested with COBOL/370, IBM documentation indicates that COBOL/370 is a superset of COBOL II and supports all programming techniques in this book. All features that differ from COBOL II are documented.

The following terms used in this book are trademarks of the International Business Machines Corporation:

MVS/XA, MVS/ESA, SAA, CICS/MVS, DB2, DATABASE 2, CICS/ESA, CICS/VSE, VSE/ESA, CICS/OS2, DisplayWrite, IBM, AD/Cycle

Preface

WHAT THIS BOOK IS

I wrote this book especially for you, the professional COBOL programmer (or the person aspiring to be a professional) who needs to learn CICS quickly. If you know COBOL, are comfortable with working with either MVS or VSE, and know a smattering of JCL, then all you need to learn to use CICS is here. I wrote this book in an MVS environment, but the CICS information still applies (i.e. the JCL examples are useless to VSE programmers). If, on the other hand, you are already a practicing CICS COBOL programmer, then you will find in this a ready, day-to-day reference to help you develop solutions to typical CICS issues. In summary, this book is a "keeper." Unlike books that help you learn the basics and then abandon you when the going gets tough, I wrote this book with the intent that it will be open on your desk, always ready to assist you in working with CICS.

Examples in this book will emphasize COBOL II and COBOL/370, although VS/COBOL (both OS/VS and DOS/VS) is also covered in all examples. With the continued migration to ESA, you need to know COBOL II to maintain your professional proficiency. This book will assist you in those aspects that affect CICS. If, on the other hand, your company still has many VS/COBOL applications, you will have all the information needed to develop applications with VS/COBOL as well. *Note*: Since COBOL/370 is a superset of COBOL II, the term *COBOL II* in this book applies to both COBOL/370 and COBOL II. Where there is a difference, I will point it out.

Additionally, all examples in this book support all current releases of CICS, whether in an MVS or a VSE environment. Where any difference exists, I will point it out. Although technical issues that are only of interest to systems programmers or other specialized technicians are ignored, those issues of probable interest to the professional mainframe application programmer will be mentioned at appropriate points. In summary, you can rely on the book to assist you in most normal application situations.

Finally, the book includes references to the most common aspects of IBM software that affect the programmer, including JCL and compile options, BMS JCL, building MAPs, and program design.

WHAT THIS BOOK IS NOT

No, this book makes no attempt to provide in-depth knowledge of all CICS commands. To do that, IBM had to write many, many reference manuals — mostly information you will never need. This book focuses on the most commonly needed features of CICS and presents examples to ensure you are proficient in their use.

Since most CICS applications use 3270-type terminals, the book limits its direction to terminals of that family, although some information is provided to assist you in pursuing other terminal environments. Does that mean this book is short-sighted? No. It means that CICS is so flexible, so varied in its implementation, that no book could possibly address all of it. The majority of CICS programmers use only a small fraction of CICS's potential, and most employers ask for no more than that. With this book, you will easily exceed such expectations.

By limiting the scope of the book, I am able to provide the information that you need to understand underlying concepts within CICS and to position you to learn more advanced topics on the job. After all, textbook examples never relate to real applications. Instead of attempting to match real applications, I consciously limited all program examples to demonstrate a concept rather than duplicate a real application.

HOW THIS BOOK IS ORGANIZED

Unlike my prior books, this book is both an introductory text and a reference manual. To achieve that, I constructed the book to consist of several separate sections. If you are a novice to CICS, be sure to begin at the beginning, carefully reading and reviewing each chapter. If you are a skilled practitioner, I encourage you still to review the first section of introductory material, if only to ensure there are no basics that were overlooked in your introduction to CICS (yes, I still encounter CICS programmers with several years' experience who don't know how BMS or CICS work). Here is an outline of how the book is structured:

SECTION 1 — CICS Fundamentals

Chapter 1: What Is CICS. This chapter presents the fundamentals of interactive processing and explains the basic functions of CICS. This is an important building block for the novice. Detailed explanations of various tables and processes are bypassed in this chapter, concentrating instead on your need to grasp the basic tenets of online transactions. More details will be presented later.

Chapter 2: Developing a Basic CICS Transaction. In this chapter you will build your first CICS application. The programming processes and transaction design fundamentals are the goal here. After reviewing this chapter, you will have the requisite skills to develop a CICS transaction.

Chapter 3: Building a MAP. This chapter will introduce you to the exciting world of screen design and developing screens for your CICS applications. Building MAPs is a critical skill in increasing your expertise in CICS.

Chapter 4: Developing Expanded Transactions. This chapter will combine topics covered so far, allowing you to develop a transaction using several programs and MAPs. Normally, this knowledge is sufficient to secure assignment to a CICS programming team. No, you won't know everything, but you will be positioned to contribute to a CICS development project. This chapter concludes Section 1 and, by this time, you should feel conversant in CICS terminology and processes. Some topics covered in this section will be repeated in later sections, as appropriate for more substantive information.

SECTION 2 — CICS Techniques

Chapter 5: COBOL/370, COBOL II and VS/COBOL. If you've read my prior book, *COBOL II Power Programmer's Desk Reference* (one for MVS, one for VSE), then you know how strongly I believe that COBOL II is the way to go. This chapter identifies some of the basics of COBOL II and highlights conversion techniques to migrate applications to COBOL II or COBOL/370. Differences among the compilers are also noted.

Chapter 6: CICS Programming Techniques. This chapter is unlike the rest. Instead of providing incremental training information, this chapter documents various CICS programming techniques that may or may not apply, depending on the particular system you are developing. This is a chapter that you should refer to periodically, as it may offer tips or ideas to assist you in developing CICS systems. This is a chapter you should read at least once, if only to know what it contains.

Chapter 7: Using the IBM-Supplied CICS Transactions. Along with CICS, IBM supplies a variety of online utility programs to assist the application programmer. Remarkably, many programmers are unaware of them or do not know how to use them. This chapter will introduce you to the ones that are most frequently used by application programmers. These utilities extend your CICS proficiency beyond developing applications to actually interacting with CICS itself. Whether you need to verify the presence of files, test a CICS command, or walk through a transaction, the power of these utilities will make it possible. If you already have some experience with CICS, you may want to read this chapter first. This chapter is most effective when sitting at a computer terminal so you will receive immediate feedback.

Chapter 8: CICS Debugging Facilities and Techniques. No, this chapter won't make you the world's best dump reader. That isn't my style. I believe that, with the right tools, you can usually solve most application discrepancies (I think that using the term *discrepancies* is preferable to using the term *bugs*, don't you?). This chapter references the previous chapter and also includes some information on IBM-supplied facilities to assist you in resolving technical difficulties.

Chapter 9: Additional MAP and Screen Techniques. This chapter is one of the shorter chapters and discusses some new approaches that are being used in designing screens. This information will assist you in developing transactions that are more user-friendly and that use more of the features of the user's terminal.

SECTION 3 — CICS Reference

Chapter 10: Compiling a CICS Program. Surprisingly, few textbooks explain this process, yet you need to know the various options if you are going to use CICS and COBOL effectively. Too many programmers use whatever everyone else uses, often preventing them from taking advantage of various documentation, performance, or debugging techniques. This chapter reviews the compile and link steps that must be used to develop a CICS program.

Appendix A: Using CICS. This is a summary of CICS control blocks, COPYbooks, and a complete listing of CICS commands. While not complete in itself, it can assist you as you read other chapters.

Appendix B: Related Publications. As with all my books, I include a summary of available QED and IBM books to help you expand your knowledge of specific topics in the world of CICS.

HOW TO READ THIS BOOK

Since this book is designed not only for the CICS novice but also for the experienced practitioner, how you approach the book will affect the benefits you receive. I focus on techniques, structure, and style. Look for these three items in each chapter and you will become a better CICS programmer (and a better application designer as well). Look only for coding examples of infinite (almost) CICS possibilities and you will be disappointed. Look instead for "How does it really work?" examples. Wherever I perceive that CICS may appear to be magic, I attempt to remove the mystery. You can never master what you do not understand. Coding by rote does not make you a master of CICS any more than a parrot's ability to speak makes it human.

The programming experience is an intense human activity, fraught with the joys and frustrations of any human experience. As such, I don't expect you to do everything as I have done it, nor should you. In fact, your employer may not allow some of my techniques, despite their advantages, so extend yourself only as you see appropriate.

Despite that last paragraph, I encourage you to attempt these techniques wherever possible. I have convinced more than one manager to change the local standards only after demonstrating that better techniques were at hand, were more efficient, and were more productive for the practicing professional.

Finally, I did not write this book for the programmers who "just want to get by." I wrote it for those many programmers who want to do it right. There will be times when I may appear opinionated (I am), dogmatic (that too), and stubborn (okay, okay, so maybe I'm a *little* stubborn). Despite that, if you follow the guidelines in this book, you will find that your programs look better, are more reliable, and you will feel like the professional that you are. If you're like most programmers that I know, you don't like writing grungy code that meets archaic programming standards. Instead, you want to program reliable, easy-to-maintain applications. If the book helps you achieve that goal, I will consider the endeavor a success.

As you read this book, make your own notes in the margins, thereby making your personal imprint on these pages. Also, don't assume any idea is wrong just because your shop isn't using it. CICS improves with each release and new features regularly replace old ones. Let me know what works for you. There is a response form in the back of the book. Yes, I want to hear from you. With your feedback, the next edition can be even better. Together, we can continue to assist programmers who are new to CICS or who need to master various technical aspects.

David Shelby Kirk
Cicero, New York

Part 1

CICS Fundamentals

What Is CICS?

CICS (for Customer Information Control System) has been around for over 20 years, making it almost as old as many of the readers of this book. Does that make it out of date? No. CICS has grown in capability and functionality every year. In working with CICS, you will be working with one of the most popular and powerful software products available today. What makes CICS fun to work with is the very flexibility it offers. Providing not only an online communication facility, CICS also provides many alternative routes to access MVS services. If you enjoy programming as I do, then you will surely enjoy the experience of working with CICS. Welcome aboard!!!

The CICS software product is operational in over 90 countries, used at over 20,000 DP shops, and runs on approximately 75 percent of all MVS installations. Considering the additional VSE sites, that easily makes CICS IBM's most popular transaction management software product. Whether you work at an MVS or a VSE shop, you will find this book a continual repository of useful information.

Developed in the late 1960s by IBM, CICS was initially used only to simplify the tedious task of integrating applications with telecommunications facilities. In those early days, each terminal required acknowledgement of its unique demands on the central processor. CICS removed that technical constraint and allowed companies to focus on their business applications instead of on telecommunications techniques. We've come a long way since those days. Today, CICS supports all IBM application platforms and is at the core of many corporate mission-critical applications. Where once it was only an oddity to have online access to the company computer, it is today a necessity. Additionally, as companies continue to want to move access out from their central site, CICS helps provide features and facilities to extend corporate data access beyond the mainframe, whether to remote processing centers or to individual PCs.

Answering the question "What is CICS?" will not be easy. Describing CICS is not unlike describing the universe. Yes, the universe is larger and more spectacular — and certainly more diverse. Still, CICS has its own share of richness, complexity, and diversity. To know it fully is to have spent a career researching its capabilities. Certainly, this book will not (and could not) explain all of its features. Since most programmers use the more readily available facilities, those will be the thrust of this book.

Also, CICS represents a *family* of software products. While this book will focus on the mainframe use of CICS, it is also available on desktop PCs. The CICS products are the following:

CICS/VSE — for the VSE/ESA environment

CICS/MVS — for the MVS/XA environment

CICS/ESA — for the MVS/ESA environment

CICS/OS2 — for the MS/DOS or OS/2 workstation environment

What ties them all together for you, the applications programmer, is that they all share the same application programming interface (API) that is the subject of this book. Your shop may still be working with versions of CICS that aren't listed above, such as CICS/DOS/VS or CICS/OS/VS. That's okay. Anytime there is an option that applies to a specific release of CICS, I'll point it out. In this book I will use the term CICS/VS when referring to the CICS/OS/VS or the CICS/DOS/VS products. The majority of what this book is about will work on all mentioned products.

CICS has succeeded because it separates various technical responsibilities into manageable components. Consider the elements in Figure 1.1. They represent significant technical issues, yet they are all transparent to the application program.

Figure 1.1 may imply that CICS only works with VSAM files. That isn't true. I limited the example to VSAM to demonstrate the functional segregation within the CICS environment. In fact, CICS can be used with other IBM products, such as IMS, DL/I, SQL/DS, and DB2.

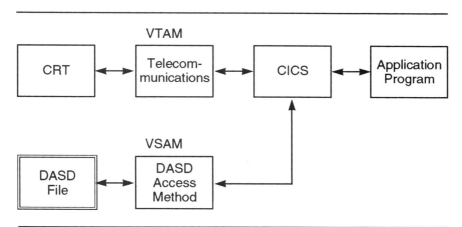

Figure 1.1. Example of segregation of function in CICS.

CICS allows the application program to focus on the business requirements instead of on scheduling access to various terminals or on controlling competition to access/update various online files. This standardizes and simplifies a company's use of online access and removes from the programmer the need to master such intricate technical details.

I assume that you, the reader, want to know enough about CICS to perform adequately in most job situations. To that goal, this book will serve you well. To the larger goal of learning all about CICS, this book will help you develop the fundamentals and the desire to pursue a more complete knowledge. This first chapter presents the basic concepts of CICS, although many CICS programmers do well even without this knowledge. Here goes...

1.1. THE CICS ENVIRONMENT

First, let's cut through the magic. CICS is a program in itself that runs under control of the operating system, either MVS or VSE. Throughout this book, I will occasionally mention the *operating system, MVS, or VSE*. For most purposes, it won't matter. Where I believe it is important, I will clarify specific differences. For now, just accept that CICS is a task running under the available operating system. See Figure 1.2.

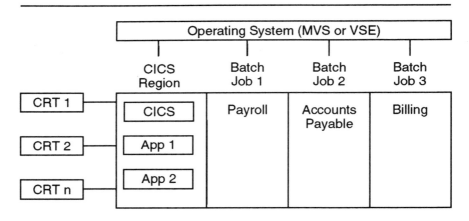

Figure 1.2. Example of a CICS environment.

In Figure 1.2, CICS is controlling two -applications across an unknown number of terminals. Concurrently, the operating system is scheduling three batch jobs. This separation allows the operating system to focus on overall system throughput while allowing CICS to focus on overall terminal management and transaction throughput. This segregation of duties is a strength of IBM's software products, allowing each to provide customer emphasis on specific processing requirements. Since CICS concentrates on the online user's needs, the operating system can concentrate on overall corporate computing requirements, letting CICS handle the hundreds (or thousands) of on-line terminal requirements.

Naturally, all of this could be done by you. Instead of using CICS, you could use the telecommunications access method (normally VTAM) and, knowing all the idiosyncrasies of every terminal, write program code to manage the terminal as well as the data. In the early 1960s, that was the only way to do it. Fortunately, you needn't do that today. The cost and time required to master such extensive hardware platforms could prevent you from ever getting the simplest transaction developed.

CICS is a software program that has evolved over two decades and can handle the details of online dialogue for you. Also, as it has evolved, it has been modified to adapt to a growing platform of hardware and software platforms, freeing you from the concern. In a later part of this book, we'll review the technical issues more in-depth than here, but CICS should never be regarded as handling a trivial task.

Online processing is the most demanding environment for computer systems, and CICS has proved itself well here. If we were to explode the information from Figure 1.1, we might see the components as shown in Figure 1.3.

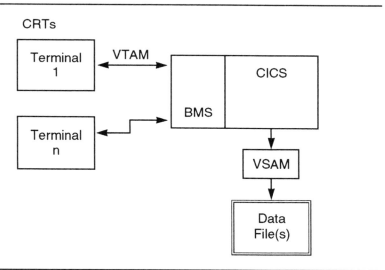

Figure 1.3. Example of CICS components.

In Figure 1.3, CICS has a major component, BMS (for Basic Mapping Services), controlling terminal data, and VSAM (for Virtual Storage Access Method) to control physical I/O to disk devices. What is significant to the programmer is that all I/O is handled by CICS. No reads, no writes, no I/O of any kind is to be handled by the application program. That is probably the most visible change to the batch programmer: All I/O is handled by the supporting software.

As you study the book, the strength of the various CICS components such as BMS will become more familiar. For now, rest assured that CICS is not one large program that is impossible to grasp. Instead, it is a family of software components that all work in support of one another.

By reading this book, you probably already have a grasp of JCL so I won't explain that concept. What you may not be familiar with is that IBM operating systems allow special tasks to be started by the computer operator with JCL. These tasks can run independently from the operating environment and can, if so programmed, support terminal users. CICS is one of such programs. Other software that fits this niche are IBM's IMS (DL/I to VSE users) and DB2 (SQL/DS to VSE users). All are programmed to provide an umbrella environment to the application programmer. Where CICS excels is that it can provide an umbrella for the other umbrellas — quite a feat!

In working with CICS, you will occasionally hear reference to various tables or other components of CICS. As I mentioned earlier, we will cover the fundamental components later, when you have better formed a mental "filing cabinet" for the various acronyms. For now, let's just focus on the environment itself and on the mechanics of getting your first CICS application working.

One of the first things to understand, and one of the major issues often overlooked, is the concept of a dialogue, whether person-to-person or person-to-computer. In most ways, they have major similarities. The next section presents an overview of a person/computer dialogue and emphasizes the aspects that affect the programmer. Pay close attention and experiment with the issues as they impact on your personal dialogues. After all, a dialogue is a dialogue, even when it doesn't involve computers.

1.2.   AN INTERACTIVE DIALOGUE

Learning CICS in itself is not the goal. Learning to program online applications that support the business requirements of the terminal user through an interactive dialogue is the real goal. CICS just makes it easier to implement such applications. In this section, we will review some basics in maintaining a dialogue. With a computer, you must be more sensitive to the requirements than you would otherwise. For example, if you worked for a telephone answering service, you probably wouldn't think it unusual to keep a pencil and pad by the phone to record each conversation and the questions or requests posed by each caller. That's logical. Well, with a computer dialogue, you face the same issues. You must develop a program that simulates the paper-and-pencil technique of always being able to recall the topics of prior conversations and what decisions were made. Let's review some typical dialogues below.

1.2.1.　Transaction Concepts

If you are new to online processing, you may wonder what type of work is conducted from terminals. Let's review a theoretical example to help you understand the business concept and the business need. The online processing computer program must participate in a conversational environment, possibly the most complex situation to handle. Consider a simple conversational environment with a person:

Customer: I want to order a sandwich. Do you serve any?

Clerk: Yes, what kind do you want?

Customer: Well, what kind do you have?

Clerk: We have almost any kind, including capicola, hamburger, cheeseburger, baconburger, tuna melt, and others.

Customer: Can I get lettuce?

Clerk: Yes, on certain sandwiches.

Customer: Okay, I want a turkey club with lettuce and cole slaw on the side.

Clerk: Oops. We don't have cole slaw.

Clearly, this isn't an ideal conversation, but it demonstrates some of the unknowns and guesses of any dialogue. People are able to cope with missing or omitted information and to recover the dialogue. Computer programs generally cannot do this. Good online programs ensure that all relevant information is communicated *before* any processing occurs. When writing a program for online use, the programmer needs to anticipate such give and take. For example, the computer program needs to remember what questions were posed, what information has already been shared, and what possibilities are available. As you progress in CICS, such skills will become almost automatic. To the degree that you can anticipate such dialogue, your programs will excel.

To summarize where we are, an online program (whether CICS or not) must retain adequate information between each dialogue so it can provide the proper information as needed by the computer user.

The easiest way to grasp this concept is probably in the airline reservation environment. Let's examine a simple example of a person inquiring about an airline flight, with the intent of making a reservation:

1. Customer inquires to a travel agent about a possible flight from Little Rock to Syracuse.

2. Travel agent keys the query via a terminal:

    FROM: Little Rock
    TO: Syracuse

3. With so little information, most programs could reply, "Yes, it's possible."

    Obviously, what is needed is more information so a dialogue can be conducted. Let's make it more specific.

1. Travel agent keys to terminal:

    FROM: Little Rock
    TO: Syracuse
    WHEN: October 2, 1992
    PASSENGERS: 2
    CLASS: Coach

2. With this information, a computer program could interrogate appropriate files and send information to the terminal operator of what flights were available on that day and if two seats were available. If the program retains the necessary information, it can be prepared for a response, such as the following:

    FLIGHT #: 625
    SEATS: 15A,15B
    CONFIRM: Yes

3. Having already presented the flight information, the online program already knows the time of the flight and needs only minor information to complete the dialogue. The program might send this request to the travel agent:

    NAME OF PASSENGER #1?:
    NAME OF PASSENGER #2?:
    FEE: $1,050.42
    HOW BILLED?:

4. This is an obvious oversimplification of booking an airline reservation, but my intent was to demonstrate some of the concepts of managing a dialogue via computers. With CICS, you can develop applications that easily retain such information and provide appropriate direction to terminal operators. All it takes is practice, practice, practice, and the ability to envision potential dialogues within the business environment — not necessarily an easy task if the business is unfamiliar to you. (If that's the case, you need to establish a personal priority to *learn the business* of your employer!!!)

As demonstrated, the successful computer transaction will remember key aspects of the dialogue. The transaction should also remember necessary elements that contribute to the appropriate solution without requiring the user to reenter the data. Naturally, the transaction has no memory of its own, so it must find ways to accomplish what was done with pencil and paper in prior years. CICS provides many options to this requirement, and we will explore several of them. For the options to be useful, you must keep in mind that most transactions consistently need to record temporary information for later recall. To the extent that you use CICS facilities to assist in this, you will have successful business applications. For example, in the previous example of securing an airline flight from Little Rock to Syracuse, the transaction remembered the city of origin, the desired destination, and the number of passengers so that information didn't need to be reentered.

In developing an online dialogue, the skilled programmer identifies the major components of the transaction and establishes means to keep the information available — and to keep the transaction simple. After all, you're not trying to win an award for artificial intelligence, are you? (Well, *are* you?) Doing that effectively requires that the programmer create various scratch pads of information for recall, where needed. If you succeed in this major design phase, your CICS transactions will always be winners, regardless of your technical mastery.

In handling such as the above dialogue, an additional strength of CICS is that it also supports multiple concurrent dialogues, just as any airline earning a profit will assuredly have many travel agents keying in transactions at the same time. The ability to handle concurrent requests for computer processing, without regard to other processing needs, is another strength of CICS. As the application programmer, you are free to focus on the business requirements instead of on the issue of managing computer resources. Handling one transaction is trying enough. Handling several hundred can be devastating if attempting to do the programming requirements alone.

Obviously, the considerations of online transactions are more complex than demonstrated here. Still, I hope you have a better grasp of the issues involved and of the contribution made by CICS to remove such issues from your application design. As we move through the book, I will periodically review these issues and how they may affect your application. For now, I encourage you to focus on your application design and programming requirements and leave the technical issues for a later discussion. Yes, we'll cover all of it.

I recall that, as a teenager, several of my friends were more interested in how a car's engine worked than in the techniques of driving a car safely. To them, driving a car was a contest of how fast the car could go in each gear. Don't follow that track of wanting to master the technical issues to the detriment of mastering the global concepts. Eventually, it will all fit. Honest.

1.2.2.   Transaction Options

The previous section introduced you to the concept of maintaining a dialogue with a terminal user. Let's review the basic structures that are most often used. While these examples represent the most common examples, I don't want to imply, either here or in any other part of this book, that the examples I present are the only ones. Programming in CICS is a challenging occupation, and I will consider all my efforts in writing this book to be a success if you are motivated to always seek new options and opportunities. For now, here are three common techniques, each with their own advantages and disadvantages, depending on the client's requirements.

The simple, nonconversational transaction. In a nonconversational transaction, the requirement is immediate and only infrequently requires further follow-up. You can usually think of nonconversational transactions as being of the "yes/no" variety. An example would be the transaction that inquires whether a given individual is a company employee. Yes, the transaction would be simple to do, and it may be all that is required for a particular department's needs. Just getting the employee number, department number, salary level, salary, years employed, and similar information could be adequate for many corporate needs. Such a transaction would involve only these steps:

1. Terminal user enters transaction code and employee name.

2. Program receives screen and embedded employee name.

3. Program checks employee database for a match.

4. If a match, display employee information and terminate transaction. Otherwise, display a message denoting that the employee was not found and terminate transaction.

An advantage of nonconversational transactions is that they make the least demands on the computing resources. They are one-time queries only — and they are usually much quicker to execute. If your client appears to need such yes/no type inquiries, consider this format. They are easier (cheaper) to develop, easier to test, easier to document, and easier to maintain. However, since nonconversational transactions perform simple functions, you may end up with many transactions to accomplish a single unit of work. If that happens, the benefit of lower cost may be defeated. As with all transaction formats, when it fits, it is an excellent fit. When it doesn't, it is a mess.

The conversational transaction. Despite the name, you will seldom encounter conversational transactions in CICS (in IMS, the opposite is true). Compare this transaction with a human dialogue:

1. The first person asks a question of a second person.

2. While the second person contemplates the question and formulates an answer, the first person waits for the response.

3. The two persons continue their dialogue, with both actively involved either as speakers or as listeners.

While the above sounds ideal, it makes unusual demands on a computer system. For example, since a CICS transaction is a program that occupies main storage, the computer suffers performance degradation while waiting for the person at the terminal to respond. Although this is ideal for real people, computers work at such impressive speeds that it is not efficient for a computer transaction to occupy main memory while waiting for human terminal users to scratch their heads, make notes with a pencil, and otherwise appear "slow" to the computer. That gives a third option, described next.

The pseudoconversational transaction. The pseudoconversational transaction is by far the most common transaction technique used for CICS systems — and the one technique you will most likely encounter at your shop. By "pseudoconversational," the technique appears to the human terminal user to be fully conversational. That's a plus.

Where it succeeds is that it removes the heavy computing demand on the mainframe. This is done by having the program relinquish control of computer resources until the user fills in the fields on the screen and presses the Enter key (or appropriate PF key, depending on the application).

The pseudoconversational technique is used consistently in this book and, most likely, by the majority of transactions at your shop. The pseudoconversational transaction relies on (1) the slowness of humans (compared to computers), and (2) the system management techniques of CICS. This is done by the following steps:

1. The transaction presents a screen of data elements to the terminal, just as other techniques do. However, instead of waiting for a response, the transaction relinquishes control of the CPU back to CICS until the user finishes entering data to the screen.

2. When the user presses Enter (or a PF key), CICS receives the data from the terminal and initiates the transaction as requested in step 1.

3. The transaction receives the screen data from CICS, processes it, and sends a response screen (possibly asking for more information) to the user.

4. The transaction again relinquishes control back to CICS, specifying the transaction (if any) that should be given control next.

5. Steps 2 through 4 continue until the transaction determines that the process has been completed (usually by something entered by the terminal user), at which time the transaction relinquishes full control back to CICS.

This give-and-take continues throughout the dialogue. The terminal user is unaware of the technical architecture, as the terminal "appears" to be in constant dialogue. Since most persons take from 10 seconds to several minutes to fill in the required data fields for a transaction (e.g., date of birth, driver's license number, street address, policy number, social security number, date of employment, and so forth), this frees CICS to use the available computer resources to support other concurrent transactions.

As you learn the technique of pseudoconversational transactions, it will become natural to you. Yes, it takes a little practice, but it also gives you more control of the total dialogue than the other options do.

For example, your program might send a screen that requests medical information. When your program relinquishes control back to CICS, you have the option of specifying the name of the transaction that is to receive control when the user is finished filling in the requested data. In this example, that might be the same medical validation program, but it could also be a different program. In summary, pseudoconversational programs are built to do only a piece of the dialogue with each iteration. When you seen an example later, it will become clearer.

1.3.   INTERACTING WITH CICS

Interacting with CICS demands that you, as a programmer, be familiar with some basic terms. Since CICS is table-driven, knowing the fundamentals of these tables will assist you in assembling relevant material about this environment. I will avoid the technical issues that a systems programmer might face but will attempt to ensure that application issues are covered. Here goes...

First, you must be using a terminal that is identified to CICS. I assume that whatever terminal you are using has been defined to CICS, and the technical processes required to do that are beyond this book. I mentioned it only to remind you that just because a terminal has access to a mainframe does not mean it can access all environments (such as IMS/DC or CICS). Assuming that your terminal is attached to a CICS region, here are some basics:

To logon: The command is CESN or CSSN. Check with your supervisor for specifics of your installation. *(CICS commands are always entered at the upper left-hand corner on a blank terminal screen.)* You will probably be prompted to enter an assigned password. From this point on, your terminal will be under the control of CICS.

To logoff: The command is CSSF. Check with your supervisor for specifics of your installation. At some shops, you must enter CSSF LOGOFF while just CSSF is sufficient elsewhere. *(Note:* I have been on systems where neither the logon nor logoff commands were needed. This is because some companies develop their own opening menu for access to their CICS transactions. This is more "user friendly" and can provide better management control.)

To execute a transaction:

a. The transaction identifier is four characters long and is defined in the PCT (Program Control Table). The PCT is important because all transaction identifiers and the programs to which they give control are defined in this table.

b. From the PCT, CICS then searches the PPT (Processing Program Table) to determine the whereabouts of the needed program (i.e., already in memory or still on DASD). This helps CICS determine whether to load the program into memory or just to make a copy available.

c. If files are accessed, their identifiers must be in the FCT (File Control Table). As with the PPT and the PCT, all table entries must be predefined so performance and recovery issues can be planned. *Note:* Placing entries in these tables is normally done by your shop's technical staff and the mechanics of that are not part of this book.

To communicate with CICS: After entering data at a terminal, a user needs some way of notifying CICS that the terminal data is "ready." That can be done by pressing a variety of keys, known as AID keys in CICS. The AID keys are the set of keys that trigger an interrupt that the mainframe can detect. Since CICS can remember which AID key was used, this information (as we shall see) can be made available to the program. AID keys are in Figure 1.4. When I refer to CICS or the application waiting for the user to finish entering data, what I really mean is that CICS is waiting for one of the AID keys to be pressed.

```
All program function (PF) keys, from PF1 through PF24
The PA1 and PA2 keys
The Clear key
The ENTER key.
FUNCTION:  AID keys are the keys that signal to CICS
           that the terminal is ready for its data to
           be processed.
```

Figure 1.4. List of CICS AID keys.

Actually, the whole process is quite straightforward. See Figure 1.5 for an example of the process. While simplistic, it represents the flow from the terminal user to the transaction. The steps represent control aspects that are a strength of CICS — and also a mark of its flexibility. Also, since CICS is table-driven, that puts responsibility on you, the programmer, to ensure that entries are made in the appropriate tables for your applications. Just because you write and compile a CICS COBOL program doesn't mean it will run. The PCT and PPT must contain their names.

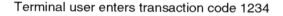

Terminal user enters transaction code 1234

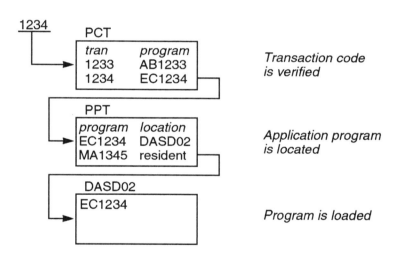

Figure 1.5. Example of CICS transaction flow.

When the user enters a transaction code, CICS confirms its validity and then checks the PCT to locate the program. Then, the program is loaded. This example oversimplifies the process, but it should reinforce the CICS process of ensuring application integrity by demanding that all transactions are predefined. The mechanics of defining these entries to CICS tables are beyond this book but are issues of which you need to be aware. (*Note:* Defining entries in the various CICS tables isn't complicated; it's just that this is normally done by the technical support staff.) Being a programmer, your primary concern with these tables is to ensure that your programs and files are defined there *before* you are ready to start testing an application. Other than that, they contribute nothing to the logic of your program.

SUMMARY

CICS is a major software component from IBM, providing online support in both VSE and MVS environments. CICS serves as a vehicle from which you can build a variety of transactions without worrying about the technical underpinnings. Your goal is to understand dialogues and how people interact with computers so that you can design and program effective applications. Look upon CICS as a tool to simplify that process, not as a software product that is complicated. If you use the first perspective, you will find CICS is a ready assistant. If you use the second, you will be forever frustrated by its technical aspects.

VOCABULARY REVIEW

At the end of each chapter, I will list some of the key terms that were introduced. Some will have been thoroughly explained; others have not received as much attention. Use the list as a guide to review concepts from the chapter. If you feel a term wasn't adequately explained, let me know about it.

CICS

VSAM

VTAM

Dialogue

Concurrent access

PPT

PCT

FCT

Nonconversational transaction

Conversational transaction

Pseudoconversational transaction

AID keys

2

Developing a Basic CICS Application

Developing a CICS application is your goal in this chapter. It will provide direction for developing a simple transaction. Since all CICS transactions share common components, the skills you learn in this chapter can be applied to a wide variety of business applications. Later, we will pursue more complex transactions and more sophisticated terminal interaction. For now, let's focus on developing that first transaction. While there are certainly differences in IBM's platforms that support CICS (e.g., MVS/ESA vs. VSE/ESA), CICS is a universal language that exploits any given platform and, unless noted, you can assume any example can be used in any MVS or VSE environment.

Also, since CICS controls the entire application environment, there can be *no files allocated within the program*. That means no configuration section and no file section. All files must be accessed via CICS commands and CICS will control the files.

Because you're probably anxious to see some "real" CICS code and listings, I have included a couple in this chapter, not for mastery, but to let you get a feeling for how CICS programs look and what additional entries they have. All information presented here on CICS will be more fully explained in later chapters.

2.1. CICS COMMAND SYNTAX

CICS commands are separate from those of the chosen programming language, but they are imbedded within the chosen language. Since this book is about COBOL, we won't review how CICS commands are processed in other languages, although the process is similar. Also, all examples will be shown in upper-case text to ensure that you can separate my comments from the actual COBOL or CICS statements. (COBOL II programmers may use lower-case text if desired, but I'll review that later.) There are also major differences in program design opportunities for COBOL II programmers, and those will be covered later in the book.

2.1.1.   Coding CICS Commands

CICS commands are coded in a blocked structure, having a beginning and an ending (similar to DB2 commands within COBOL). The format may seem strange to the uninitiated, but it fits well within the framework of COBOL II's scope terminator concept. (COBOL II allows certain statements to end without a period. You'll see some examples later.)

The most visible aspect of CICS commands is that they all have a common framework. Here is the basic format:

```
EXEC CICS
    function
    [ options ]
END-EXEC
```

This structure provides a boundary for the CICS commands and, provided that you always code the prefix (EXEC CICS) and the scope terminator (END-EXEC), these commands will be properly translated within the logic of your program.

The various options of each command are either stand-alone variables that require no modification or are keyword variables that will require a parameter in parentheses. When a variable is optional, I will show it in brackets ([]). When a variable has multiple mandatory choices, I will show it in braces ({}). Where there are multiple-choice options, I will separate each by a |. Where a variable may only be used with another variable, I will nest the brackets. Here is an example:

```
EXEC CICS
    RETURN
    [TRANSID (name)
    [COMMAREA (dataname)
    [LENGTH   (datavalue)]]]
END-EXEC
```

The above example is the command that returns control to CICS. It is the first command you need to know. (We'll review it in appropriate detail later. For now, let's just review the syntax.) In this example, all variables are followed by a parameter, so you know there are no stand-alone variables for this command. Look carefully at the brackets and you will notice that the LENGTH variable may be used only when COMMAREA is specified, and that COMMAREA may be specified only when TRANSID is used. Also, whenever you see a variable, it can usually be either a data-name or a literal. Here are some possible ways to code the RETURN command, using the above syntax:

```
EXEC CICS
      RETURN
END-EXEC
EXEC CICS
      RETURN
      TRANSID ('A420')
END-EXEC
EXEC CICS
      RETURN
      TRANSID (WS-TRANID)
      COMMAREA(WS-WORKAREA)
END-EXEC
EXEC CICS
      RETURN
      TRANSID ('INQT')
      COMMAREA(COMM-WORK)
      LENGTH  (48)
END-EXEC
```

Along with learning CICS commands, you will need to learn what condition codes occur with various commands. For example, a READ command might be issued for a nonexistent file or for a file where the desired record does not exist. Handling such errors is also a part of writing CICS programs. To keep things simple, we will postpone reviewing condition codes for now.

2.1.2.   CICS Command Data Arguments

In the prior section, you saw that CICS command keywords often require that an argument value be specified; for example, LENGTH (datavalue). You aren't always free to decide what this format may be. For example, some items must be defined as COMP or COMP-3, so you need to look carefully at each CICS command before assuming you know how to code it.

Data options. There are also some keywords where you may either code an alphanumeric or numeric literal (depending on the context) or the dataname of a field that contains the value. For example, if you reviewed the previous examples of the RETURN statement, you saw that TRANSID was a literal in one example ('A420') and a dataname in another (WS-TRANID). To help you figure out your options, here is what I will use within syntax definitions in the book:

> *dataname* — Dataname containing the value is the only option; in other words, no literals.

> *pointer* — A variable that is a specific data address pointer (covered later in the book).

> *anything else* — The argument may be either a literal or a dataname.

To see how that looks, let's review the earlier example of the RETURN statement to see what else was imbedded in the syntax besides the keyword names. As you review it, you now see that TRANSID and LENGTH may be either literals or datanames, whereas COMMAREA must always be a dataname.

```
EXEC  CICS
      RETURN
      [TRANSID   (name)
      [COMMAREA  (dataname)
      [LENGTH    (datavalue)]]]
END-EXEC
```

Numeric format options. When you code a numeric literal, the format isn't important, as the CICS translator (covered in topic 2.1.4) converts the literal to the proper format. However, when you code a dataname for a numeric value, the named data area must be one of three possible formats:

- For halfword binary items — PIC S9(4) COMP

- For fullword binary items — PIC S9(9) COMP or PIC S9(8) COMP

- For packed-decimal items — PIC S9(7) COMP-3.

These definitions automatically impose restrictions on whatever command in which they are used. For example, if a dataname is used for the LENGTH keyword, it must be halfword binary. That means the highest value for LENGTH is 32,767 (the largest achievable number in a binary halfword). In practice, IBM recommends that the maximum amount never be used, keeping all data lengths under 24K for full compatibility.

You will also find that some commands that allow fullword binary items impose restrictions that have no bearing on the capacity of a binary fullword. If your application needs to specify a value greater than 32K, always check the specifics of the CICS command for the version of CICS that you are using (i.e., CICS/ESA allows more flexibility than CICS/MVS or CICS/VS). One, the command may not allow a value larger than 32K. Two, it may allow it in unusual formats.

For example, the GETMAIN command (covered later) allows a LENGTH value of 65,535, but it must be in a binary halfword. If you're up on your binary arithmetic, you know that a binary halfword is 16 bits, one bit for the sign and 15 for data. Storing a number larger than 32,767 would require that the sign bit be used for data. (IBM documentation refers to this as "unsigned halfword binary format.") Doing that with COBOL would require trickery, since a MOVE statement would cause truncation of the high-order bit.

Old-timers using CICS may feel I spent too much time on this topic, since "everyone knows you should never use large amounts of memory." I admit that, for many years, CICS books, instructors, and technicians encouraged programmers to do everything possible to keep memory demands low. Now, with CICS/ESA and MVS/ESA's hyperspace capabilities, CICS programmers need to rethink their traditionally conservative memory management techniques.

If you're just getting your feet wet with CICS, keep all numeric values under 24K (per IBM's recommendation) and don't fret about it. When you have more experience and are designing a new or revamped application, come back and reread this.

2.1.3. CICS Command Style Issues

Throughout this book, you will see a variety of formats for CICS commands, with all examples emphasizing structure and commonality, as shown above. This is a style issue and has no effect on the command logic. For example, a CICS command to read a file might appear as follows:

```
EXEC CICS
     READ FILE    (PAYROLL)
          INTO    (WS1-PAYROLL-REC)
          LENGTH  (WS1-PAYREC-LEN)
          NOHANDLE
          RESP    (CICS-RESP-CODE)
END-EXEC
```

The command would also work if written as follows:

```
EXEC CICS READ FILE(PAYROLL) INTO(WS1-PAYROLL-REC)
LENGTH(WS1-PAYREC-LEN) NOHANDLE RESP(CICS-RESP-CODE)
END-EXEC
```

That works, but it is difficult to read. Your shop may have its own standards on how to write CICS commands and, so long as there is a meaningful structure, it will improve readability. For example, two common formats that I have seen are slightly different from the one shown above for the READ command:

```
EXEC CICS READ FILE    (PAYROLL)
               INTO     (WS1-PAYROLL-REC)
               LENGTH   (WS1-PAYREC-LEN)
               NOHANDLE
               RESP     (CICS-RESP-CODE)
END-EXEC

EXEC CICS READ FILE     (PAYROLL)
               INTO     (WS1-PAYROLL-REC)
               LENGTH   (WS1-PAYREC-LEN)
               NOHANDLE
               RESP     (CICS-RESP-CODE)
               END-EXEC
```

As you read further into this book, you will find that I believe strongly that style and structure contribute noticeably to good program design. All program examples in the book follow top-down decomposition techniques (if you're used to using GO TOs, there are none in this book except in examples where I'll show you some old CICS techniques that I don't recommend). As I mentioned earlier in the book, I focus on techniques, structure, and style. Learning CICS is similar to learning other computer languages. Knowing and using CICS is also similar to knowing and using other computer languages. Just because you know how to code CICS statements, though, doesn't mean your programs are well designed or easy to maintain. That will be a constant focus.

2.1.4.   Converting CICS Commands to COBOL

You're possibly wondering, "How do the CICS commands get converted into executable instructions when they clearly violate COBOL coding conventions?" I hope that thought crossed your mind, since CICS commands follow different rules than COBOL. Well, the answer is that the CICS commands are converted into appropriate COBOL instructions by an IBM-supplied translator program. In the COBOL compiler listing, you will see the CICS commands appearing as comments, followed by the generated COBOL code. In most cases, it will be one or more MOVE instructions followed by a CALL statement to a CICS module supplied by IBM. The following is an example of a CICS command as it might appear in a COBOL program listing:

```
*EXEC  CICS
*       RETURN
*END-EXEC
        MOVE  '        00053      ' TO  DFHEIV0
        CALL 'DFHEI1' USING DFHEIV0
```

Don't concern yourself with the generated code. I only present it here to remove any magic that may exist. Focus instead on the function of the CICS command itself. For example, the displayed command above returns control to CICS. The fact that the numeric value of 00053 is moved to a field called DFHEIV0 is meaningless to me and should also be to you. The developers of CICS wrote the software to use various values and parameters to communicate your instructions to CICS. The next section will provide more information on the mechanics of compiling a CICS program. If you're used to always having the COBOL compiler directly process your source programs, you will find the process for CICS is unique.

2.2.   STEPS TO COMPILE AND LINK A COBOL CICS PROGRAM

The prior section explained that CICS commands were imbedded within a COBOL program and needed to be converted into acceptable COBOL code. That is done by the IBM-supplied CICS translator. As the programmer, you write the CICS commands within the COBOL program where the commands are logically appropriate. (You will find that CICS commands fit well within the COBOL program structure.)

2.2.1. The Compile Process

The compile process is a three-step procedure (IBM's JCL PROCEDURE for MVS is DFHEITCL, documented later in the book. The JCL PROCEDURE for VSE is DFHECP1$.). See Figure 2.1 for an example of the process for both MVS and VSE.

In Figure 2.1, the first step reads the COBOL program with embedded CICS commands. It checks the syntax of the CICS commands and prints any errors on the output listing. The listing printed from this step shows the program exactly as the programmer wrote it. The translator modifies the program by changing all CICS commands to comment statements and inserts appropriate MOVE and CALL statements to accomplish the desired function. This is the version you will see in a COBOL compiler listing. (The translator will make certain adjustments if the JCL notifies it that the program will be processed by the COBOL II compiler. The steps to do that are covered later.) This listing does more than just check for syntax errors on EXEC CICS commands. It also supports an IBM debugging facility called the Execution Diagnostic Facility (EDF) that we will cover later.

The second step is the traditional COBOL compile (either VS/COBOL or COBOL II). The compiler is unaware of the preceding step and processes the COBOL program normally. (*Note:* While the preceding sentence is correct, code generated by COBOL II is sensitive to the CICS environment.) Since the CICS commands are now just comment statements, they are ignored by the COBOL compiler. In the COBOL listing, you will see not only the COBOL code that was written by you but also the COBOL code (both DATA DIVISION and PROCEDURE DIVISION) that was generated by the CICS translator. (*Reminder:* All references in this book to COBOL II also apply to COBOL/370. Differences will be noted.)

Don't expect that you will ever understand the functions of all of the generated code. This is because the translator inserts WORKING STORAGE elements that *might* be needed by the CICS commands, plus potentially useful entries in the LINKAGE SECTION. Since you might be wondering what type of modifications are made by the translator, I have included here a listing of a COBOL program that does nothing except return to CICS (or an invoking program within CICS).

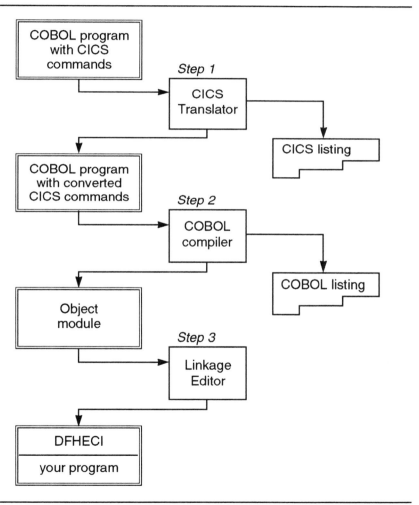

Figure 2.1. Example of CICS compile steps.

2.2.2.   A Sample Program Compile Listing

While the program itself is worthless (except as a stub program in a structured development environment), it allows you to see all the modifications made to the program by the translator. Remember, the translator is only providing work areas for the various CICS commands that *might* be in your program. Since there are differences for VS/COBOL and COBOL II environments, I include examples for both compilers. I will not elaborate on the differences yet, because you aren't yet ready to handle that. When we review VS/COBOL vs. COBOL II, I'll come back for a more thorough explanation. For now, I only want you aware of the changes that occur to your program when it is processed by the CICS translator. (*Note:* Figure 2.2 is the program as written; Figure 2.3 is the translated version for VS/CO-BOL; Figure 2.4 is the translated version for COBOL II.)

Remember what I said in the previous paragraph about your not needing to understand all the meanings in the figures shown. I present this information here so you can remove the mystery of the COBOL-to-CICS interface. It's done in traditional ways, using data fields and CALL statements. The differences you will see are important in how each compiler supports (or doesn't support) IBM's extended architecture. Most programmers are surprised by the mysterious modifications that occur to their program; some even attempt to insert the items themselves (which is wrong). In future months, you may want to revisit these figures for review to refresh your knowledge of the various pieces.

```
IDENTIFICATION DIVISION.
PROGRAM-ID.    STUBPROG.
*AUTHOR.    DAVID S. KIRK.
ENVIRONMENT DIVISION.
DATA DIVISION.
WORKING-STORAGE SECTION.
LINKAGE SECTION.
01  DFHCOMMAREA PIC X(1).

PROCEDURE DIVISION.
1.   EXEC CICS RETURN END-EXEC.
     GOBACK.
```

Figure 2.2. Sample stub program.

The sample stub program in Figure 2.2 does nothing except return control to CICS. I've used it many times when doing top-down development and needed to access a program that hadn't yet been written. For now, notice that there are no entries for the ENVIRONMENT DIVISION or the FILE SECTION. (Actually, the ENVIRONMENT DIVISION statement is not required for CICS applications, and I usually omit the statement entirely.) If you're wondering what the DFHCOMMAREA item is for, I'll get to it shortly. (The DFHCOMMAREA isn't used in this program, but I include it for consistency.) Our goal in this section is to help you see that (1) a CICS program looks a bit different from other programs, and (2) the CICS translator will modify it prior to the compile step. Notice how much the program grows in Figure 2.3. (In case you're wondering why I have a GOBACK statement in the program, I placed it there to prevent the COBOL compiler from generating a warning message about there not being any termination statement (STOP RUN, GOBACK, EXIT PROGRAM). In a properly designed program, the statement should never be executed. (Also, by having the RETURN statement and the GOBACK statement, I preserve compatibility with both VS/COBOL and with COBOL II, but that's a later chapter.)

```
CICS/MVS COMMAND LANGUAGE TRANSLATOR VERSION 2.1
*OPTIONS IN EFFECT*
  CICS
  DEBUG
NOFE
  SPIE
  EDF
  LINECOUNT(60)
  TABLE(DFHEITAB)
  SOURCE
NOVBREF
  OPTIONS
  FLAG(W)
  SEQ
  APOST
NONUM
  OPT
  SPACE(1)
```

Figure 2.3. Sample CICS translate/compile/link for VS/COBOL.

```
LANGLVL(2)
LINE  SOURCE  LISTING

00001 A.  ==>  IDENTIFICATION DIVISION.
00002          PROGRAM-ID.  STUBPROG.
00003          *AUTHOR.   DAVID S. KIRK.
00004          ENVIRONMENT DIVISION.
00005          DATA DIVISION.
00006          WORKING-STORAGE SECTION.
00007          LINKAGE SECTION.
00008          01  DFHCOMMAREA PIC X(1).
00009
00010          PROCEDURE DIVISION.
00011          1. EXEC CICS RETURN END-EXEC.
00012             GOBACK.
NO MESSAGES PRODUCED BY TRANSLATOR.


PP 5740-CB1 RELEASE 2.4        IBM OS/VS COBOL

00001          IDENTIFICATION DIVISION.
00002          PROGRAM-ID.  STUBPROG.
00003          *AUTHOR.   DAVID S. KIRK.
00004          ENVIRONMENT DIVISION.
00005          DATA DIVISION.
00006          WORKING-STORAGE SECTION.
00007 B.  ==>  01  DFHLDVER PIC X(22) VALUE 'LD TABLE DFHEITAB 210.'.
00008          01  DFHEIDO PICTURE S9(7)  COMPUTATIONAL-3 VALUE ZERO.
00009          01  DFHEIBO PICTURE S9(4) COMPUTATIONAL VALUE ZERO.
00010          01  DFHEICB PICTURE X(8)  VALUE IS '        '.
00011
00012          01  DFHEIV16   COMP PIC S9(8).
00013          01  DFHB0041   COMP PIC S9(8).
00014          01  DFHB0042   COMP PIC S9(8).
00015          01  DFHB0043   COMP PIC S9(8).
00016          01  DFHB0044   COMP PIC S9(8).
00017          01  DFHB0045   COMP PIC S9(8).
00018          01  DFHB0046   COMP PIC S9(8).
00019          01  DFHB0047   COMP PIC S9(8).
00020          01  DFHB0048   COMP PIC S9(8).
```

Figure 2.3. (cont'd). Sample CICS translate/compile/link for VS/COBOL.

```
00021              01  DFHEIV11    COMP  PIC  S9(4).
00022              01  DFHEIV12    COMP  PIC  S9(4).
00023              01  DFHEIV13    COMP  PIC  S9(4).
00024              01  DFHEIV14    COMP  PIC  S9(4).
00025              01  DFHEIV15    COMP  PIC  S9(4).
00026              01  DFHB0025    COMP  PIC  S9(4).
00027              01  DFHEIV5     PIC  X(4).
00028              01  DFHEIV6     PIC  X(4).
00029              01  DFHEIV17    PIC  X(4).
00030              01  DFHEIV18    PIC  X(4).
00031              01  DFHEIV19    PIC  X(4).
00032              01  DFHEIV1     PIC  X(8).
00033              01  DFHEIV2     PIC  X(8).
00034              01  DFHEIV3     PIC  X(8).
00035              01  DFHEIV20    PIC  X(8).
00036              01  DFHC0084    PIC  X(8).
00037              01  DFHC0085    PIC  X(8).
00038              01  DFHC0320    PIC  X(32).
00039              01  DFHEIV7     PIC  X(2).
00040              01  DFHEIV8     PIC  X(2).
00041              01  DFHC0022    PIC  X(2).
00042              01  DFHC0023    PIC  X(2).
00043              01  DFHEIV10    PIC  S9(7)      COMP-3.
00044              01  DFHEIV9     PIC  X(1).
00045              01  DFHC0011    PIC  X(1).
00046              01  DFHEIV4     PIC  X(6).
00047              01  DFHC0070    PIC  X(7).
00048              01  DFHC0071    PIC  X(7).
00049              01  DFHC0440    PIC  X(44).
00050              01  DFHDUMMY    COMP  PIC  S9(4).
00051              01  DFHEIV0     PICTURE  X(29).
00052              LINKAGE  SECTION.
00053  C.  ==>     01  DFHEIBLK.
00054              02  EIBTIME     PIC  S9(7)      COMP-3.
00055              02  EIBDATE     PIC  S9(7)      COMP-3.
00056              02  EIBTRNID    PIC  X(4).
00057              02  EIBTASKN    PIC  S9(7)      COMP-3.
00058              02  EIBTRMID    PIC  X(4).
00059              02  DFHEIGDI    COMP  PIC  S9(4).
```

Figure 2.3. (cont'd). Sample CICS translate/compile/link for VS/COBOL.

```
00060          02 EIBCPOSN  COMP PIC S9(4).
00061          02 EIBCALEN  COMP PIC S9(4).
00062          02 EIBAID    PIC X(1).
00063          02 EIBFN     PIC X(2).
00064          02 EIBRCODE  PIC X(6).
00065          02 EIBDS     PIC X(8).
00066          02 EIBREQID  PIC X(8).
00067          02 EIBRSRCE  PIC X(8).
00068          02 EIBSYNC   PIC X(1).
00069          02 EIBFREE   PIC X(1).
00070          02 EIBRECV   PIC X(1).
00071          02 EIBFIL01  PIC X(1).
00072          02 EIBATT    PIC X(1).
00073          02 EIBEOC    PIC X(1).
00074          02 EIBFMH    PIC X(1).
00075          02 EIBCOMPL  PIC X(1).
00076          02 EIBSIG    PIC X(1).
00077          02 EIBCONF   PIC X(1).
00078          02 EIBERR    PIC X(1).
00079          02 EIBERRCD  PIC X(4).
00080          02 EIBSYNRB  PIC X(1).
00081          02 EIBNODAT  PIC X(1).
00082          02 EIBRESP   COMP PIC S9(8).
00083          02 EIBRESP2  COMP PIC S9(8).
00084          02 EIBRLDBK  PIC X(1).
00085          01 DFHCOMMAREA' PIC X(1).
00086
00087 D. ==>  01 DFHBLLSLOT1 PICTURE X(1).
00088          01 DFHBLLSLOT2 PICTURE X(1).
00089 E. ==>  PROCEDURE DIVISION USING DFHEIBLK DFHCOMMAREA.
00090 F. ==>      CALL 'DFHEI1'.
00091              SERVICE RELOAD DFHEIBLK.
00092              SERVICE RELOAD DFHCOMMAREA.
00093 G. ==>  *EXEC CICS RETURN END-EXEC.
00094          1. MOVE ' 00011   ' TO DFHEIVO
00095              CALL 'DFHEI1' USING DFHEIVO.
00096              GOBACK.
```

Figure 2.3. (cont'd). Sample CICS translate/compile/link for VS/COBOL.

```
MVS/DFP VERSION 3 RELEASE 2 LINKAGE EDITOR
JOB DKIRK#01      STEP CICS          PROCEDURE LKED
INVOCATION PARAMETERS - SIZE=(2000K,900K),XREF,LIST
ACTUAL SIZE=(1972224,903168)
IEW0000      INCLUDE SYSLIB(DFHECI)


CONTROL SECTION
  NAME        ORIGIN     LENGTH
DFHECI          00          48
STUBPROG        48         696


ENTRY ADDRESS          48
TOTAL LENGTH           6E0
** STUBPROG DID NOT PREVIOUSLY EXIST BUT WAS ADDED AND HAS
   AMODE 24
** LOAD MODULE HAS RMODE 24
** AUTHORIZATION CODE IS          0.
```

Figure 2.3. (cont'd). Sample CICS translate/compile/link for VS/COBOL.

In reviewing Figure 2.3, you see that the program grew a lot. Actually, this is the sum total of what is automatically added to every CICS program. It looks like a lot of additional statements only because my program was so small. Let's review some of the items (my comments are marked by ==> in the listing).

First, locate note A (A. ==>). It is pointing to the translator listing which shows the program as written. This listing is useful because it will flag any incorrectly coded EXEC CICS commands. I like this listing also because it is the only listing that shows me what I wrote. This listing is also of some benefit for some basic debugging that I'll cover later.

Next, see note B. These data fields from line 7 through 51 are inserted by the translator *after* your last WORKING-STORAGE entry. They are placed there automatically because at least one of them is used by every possible EXEC CICS command. If you examine statements 94 and 95, you will see that my translated program uses only one of those fields, DFHEIV0. With a larger program, using more commands, more of the fields would have been used. You never need to know what these fields are for. *Just leave them alone.* (For that matter, you should always avoid modifying *any* of the inserted data elements. They are there to be used by the generated CICS statements and unpredictable results could occur if you modified their contents.)

Now examine note C. This is the Execute Interface Block (EIB) and is always inserted as the *first entry* in the LINKAGE SECTION. These fields will be useful to your application because CICS inserts information into them before giving control to your program. For example, if you need to know what position the cursor occupied on the screen at the time the screen contents were read by CICS, that information is in the EIB. Also, you will often want to know what key the user pressed that caused CICS to regain control from the terminal. (Keys that do this are called AID keys in CICS terminology. The AID keys are all of the function keys, the Enter key, the Clear key, and the PA1 and PA2 keys.)

Note D is informational only. You will see these two entries inserted as the last two entries in the LINKAGE SECTION for VS/COBOL programs. They're just some addressability pointers that don't affect you. Ignore them. You won't see them in COBOL II programs.

Note E points to the only COBOL statement that the translator modifies. The PROCEDURE DIVISION statement was modified to show it was being passed addressability to the EIB area and the previously referenced DFHCOMMAREA. These are the only two 01-level areas in the LINKAGE SECTION that can be immediately addressed by you. If, for any reason, your application needs other 01-level entries in the LINKAGE SECTION, you will need to provide that in your procedural code. We'll cover it later in the book. (*Note*: The DFHCOMMAREA is for your application's use. How it is used will be presented later.)

Note F points to 3 instructions that are inserted by the translator if a VS/COBOL program is being compiled with the OPTIMIZE option, which is the normal choice. The SERVICE RELOAD statement has meaning only for VS/COBOL programs and reestablishes addressability to data areas. Yes, we'll cover this at the appropriate point.

Note G is simply an example of how a translated CICS instruction appears. Notice how both statements 90 and 95 CALL the CICS interface module, DFHEI1. You will see a CALL to this module in virtually every translated CICS command. This is how your program actually "talks" to CICS. There ain't no magic!

Finally, review the abbreviated listing from the Linkage Editor. Notice that a CICS module, DFHECI, appears at the beginning of your program. Most (all?) shops have set their compile/link JCL to ensure this happens without your needing to be aware of it. I mention it here in case you, like me, often like to code your own Linkage Editor commands. In reviewing Figure 2.4 (the COBOL II version of Figure 2.3), you will see only subtle differences. There are major improvements in programming with COBOL II and several CICS differences that won't be apparent here. Still, the fundamental interface you see here remains constant.

```
CICS/MVS COMMAND LANGUAGE TRANSLATOR VERSION 2.1
OPTIONS SPECIFIED:-COBOL2
*OPTIONS IN EFFECT*

    CICS
    DEBUG
NOFE
    SPIE
    EDF
    LINECOUNT(60)
    TABLE(DFHEITAB)
    SOURCE
NOVBREF
    OPTIONS
    .FLAG(W)
    SEQ
    APOST
NONUM
    OPT
    SPACE(1)
    LANGLVL(2)
    COBOL2
LINE            SOURCE LISTING

00001           IDENTIFICATION DIVISION.
```

Figure 2.4. Example of translate/compile/link for COBOL II.

```
00002          PROGRAM-ID.  STUBPROG.
00003          *AUTHOR.  DAVID S. KIRK.
00004          ENVIRONMENT DIVISION.
00005          DATA DIVISION.
00006          WORKING-STORAGE SECTION.
00007          LINKAGE SECTION.
00008          01 DFHCOMMAREA PIC X(1).
00009
00010          PROCEDURE DIVISION.
00011          1. EXEC CICS RETURN END-EXEC.
00012             GOBACK.
```

```
PP 5668-958 IBM VS COBOL II Release 3.2
Invocation parameters:
TRUNC(BIN),LIB,SIZE(2000K),BUF(32760),OPT,RES,RENT
PROCESS(CBL) statements:
    CBL RENT,RES,NODYNAM,LIB              <== Note A
Options in effect:
    ADV
    APOST
   NOAWO
    BUFSIZE(32760)
   NOCMPR2
   NOCOMPILE(S)
    DATA(31)
   NODBCS
   NODECK
   NODUMP
   NODYNAM
   NOEXIT
   NOFASTSRT
   NOFDUMP
    FLAG(I,E)
   NOFLAGMIG
   NOFLAGSAA
   NOFLAGSTD
    LANGUAGE(EN)
    LIB
    LINECOUNT(60)
```

Figure 2.4. (cont'd). Example of translate/compile/link for COBOL II.

```
       NOLIST
       NOMAP
       NONAME
       NONUMBER
         NUMPROC(MIG)
         OBJECT
       NOOFFSET
         OPTIMIZE
         OUTDD(SYSOUT)
         RENT
         RESIDENT
         SEQUENCE
         SIZE(2048000)
         SOURCE
         SPACE(1)
       NOSSRANGE
       NOTERM
       NOTEST
         TRUNC(BIN)
       NOVBREF
       NOWORD
       NOXREF
         ZWB
000001          IDENTIFICATION DIVISION.
000002          PROGRAM-ID.   STUBPROG.
000003          *AUTHOR.   DAVID  S.  KIRK.
000004          ENVIRONMENT DIVISION.
000005          DATA DIVISION.
000006          WORKING-STORAGE SECTION.
000007          01 DFHLDVER PIC X(22) VALUE 'LD TABLE DFHEITAB 210.'.
000008          01 DFHEIDO PICTURE S9(7) COMPUTATIONAL-3 VALUE ZERO.
000009          01 DFHEIBO PICTURE S9(4) COMPUTATIONAL VALUE ZERO.
000010          01 DFHEICB PICTURE X(8) VALUE IS '          '.
000011
000012          01 DFHB0040    COMP PIC S9(8).
000013          01 DFHB0041    COMP PIC S9(8).
000014          01 DFHB0042    COMP PIC S9(8).
000015          01 DFHB0043    COMP PIC S9(8).
```

Figure 2.4. (cont'd). Example of translate/compile/link for COBOL II.

```
000016          01  DFHB0044    COMP  PIC  S9(8).
000017          01  DFHB0045    COMP  PIC  S9(8).
000018          01  DFHB0046    COMP  PIC  S9(8).
000019          01  DFHB0047    COMP  PIC  S9(8).
000020          01  DFHB0048    COMP  PIC  S9(8).
000021          01  DFHB0020    COMP  PIC  S9(4).
000022          01  DFHB0021    COMP  PIC  S9(4).
000023          01  DFHB0022    COMP  PIC  S9(4).
000024          01  DFHB0023    COMP  PIC  S9(4).
000025          01  DFHB0024    COMP  PIC  S9(4).
000026          01  DFHB0025    COMP  PIC  S9(4).
000027          01  DFHC0040    PIC  X(4).
000028          01  DFHC0041    PIC  X(4).
000029          01  DFHC0042    PIC  X(4).
000030          01  DFHC0043    PIC  X(4).
000031          01  DFHC0044    PIC  X(4).
000032          01  DFHC0080    PIC  X(8).
000033          01  DFHC0081    PIC  X(8).
000034          01  DFHC0082    PIC  X(8).
000035          01  DFHC0083    PIC  X(8).
000036          01  DFHC0084    PIC  X(8).
000037          01  DFHC0085    PIC  X(8).
000038          01  DFHC0320    PIC  X(32).
000039          01  DFHC0020    PIC  X(2).
000040          01  DFHC0021    PIC  X(2).
000041          01  DFHC0022    PIC  X(2).
000042          01  DFHC0023    PIC  X(2).
000043          01  DFHD0040    PIC  S9(7)  COMP-3.
000044          01  DFHC0010    PIC  X(1).
000045          01  DFHC0011    PIC  X(1).
000046          01  DFHC0060    PIC  X(6).
000047          01  DFHC0070    PIC  X(7).
000048          01  DFHC0071    PIC  X(7).
000049          01  DFHC0440    PIC  X(44).
000050          01  DFHDUMMY    COMP  PIC  S9(4).
000051          01  DFHEIVO     PICTURE  X(29).
000052          LINKAGE  SECTION.
000053          01  DFHEIBLK.
000054          02  EIBTIME     PIC  S9(7)  COMP-3.
```

Figure 2.4. (cont'd). Example of translate/compile/link for COBOL II.

```
000055          02  EIBDATE    PIC  S9(7)  COMP-3.
000056          02  EIBTRNID   PIC  X(4).
000057          02  EIBTASKN   PIC  S9(7)  COMP-3.
000058          02  EIBTRMID   PIC  X(4).
000059          02  DFHEIGDI   COMP  PIC  S9(4).
000060          02  EIBCPOSN   COMP  PIC  S9(4).
000061          02  EIBCALEN   COMP  PIC  S9(4).
000062          02  EIBAID     PIC  X(1).
000063          02  EIBFN      PIC  X(2).
000064          02  EIBRCODE   PIC  X(6).
000065          02  EIBDS      PIC  X(8).
000066          02  EIBREQID   PIC  X(8).
000067          02  EIBRSRCE   PIC  X(8).
000068          02  EIBSYNC    PIC  X(1).
000069          02  EIBFREE    PIC  X(1).
000070          02  EIBRECV    PIC  X(1).
000071          02  EIBFIL01   PIC  X(1).
000072          02  EIBATT     PIC  X(1).
000073          02  EIBEOC     PIC  X(1).
000074          02  EIBFMH     PIC  X(1).
000075          02  EIBCOMPL   PIC  X(1).
000076          02  EIBSIG     PIC  X(1).
000077          02  EIBCONF    PIC  X(1).
000078          02  EIBERR     PIC  X(1).
000079          02  EIBERRCD   PIC  X(4).
000080          02  EIBSYNRB   PIC  X(1).
000081          02  EIBNODAT   PIC  X(1).
000082          02  EIBRESP    COMP  PIC  S9(8)
000083          02  EIBRESP2   COMP  PIC  S9(8).
000084          02  EIBRLDBK   PIC  X(1).
000085       01 DFHCOMMAREA PIC  X(1).
000086
000087       PROCEDURE  DIVISION  USING  DFHEIBLK  DFHCOMMAREA.
000088       *EXEC  CICS  RETURN  END-EXEC.
000089       1.  MOVE  '  00011        TO  DFHEIVO
000090           CALL  'DFHEI1'  USING  DFHEIVO.
000091           GOBACK.
*  Statistics  for  COBOL  program  STUBPROG:
```

Figure 2.4. (cont'd). Example of translate/compile/link for COBOL II.

```
*   Source records = 91
*   Data Division statements = 77
*   Procedure Division statements = 3
End of compilation 1, program STUBPROG,   no statements flagged.
Return code 0

 MVS/DFP VERSION 3 RELEASE 2 LINKAGE EDITOR
 JOB DKIRK#02    STEP CICS        PROCEDURE LKED
 INVOCATION PARAMETERS - SIZE=(2000K,900K),XREF,LIST,RENT
 ACTUAL SIZE=(1972224,905216)
IEW0000        INCLUDE SYSLIB(DFHECI)

 CONTROL SECTION
   NAME       ORIGIN   LENGTH
   DFHECI        00       48
   STUBPROG      48      3EC
   IGZEBST  *   438      1A8

ENTRY ADDRESS          48
TOTAL LENGTH           5E0
** STUBPROG DID NOT PREVIOUSLY EXIST BUT WAS ADDED AND HAS AMODE 31
** LOAD MODULE HAS RMODE ANY
** AUTHORIZATION CODE IS          0.
**MODULE HAS BEEN MARKED REENTERABLE, AND REUSABLE.
```

Figure 2.4. (cont'd). Example of translate/compile/link for COBOL II.

Yes, Figure 2.4 is almost identical to Figure 2.3, but look for the differences. First, you may see in note A that there is a PROCESS statement in effect during the COBOL compile (sometimes referred to as a CBL statement, as COBOL II allows either spelling). If PROCESS statements are new to you, don't worry. They are a means to specify COBOL compile options. We'll review them briefly in this book, as my main purpose in pointing this out is that the translator inserts this statement to ensure that you don't use different COBOL compile options than those specified (RENT, RES, NODYNAM, LIB). For more information on specific COBOL II facilities and techniques, you will want a copy of one of my other books, *COBOL II Power*

Programmer's Desk Reference. (There are two books in the series; one addresses MVS and the other addresses VSE). Also, don't worry about remembering the compile options yet. We will get to it at the right time.

Next, compare the two figures and notice that several of the items that were in Figure 2.3 are absent from Figure 2.4. Why? COBOL II was written by IBM to work hand in hand with CICS. For that reason, it doesn't need some of the commands that were used in earlier compilers. This difference also is apparent in the Linkage Editor listing, where you will notice the AMODE and RMODE are different from that produced by VS/COBOL. As you learn about AMODE and RMODE in this book, you will appreciate the difference — and the opportunity — of COBOL II. There are several programming differences also. We'll cover them thoroughly. If you are new to COBOL II or involved in converting from VS/COBOL to COBOL II, that information will be useful.

While most of the importance of the contents of Figures 2.3 and 2.4 is meaningless to you at this time, all the hints you will eventually need to fully understand the CICS-COBOL interface are in the previous three figures. There is no magic here, only practical code. There is still an additional option that can be done with COBOL II that affects the entries inserted by the translator, but the concept is too new for this part of the book. Now, let's move on. We've looked at some CICS basics. Now let's get back to designing the program itself.

2.3.   BASIC PROGRAM DESIGN FOR A TRANSACTION

Transaction design requires all of the steps that are normal in any project except that the steps are more demanding. You can develop CICS transactions that work, yet don't conform to everything in this section. Many programmers, unfortunately, do just that. Since you're reading this book because you want to be better than that, stay with me. Good CICS programs are the result of clean design. So let's review some design issues first. In this section, I've prepared seven basic steps that cover most issues for simple CICS transactions. Obviously, there are entire books that cover this concept more thoroughly, but this should be sufficient to help you develop quality programs. The quality factor is especially important because most CICS transactions interact with people; batch programs don't.

Whereas a user may not be upset about the specific locations of fields on a printed report from a batch application, their location, structure, and interaction from a terminal are a very different matter. You've probably had experience with software that is accessed from a terminal, and you know how frustrating it can be to work with software that gives poor feedback, has data fields that are poorly organized on the terminal screen, or that simply requires too much input before giving you the information you desire.

In designing an online transaction, there are several steps that will ensure quality. I list them here. By the way, by *quality* I don't mean the world's best program, whatever that is. Instead, I use the word *quality* to emphasize that programs should do what the user needs and requests. For example, if the user doesn't need help screens, then adding them does *not* improve quality — it only increases costs. Surprisingly, many programmers with whom I've worked believe that quality means doing your very best. It doesn't. It means doing what the customer needs and requests. My neighbor, for example, feels that quality lawn mowing must be done diagonally. That's great, but, to me, it takes too much time. For me, quality means that the weeds are no higher than the grass. While he might pay extra for the pretty diagonal stripes in the lawn, I would not. Neither of us is wrong; we just have different requirements.

To ensure quality in your transactions, follow these steps (or similar ones, depending on your company's requirements):

2.3.1.   Specifications

Get clear, written specifications for the work environment. This may require that you interview users or help them assess how the terminal application is used. Look on it as a positive opportunity to understand the real needs and how the application will be used.

Written specifications ensure that you and the customer know exactly what is required. There are few frustrations more irritating to a programmer than to have developed a working application and then to have the user exclaim the traditional statement, "It's just what I asked for, but not what I want."

You can positively influence this process by discussing with the users what they need to accomplish the business issues. Issues such as rapid response, assumptions by their customers, or common practices in their business may affect your system design. For example, if you were designing an online policyholder administration system for an insurance company, it would be beneficial for you to learn what types of transactions would have high volume and what types would have low volume. This affects not only the screen design, but performance considerations as well.

2.3.2. Data and Transaction Flow

Review the data and transaction flow with the prospective user. Often, a user will ask for a particular transaction without fully understanding the impact it will have on the department's staff. By walking through the possible dialogue the user will have with the transaction, you may surface bugs or inconsistencies. Yes, it may mean more work in developing the transaction, but it also represents less work in future maintenance.

For example, a user may request that the system have a menu structure that requires that a terminal user respond to four or five menus before any real work is done. Clearly, such a design would tax the patience of any person who worked at a computer terminal for more than even one hour a day. Yes, the first time it seems friendly and easy to use, but, unfortunately, such designs become tiresome within minutes. (Do you remember when you first learned to use ISPF or a similar product? At first, the menus seemed helpful. Soon, you were anxious to learn the shorthand commands that bypassed the menus because you no longer needed to evaluate all the options. So it will be with your own users.)

One approach is to develop transaction flow diagrams. Such diagrams aren't intended to be permanent documentation for the system, but may assist a user in understanding the many complexities and demands the transaction makes on the terminal user. For example, consider Figure 2.5.

In Figure 2.5, the first step may be a company-wide application menu, providing not only application information but application security as well. The second step is usually an application-specific menu that offers the various processing options for a specific application. The third step (often missing) is a menu to control the various mechanics of the application, providing control to such mechanics as adding new records or changing existing records. Steps below this level are usually specific functions for a given application, such as adding or deleting a specific data record.

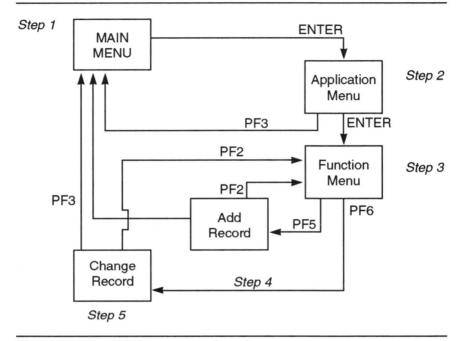

Figure 2.5. Sample transaction flow diagram.

A variant of the above is the screen flow diagram. While it is similar to the transaction flow diagram, it focuses instead on the user and the sequence in which the user will work with screens. This can be helpful in assisting a ·user to design a transaction, as it helps the user to see the order in which screens are presented and the total number of screens that must be viewed to complete a unit of work.

Figure 2.6 is intended to represent a typical transaction struc-ture and help you develop your own screen data flows. The goal is to show all screens that the user might see and the order in which the screens are seen. In Figure 2.6, the user signs onto a menu applica-tion and, from that menu, selects a submenu. From the submenu, the user selects either the add or the update menu. Each of those menus in turn invoke subordinate processing programs. With CICS, each box can be a separate program, thereby isolating programming complex-ity and improving reusability of applications.

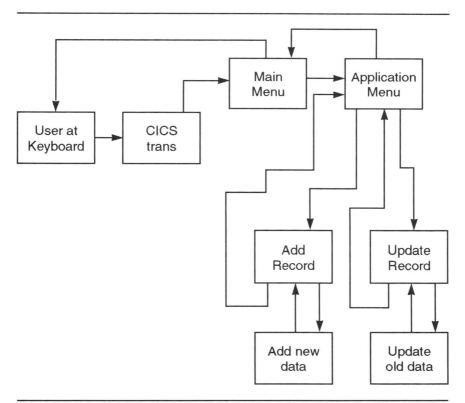

Figure 2.6. Example of screen data flow.

2.3.3. Screen Design

Design the screens and walk through the screens with the users, letting them see what will be presented to the staff. This might be done on paper, on the mainframe terminal (most companies have simple software that can display sample screens), or with a PC. Having application logic to support the screens is not important; having screens that simulate the proposed application is. While this is a simple, low-cost activity, many companies don't do it. If there are several screens for the system, or if there are hundreds of persons affected by the system, this process alone can ensure a successful system. Developing a well-programmed system is meaningless if the users aren't trained or are unaware of the system's purpose. Tripling the time you spend in this step may reduce your implementation costs significantly.

Although screen design will be covered again in a later chapter, you should start envisioning the screen as being broken into several components, including the components identified in Figure 2.7A.

```
Information component:   This should provide the data
                         elements that are required for
                         the application.  Data fields
                         should be organized in a way
                         that simplifies use of the
                         screen.

Control component:       This should provide information
                         on the user's options in
                         managing the dialogue and
                         should be consistent with other
                         applications at your company.
                         This should include consistent
                         use of function keys and other
                         control information.

Feedback component:      This section of the screen
                         should be a fixed location
                         where the user can always find
                         informational messages or
                         notification of errors.
```

Figure 2.7A. Screen construction concepts, part 1.

As seen in Figure 2.7B, there are three basic components (or areas) to any screen: the one that shows the user the desired data, the one that shows the user how to manage the transaction, and the one that provides feedback to the user. Too often, all emphasis is on the information component, with little or no information provided on how to manage the transaction or explanations of errors that are in the data. (Have you ever experienced the frustration of accidentally initiating a transaction and not being able to terminate it, or entering incorrect data and not knowing it?) When the machine is in control,

people feel uncomfortable. At the very least, you should always ensure that your transactions give adequate instruction to terminate
the function and notification about incorrect data.

```
XYZ0010                 XYZ  Sock  Company
• • • • • • • • • • • • • • • • • • • • • • • • • • • • • • • • •
•                        First            Last          •
•                                                        •
• Customer  name: _____   _____        •
•                                                        •
• Street: _____           •
•                                                        •
• City: _____   St: ____  Zip: _____         •
•                                                        •
• Shoe size: _____   Sex: ___                          •
• • • • • • • • • • • • • • • • • • • • • • • • • • • • • • • • •
            Information  component  ────────────►▲
            Control  component  ───────────────────┐
   | ◄────── Feedback  component  ────────────────►| ▼
• • • • • • • • • • • • • • • • • • • • • • • • • • • • • • • • •
• PF1=Help  PF3=Exit  PF4=Add  PF5=Update  PF6=Delete •
• PF7=Show  sizes                                        •
• • • • • • • • • • • • • • • • • • • • • • • • • • • • • • • • •
```

Figure 2.7B. Screen construction concepts, part 2.

Figure 2.7 shows the basic concepts only. If you've worked with
products such as ISPF, you know the value of consistent placement
of data elements and the consistent use of function keys. These two
elements are only the foundation of screen design. More specifics will
be covered later.

Finally, in recent years IBM has introduced a concept known as
SAA (for System Application Architecture). SAA is a strategic effort
to help computer professionals design applications that are portable
across multiple computer platforms. While that isn't our goal here,
one of the components of SAA is CUA (Common User Access). What
makes CUA exciting is that it is a recommended approach to building
transaction screens, ensuring a common set of techniques and structure across many applications. While CUA hasn't caught on at many
companies yet, it offers a rethinking of many traditional CICS screen
design techniques. We will cover some CUA techniques later in the

book after you are more familiar with the basics and with traditional CICS screen designs (which are what your company probably uses).

2.3.4.   CICS Mechanics

When you reach this step, you have identified all the components for a CICS transaction. You have worked with user departments and others that are affected by the given transaction design. The users have agreed to the screen flow, the screen designs, and the processing specifications. The work done to this point will be the major factor in the success of your transaction. If you received good user involvement in the design, your system should be successful. (*Hint*: Don't quit now. Keep the users involved as you develop and test the new transaction, showing them each new piece. Otherwise, users may forget what the transaction was to look like or to do.) After approval, establish the CICS mechanics through whatever forms or procedures are in use at your company.

By "CICS mechanics," I am referring to the many technical steps that are needed to ensure that CICS is ready for your new programs when they have been written and you want to start testing. Since you have all the specifications and screens identified, you need to establish names to CICS for them and select a transaction code for the transaction.

From an earlier section, you know that several CICS tables require this information. In this step, you need to ensure that all program names, transaction identifiers, and file identifiers are predefined to your CICS environment (e.g., PPT, PCT, FCT). By coordinating this in advance, you ensure that your initial testing is not postponed because of technical difficulties.

This book doesn't explain these technicalities in detail, because the process varies from shop to shop. At many companies, the systems programmers update these tables from preprinted forms that you fill out. This requirement ensures that standards and other controls are followed. Work within the system and you'll be more successful — and less annoying — than those who make their technical requests at the last moment and then complain when their own procrastination affects their project.

In this section, I mentioned program names, transaction identifiers, and file identifiers. You know what a program name is if you've previously created a load module (MVS) or a phase (VSE). Every load module or phase that CICS will interact with must be defined to the Processing Program Table (PPT).

A file identifier is similar, being a name of up to eight characters that defines the entry in the File Control Table (FCT) for a given file. (The actual file dataset name is kept in the FCT.) The file identifier is what you will reference in CICS I/O commands. Every file that will be used must have an entry in the FCT.

Finally, there is the transaction identifier. This is a four character code that is unique for each program that receives control from CICS. The transaction code and the program it invokes must both be defined in the PCT. As we'll see, many CICS programs do not need a transaction identifier as they are designed to only receive control from other application programs, never from CICS directly. This will become clear as we see examples.

2.3.5.   Screen Development

Develop the MAPs for all intended screens. MAP refers to the use of the CICS tool, BMS (Basic Mapping Support), that creates the mapping of any given CICS screen. While separate from programming, this process should always precede the programming process to ensure that the user's intended system matches your interpretation. This also gives you the opportunity to show the users exactly what their screens will look like before committing to code (displaying CICS screens without programs is via a CICS utility program, CECI covered in topic 7.5). Also, MAP is a term frequently used by programmers when referring to any screen format.

In developing the MAPs, you may uncover a need for additional information that didn't surface earlier. This is because, in developing MAPs, you must specify whether data fields are alphanumeric or numeric, what COBOL PICTURE clauses should define them as the data is entered, and what COBOL PICTURE clauses should define them as they are displayed back on the screen to the user. This happens because, as BMS develops the machine-level module for CICS to use when displaying and retrieving data from your application screen, it also produces COBOL 01-level data descriptions that you can COPY into your COBOL application.

Also, depending on what type terminals your users use, you may want to clarify what features of the terminals should be used, such as color or highlighting. For example, if a terminal has extended color capability, you will improve the effectiveness of the transaction by using different colors for different sections of the screen or different functions (e.g., flagging fields in error in the color red.) Since some of that is beyond the needs of the new CICS programmer, I won't touch on all of these features in this book but will cover the most frequent options. Again, because this is a learning book, I have BMS in two different chapters, one for basics and a later one that addresses more screen design techniques.

Since our first transaction won't require retrieving formatted data from a screen, we will cover the basic use of BMS in Chapter 3. Although many textbooks present BMS immediately, I postponed this topic because I want you already to have seen/written a complete CICS transaction before coping with BMS.

2.3.6.   Top-Down Specifications

Develop top-down, structured programming specifications for each transaction. This should include a data flow of the transaction itself, allowing the user to see how the screen-to-screen flow will occur (see Figure 2.5). You may learn from the screen flow, also. *Note*: Many programmers who are proficient with CICS feel that structured programming is inefficient. Don't believe them. Yes, structured programming may require that the resulting application use slightly more computer resources (although not necessarily), but that will never match the cost of unstructured program development.

When I speak of top-down decomposition, I refer to the process of breaking each specification down into control and action components. While the specifics of applying this to a sample CICS application are covered later in this chapter, always strive to put control statements higher in your program structure and action/process statements lower. A properly decomposed program tends to have many small paragraphs resembling an organization chart.

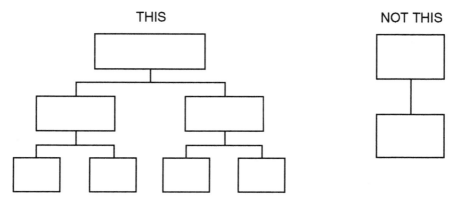

This is usually accomplished by deciding *what* must be done, not *how* it must be done. While this topic is more thoroughly covered in my *Power Programming* books, here are some general guidelines:

1. Decompose specifications or processes into subordinate processes. For example, a box in original design specifications might state "Send reply screen." Such a process might easily be decomposed into this:

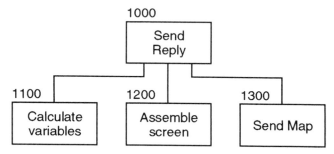

Notice also how each box name begins with a verb and how, cumulatively, the three lower boxes represent the function stated in the higher box. By combining the number at the top of the box with the verb, you can formulate meaningful paragraph names. What COBOL code is in the higher box? Probably some PER-FORM statements and some IF statements to check status of the results from the PERFORMed paragraphs. This approach is much easier to debug than where a programmer does it all in one paragraph. *Note*: In this book, you will typically find that I label the first paragraph as just "1." No verb, no fancy explanation. Why? Because, for the name of the first paragraph to follow the guideline of identifying the decomposition to follow would require that the name be many paragraphs long. Normally, such documentation is available elsewhere.

2. Ensure that each box on your structure chart represents only one COBOL paragraph. See the above for an example. If a box represents a PERFORM THRU structure, the structure becomes lost and soon disappears entirely.

3. Isolate functions. Again, see the previous example. Whenever you have several functions together, maintenance of the program suffers. Also, programmers who want their program to look structured and follow the second guideline will often write long, multiple-page, nested IF statements. I have nothing against nested IF statements, but they should be used for a single function.

4. Separate one-time processes from repetitive processes. You will see how useful this is in a CICS program shortly. The problem with mixing one-time and repetitive processes is that you invariably must set switches to ensure you don't do a one-time process twice.

5. Use structured programming techniques. If you follow the first four guidelines, you're probably on safe ground, but I still encounter programmers who write code that doesn't have one-entry and one-exit for the program itself and for each paragraph. How do you know if you are really doing structured programming? Here's a simple checklist, possible only with COBOL II:

   a. No GO TO statements, not even to an EXIT statement
   b. No EXIT statements (gotcha!)
   c. One paragraph, one period. (That's right, a paragraph should be just one sentence — not one statement, one sentence.)
   d. The exit for the program should be from within the first paragraph.
   e. No use of PERFORM THRU, as that automatically declares that you anticipate multiple functions will be executed (and violates rules a and b above).

6. Be consistent in developing structure charts. Notice the numbering used in the example in guideline one. My recommendation is to use a number for subordinate paragraphs that includes the first digit of the higher level. I suggest that the highest-level paragraph be numbered 0 or 1, the next level increment by 1000, the next level by 100, and the next level by 10. That would give a sample leg of a structure chart as follows:

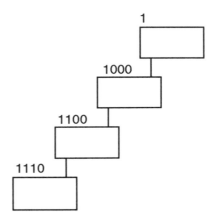

This type of numbering standard ensures that the parentage for any paragraph is immediately obvious. (I realize that your company may have its own standards, and I'm not encouraging you to not follow them. Still, if your company's standards do not make the family tree of any paragraph immediately obvious, maybe your company should be the one that changes.)

Clearly, top-down development is a major component of your success and will be demonstrated in sample programs. While this may seem "old hat" to you, many CICS transactions which you will encounter at your shop violate many of these guidelines. There are still CICS programmers who do it consciously, wanting to extract every possible CPU cycle to reduce response time. Some early books and articles used terms such as working set and locality of reference to help programmers ensure as much code as possible was crammed together for efficiency. These were techniques to reduce the overhead caused by virtual storage paging (an operating system function). In the 1970s, this may have been useful, but the concern is irrelevant today.

What these early techniques ignore is the cost of maintenance and development. There's no reason novice CICS programmers can't produce a reasonably efficient CICS transaction on their first assignment. Don't let the "efficiency technicians" get you down.

2.3.7. Application Development

Finally, it's time to write and test each transaction. There are various tools on the market, including some from IBM, to assist you in trapping errors. This can assure you that the application is working properly. A well-designed system should not abend and should at least perform the business requirements. Actually, testing online applications is usually easier than testing batch applications because you can enter a variety of data quickly and get direct feedback on whether the data was accepted or not.

By following these seven steps, your programs should start to stand out from others who ignore application documentation or who don't like to work hand in hand with the user. Always remember that it is only the user who can say your application was successful. Stay close to their needs and your systems will always be a success.

Figure 2.8 summarizes the seven key steps. After you are comfortable with coding and executing CICS programs and MAPs, I encourage you to reread this section of the book. I value the information here because I can use it for CICS, for batch, or for any interactive design approach used with user personnel.

```
1.    Get clear written specifications for the work
      environment.
2.    Review the data and transaction flow.
3.    Design the screens and walk through with the
      user.
4.    After approval, establish the CICS mechanics.
5.    Develop the MAPs for all intended screens.
6.    Develop top-down, structured programming
      specifications.
7.    Write and test each transaction.
```

Figure 2.8. Steps to ensure quality in application development.

2.4.   DEVELOPING A SIMPLE TRANSACTION

Finally, your first transaction. Our goal here is to get a simple CICS program written and executed. To accomplish that, we will bypass the added complexity of MAPs. While that is not the normal approach, it will get your first transaction operational more quickly and may give you some ideas on ways to simplify other transactions on which you may work. Yes, MAPs make a transaction more friendly but also more complex. If you need to develop a simple transaction for a limited audience, going without MAPs (at least for parts of the transaction) can be a timesaver.

This first transaction will be nonconversational, it will receive data from the terminal, formulate a response, send the response, and then terminate. This can be a productive transaction environment but, for whatever reason, isn't common in CICS shops.

2.4.1.   The Basic Transaction

In this, our basic transaction, the specification will be a simple yes/ no response. While simple, the transaction has opportunities for many situations where more complicated programming isn't justified.

The dialogue should always be reviewed first. After all, if the dialogue doesn't make sense, the transaction won't either. In our sample situation, the terminal user simply wants confirmation of the employee status of a given individual. Assuming that a company keeps an employee database based on social security number, one should be able to inquire by social security number and determine whether the person is a current employee or not. (*Note*: The actual logic of reading the employee file and determining employee status is irrelevant to the example, so the code for it is omitted from the examples.)

Accomplishing this could be done with a fancy menu and prompts, but let's take the simple route. The user will type in the social security number and the transaction will return an explanatory statement. Nothing more, nothing less.

Basic data flow:

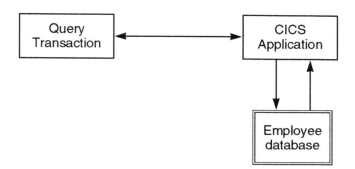

Executing this simple transaction requires that the social security number be available on screen and that the response be accessible. No problem. Doing that requires only two CICS commands. The basic syntax for each of them is in Figure 2.9.

Naturally (?), these are only the basics of these two commands. As you will find further on, CICS commands have a rich variety of features and far exceed the limited offerings shown here. The examples shown here are only for our initial experiments. In later sections, we will expand on these fundamentals. (*Note*: As demonstrated, CICS normally needs to know the name of any involved data area plus the length of the data area. When using COBOL II, you will sometimes find that the LENGTH parameter is not needed. Since COBOL II is sensitive to CICS, you will see some differences in this book about how commands must be structured with and without COBOL II.)

```
FUNCTION:    Receives data directly from screen into
             program. Does not use MAP.
  EXEC CICS
        RECEIVE
        [INTO    (dataname)]    <== receiving area
        LENGTH  (dataname)      <== length of
  END-EXEC                          receiving area

FUNCTION:    Sends line(s) of text to a terminal.
             Being unformatted, no MAP is used.
  EXEC CICS
        SEND TEXT
        FROM    (dataname)      <== name of data area
        [LENGTH (length)]       <== not required for
  END-EXEC                          COBOL II
```

Figure 2.9. Example of CICS commands without MAPs.

CICS RECEIVE command. The first example is a CICS command that receives data from a terminal but in unformatted mode. That means that the CICS command reads data directly from the screen. The keyword INTO identifies the name of the data area (normally an 01-level entry) where CICS is to place the received data. The LENGTH keyword identifies the name of a data area that contains the length of the receiving area. The LENGTH data area must be PIC S9(4) COMP. Here is an example:

```
01  WS-INPUT-FIELD.
    05  WS-TRAN-FIELD PIC  X(4).
    05  PIC X.
    05  WS-DATA-FIELD PIC  X(15).

01  INPUT-LENGTH-FLD  PIC  S9(4) COMP VALUE +20.
           .
           .
           .
    EXEC CICS RECEIVE
           INTO    (WS-INPUT-FIELD)
           LENGTH  (INPUT-LENGTH-FLD)
    END-EXEC
```

Did you notice that the LENGTH keyword is different for the RECEIVE and SEND? You should note the difference. One is a dataname and the other can be either a dataname or a literal. Why the difference? The difference exists because *any CICS command that causes data to be placed into your program must have a data area where CICS can store the length of the actual data received.* In the above example, the program specified a length of 20. After the CICS command has executed, the value in INPUT-LENGTH-FLD will be the number of bytes actually received, which could be less (an acceptable situation) or more than 20 (not normally acceptable, since the data area isn't large enough to store the data.) (*Reminder*: If that 05 level entry with no name is bothering you, remember that I will occasionally intermix COBOL II constructs in the book. COBOL II does not require FILLER for such entries.)

If this command is executed as the first CICS command in your program, it will read whatever you typed in to execute the program. For example, let's assume the transaction identifier is C123. To execute the transaction would require that you type in C123 and press Enter. Simple. However, it also demonstrates that *anything* else that you type in could also be read by the transaction. This flexibility lets you allow the user to specify additional information, since the transaction can directly retrieve it. For example, assume the user wants to inquire about a person with the social security number of 555-12-1234. Here is what the screen would look like after entering the transaction AND the social security number (see Figure 2.10).

```
C123,555-12-1234
```

Figure 2.10. Example of variable data with transaction code.

When the RECEIVE command is executed, the following information is retrieved into the program's I/O area:

```
C123,555-12-1234
```

As you can see, the data consists not only of the social security number but the transaction identifier *and* the comma. To process the data, the transaction would have needed a data area defined something like the following:

```
01   DATA-AREA.
     05   TRANS-ID  PIC  X(4).
     05   FILLER    PIC  X.
     05   SSN       PIC  X(11).
```

The CICS command to retrieve the data would be the following:

```
EXEC CICS
     RECEIVE
     INTO (DATA-AREA)
     LENGTH (LEN-FLD)
END-EXEC
```

Simple? I think so, too. This command simply reads whatever was entered on the screen and stores it. Although a simple program, I encourage you to develop it.

Likewise, the response command (SEND TEXT) is simple. It consists merely of the text that must be presented at the user terminal. A sample format might be the following:

```
01   RESPONSE-AREA.
     05   FILLER    PIC  X(22)    VALUE
          'SSN search results:    '.
     05   RESP-STATUS    PIC  X(10).
```

CICS SEND TEXT command. The SEND TEXT command sends a string of text characters, unformatted, to the screen. This is useful if you are not using formatted screens, or if you just want a termination message to be written to the screen. The keyword FROM identifies the data area that contains the text to be sent. The LENGTH keyword specifies the length of the data area. As identified earlier, the LENGTH keyword may be either a literal or a data area for CICS commands that do not move data into the applications data areas. Therefore, the LENGTH keyword could be a numeric literal or the dataname of a numeric field. If the dataname option is used, the LENGTH field must be defined as PIC S9(4) COMP.

Assuming that the program verified the SSN status first and then moved the appropriate value to RESP-STATUS, a sample response might be the following:

```
MOVE  'Employee'  TO  RESP-STATUS
EXEC  CICS
      SEND  TEXT
      FROM  (RESPONSE-AREA)
      LENGTH  (32)
END-EXEC
```

Is it starting to look simple? I hope so. What follows is the simple and complete CICS program (the read of the file is slightly more involved, but only marginally). Making the program more bullet-proof will require some additional instructions, but I omit them here to present the fundamental CICS functions.

Incidentally, did you notice in the above example that I used upper- and lower-case text for the response? Most people prefer text that is a combination of upper and lower case to text that is all upper case. (Can you imagine reading this book if every word were upper case? Within minutes you would find it tiring.) Despite the obviousness of this, most programmers still design online screens and associated messages using all upper case. Keep this in mind as we continue through the book.

2.4.2. The Sample Program

Not surprisingly, the program hasn't much logic. Despite its simplic- ity, you will learn a lot about CICS if you write, compile, and execute such a transaction. After all, your knowledge is the only reason we're working on this, isn't it? And going through the motions of developing and testing a simple transaction will add many subtle skills to your inventory. Much of the magic disappears as you do it yourself. (*Please note*: This early program (and some others to follow) do *not* represent recommended practices for the professional programmer. They are solely intended to demonstrate the basic functions of CICS applica- tions. A quality CICS program does extensive validation of input and checks for possible conditions that could occur. At this time, including that extra logic would prevent you from seeing the underlying structure. We'll add the extra logic shortly.)

The program is presented in several flavors to represent various programming techniques. This is a nonconversational transaction (it responds only once and then terminates). Nonconversational transac- tions aren't popular today because it takes so many to complete a unit of work. Their strength, however, is that they consume the least computer resources. They also are the only transactions where it is often feasible to code them as one l-o-n-g paragraph, since there is minimal need for structure. See Figure 2.11 for examples of the design structure for nonconversational programs.

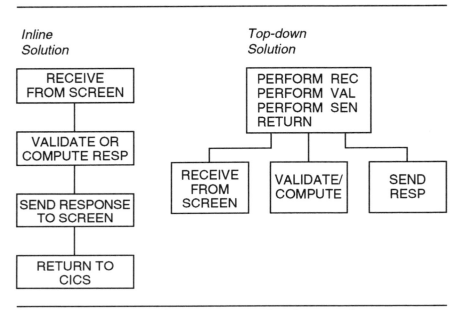

Figure 2.11. Structures for non-conversational transaction.

I picked a nonconversational transaction for your first program because it is the simplest. To review the program, see Figures 2.12, 2.13, and 2.14 for examples of various approaches to this problem. (Remember, none of these represents a complete solution to the vagaries of online systems, which would include appropriate measures to cope with unanticipated I/O or programming errors. We will study such additions later, after the basics are in place.)

Figure 2.12 is the simplest of CICS programs, receiving information, validating it (not shown for purposes of simplicity), sending a response to the terminal, and then returning control to CICS. This example (as are Figures 2.13 and 2.14) is *not conversational*, as it terminates after each inquiry. Since most of your CICS programs will be conversational (pseudoconversational, actually), don't look to this program as a model. Also, all program examples in this book will have upper case for all COBOL statements. I do this to ensure that COBOL statements are clearly defined. If you are using COBOL II, you may code the statements in lower case if desired.

Figure 2.13 is identical to Figure 2.12, except that it uses some minor features of COBOL II. Since I prefer COBOL II in all ways, I will strive to ensure you see differences in key examples.

From these examples, I hope you got the gist of a simple nonconversational transaction. The program must receive data, validate the data, and send a response. In conversational transactions, the program must also keep appropriate information available for the next part of the dialogue.

While all of the examples in Figures 2.12 through 2.14 work fine, none of them are capable of responding to routine user errors. So, while you need to appreciate the basic structure, remember that we need to add some "armor-resistant code" as we develop professional transactions. (Okay, okay, yes I do have a preference among the three examples. Figure 2.14 represents top-down decomposition, a technique that will always improve the quality of your code. Perfect? No. Strategic and bullet-resistant? Without a doubt.)

Reminder: If COBOL II is new to you, review the differences in the various examples. While the logic and approach are intentionally identical, there are minor differences. For example, FILLER is not required with COBOL II. Also, IF statements may be ended with END-IF instead of a period. Small differences, yes, but major differences in style and concept. Throughout the book, I will demonstrate differences in VS/COBOL and COBOL II. In most cases, the main difference will be that VS/COBOL only supports ANSI 74 standards, whereas COBOL II supports the ANSI 85 standard. Complete explanations of differences are in my *COBOL II Power Programming* books (one for MVS, one for VSE), available from QED.

Although the SSN validation was omitted (because it was just traditional application programming), I encourage you to develop this simple application to help you begin to feel that you really do know the CICS environment. I assure you that, no matter how simple the transaction, you will learn many aspects of your shop's use of CICS.

Expansion of example. If a simple file structure already exists at your shop, you might be able to use it for simple inquiry in a later extension of this sample program. For example, if your company has a file that contains employee information and is organized by employee number, the sample program could be easily expanded to use it.

```
IDENTIFICATION DIVISION.
PROGRAM-ID.   SAMPLE.
DATA DIVISION.
WORKING-STORAGE SECTION.

01   RESPONSE-AREA.
     05   FILLER   PIC X(21)   VALUE
          'SSN search results:   '.
     05   RESP-STATUS    PIC X(15).

01   DATA-AREA.
     05   TRANS-ID PIC X(4).
     05   FILLER   PIC X.
     05   SSN      PIC X(11).

01   DATA-LENGTH   PIC S9(4)   COMP   VALUE   +16.

LINKAGE SECTION.
PROCEDURE DIVISION.
1.   EXEC CICS
               RECEIVE
               INTO   (DATA-AREA)
               LENGTH (DATA-LENGTH)
     END-EXEC

     PERFORM CHECK-VALID-SSN            <=== not shown
     IF VALID-SSN                       <=== not shown
        MOVE 'Valid employee' TO RESP-STATUS
     ELSE
        MOVE 'Not an employee' TO RESP-STATUS.
     EXEC CICS
               SEND TEXT
               FROM   (RESPONSE-AREA)
               LENGTH (36)
     END-EXEC
     EXEC CICS
               RETURN
     END-EXEC
     GOBACK.
```

Figure 2.12. Sample of inline approach to basic program.

```
IDENTIFICATION DIVISION.
PROGRAM-ID.   SAMPLE.
DATA DIVISION.
WORKING-STORAGE SECTION.

01 RESPONSE-AREA.
   05          PIC X(21)    VALUE
        'SSN search results:   '.
   05  RESP-STATUS    PIC X(15).

01 DATA-AREA.
   05  TRANS-ID  PIC X(4).
   05            PIC X.
   05  SSN       PIC X(11).

01 DATA-LENGTH   PIC S9(4)   COMP   VALUE   +16.

LINKAGE SECTION.
PROCEDURE DIVISION.
1. EXEC CICS
           RECEIVE
           INTO    (DATA-AREA)
           LENGTH (DATA-LENGTH)
   END-EXEC

   PERFORM CHECK-VALID-SSN            <=== not shown
   IF VALID-SSN                       <=== not shown
      MOVE 'Valid employee' TO RESP-STATUS
   ELSE
      MOVE 'Not an employee' TO RESP-STATUS
   END-IF
   EXEC CICS
           SEND TEXT
           FROM (RESPONSE-AREA)
   END-EXEC
   EXEC CICS
           RETURN
   END-EXEC
   GOBACK.
```

Figure 2.13. Inline COBOL II approach to basic program.

```
IDENTIFICATION DIVISION.
PROGRAM-ID.   SAMPLE.
DATA DIVISION.
WORKING-STORAGE SECTION.

01   RESPONSE-AREA.
     05          PIC X(21)    VALUE
          'SSN search results:   '.
     05   RESP-STATUS    PIC X(15).

01   DATA-AREA.
     05   TRANS-ID   PIC  X(4).
     05              PIC  X.
     05   SSN        PIC  X(11).

01   DATA-LENGTH     PIC S9(4)   COMP   VALUE   +16.

LINKAGE SECTION.
PROCEDURE DIVISION.
1.   PERFORM 100-RECEIVE-DATA
     PERFORM 200-VALIDATE-DATA
     PERFORM 300-SEND-RESPONSE
     EXEC CICS
            RETURN
     END-EXEC
     GOBACK.

100-RECEIVE-DATA.
     EXEC CICS
            RECEIVE
            INTO   (DATA-AREA)
            LENGTH (DATA-LENGTH)
     END-EXEC.

200-VALIDATE-DATA.
     PERFORM CHECK-VALID-SSN              <=== not shown
     IF VALID-SSN                         <=== not shown
        MOVE 'Valid employee' TO RESP-STATUS
```

Figure 2.14. Sample of top-down approach to basic program.

```
ELSE
    MOVE 'Not an employee' TO RESP-STATUS
END-IF.

300-SEND-RESPONSE.
    EXEC CICS
             SEND TEXT
             FROM (RESPONSE-AREA)
             LENGTH (36)
    END-EXEC.
```

Figure 2.14. (cont'd). Sample of top-down approach to basic program.

The sample program presented in this section does not represent the majority of CICS transactions, although it could probably replace many of them at less cost. I offer it to you for practice in learning CICS without the added burden of mastering BMS for developing MAPs. One skill at a time is my motto (or rather, one of my many mottos).

As I mentioned previously, the structure of nonconversational transactions is sufficiently different from most transactions that you should not use it as a model. As you begin to develop conversational (whether pseudo or not) transactions, you will see major differences.

Since we haven't covered JCL yet, see your supervisor, teacher, or coach for appropriate JCL for your shop. That ensures that you don't have to figure out the compile process. Also, don't forget the prior topic on CICS mechanics. If CICS is not aware of your program name and desired transaction code, it won't allow the program to run. So get your load module (MVS) or phase (VSE) name defined in the PPT, along with a transaction identifier in the PCT (these are normally assigned according to company standards, since they are only four characters long).

2.5. DEVELOPING A SIMPLE PSEUDOCONVERSATIONAL TRANSACTION

After developing a simple nonconversational transaction, let's transform it into a pseudoconversational program. No, it won't accomplish much, but our goal is to give you practice in the fundamentals. Once mastered, you can build major CICS systems from these fundamentals.

The pseudoconversational transaction stands apart from other CICS transactions in that it allows CICS to manage the environment. That requires that you understand some additional basics of CICS.

2.5.1. A Simple Pseudoconversational Transaction

Whether a transaction uses a menu or not, if it is conversational, there are certain basics that apply. First, let's review conversational versus pseudoconversational. In most shops, you will use pseudoconversational and *all* conversations in this book will be in pseudoconversational format.

Conversational transactions concepts. In a conversational transaction, the program issues a SEND command to the terminal, followed by a RECEIVE command, so the program sits in main memory waiting while the terminal user types in a response. There are valid situations where this is a proper approach, but it consumes unnecessary system resources for most applications. Since the transaction never relinquishes control, it creates a burden on the system.

Pseudoconversational transactions concepts. Pseudoconversational transactions are those that appear to be conversational but aren't. After issuing a SEND to the terminal, the pseudoconversational transaction relinquishes control to CICS, giving the necessary information on what program should receive control after the terminal user finishes typing in data. This technique will get more review in other sections, but a sample structure is in Figure 2.15. CICS is included in the figure to remind you that it plays an important role in such transactions. (CICS is involved with nonconversational transactions too, but only to initiate and terminate them.) With pseudoconversational transactions, CICS is used to manage the dialogue.

The main difference between Figure 2.15 and the structure in Figure 2.11 is that CICS is used to control subsequent responses. Where nonconversational transactions simply terminate and give control back to CICS, pseudoconversational transactions realize that a reply is needed and, instead of waiting for the reply, return control of the CPU to CICS. What makes them programmatically different from nonconversational transactions is in *how* they return control.

For the structure in Figure 2.15 to work, we need some extensions to the RETURN command. Up to this point, the RETURN command simply returned control to CICS, permanently ending the dialogue. Now we want control to be returned to CICS but only until another terminal response is received. That means we need some additional variables in the RETURN command. The new variables specify that CICS is to give control to the TRANSID specified (normally the same program, but not necessarily) and to give the storage area specified in COMMAREA to that program.

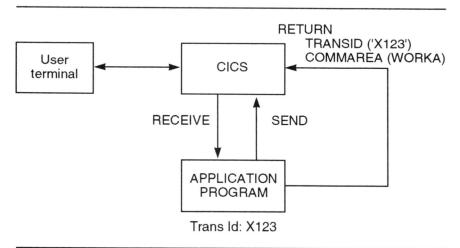

Figure 2.15. Pseudoconversational structure.

Using TRANSID. Up to now, I've mentioned the transaction identifier (TRANSID) a few times, but it may still be unclear. A program must have a TRANSID *only* if it will be given control directly from CICS. Otherwise, a program only needs to be defined in the PPT (the PCT is used for transaction ids). For example:

- If a program is initiated by a person sitting at a terminal, a TRANSID is needed.

- If a program is pseudoconversational and relinquishes control to CICS, requesting that it be given control when the user finishes entering data (specified with the RETURN command and TRANSID option), a TRANSID is needed.

While we haven't covered it yet, there are times when a program transfers control to another program during the dialogue. Since the transfer is from one program to another, no TRANSID is needed (unless that program fits one of the above two situations, also). This will become clearer as we proceed.

Using the COMMAREA. A consideration that will affect your program design is that, when CICS gives control to your program, it *always* initializes your program to its unused state (i.e., all WORKING-STORAGE entries contain the values that were specified at compile time). This means that, after SENDing a response to a terminal and executing the RETURN command with the TRANSID option, everything your program stored in WORKING-STORAGE is lost. There are several ways to keep the information accessible for subsequent dialogues with the same terminal, and the COMMAREA is the most commonly used.

The COMMAREA (specified as DFHCOMMAREA) is important, as it is a major facility that allows the application program to store variables that it will need later and is also used by programs to determine if the program is having its first contact with the user or is having a subsequent contact. The COMMAREA does not exist on the first execution of a transaction and it is the responsibility of the program, using the RETURN command, to identify a data area that CICS should copy and retain for subsequent executions. I say *copy* because the program will be reinitialized for the next use and the original data area will no longer contain the data. Unless the program stores any key information in the COMMAREA, it will have no idea of what has transpired to this point.

You will find the COMMAREA very important as you develop applications and need to keep information from one SEND to the next. The COMMAREA will always be returned to the program in the LINKAGE SECTION. (Remember the example compile listings in the previous section, Figures 2.3 and 2.4, where I mentioned that all the information necessary would eventually be found there? If you never developed the first sample program, you might want to revisit those listings to review the location of DFHCOMMAREA.)

In learning CICS, you also need to learn the maximum sizes of various data areas, as CICS uses fixed internal storage fields to contain these addresses. For example, a two-byte field can contain a binary address up to 32K, whereas a four-byte field can contain a binary address up to two gigabytes. Most CICS addresses are two-byte fields, including the internal address of the COMMAREA. That means that you cannot store more than 32,000 bytes of data in the COMMAREA, although you will rarely see a COMMAREA for a program that is larger than 1000 bytes, and many are only 10–20 bytes.

Small COMMAREAs exist because many companies have standards that restrict your setting the size of the COMMAREA. These standards were developed because CICS is sensitive to memory availability and everything you do that increases memory requirements for a transaction reduces the amount of memory available for other transactions. COBOL II did much to relieve this concern and, as more companies move to COBOL II, I expect this concern to lessen.

Using the EIB area. While we haven't covered it yet, the EIB (Executive Interface Block) is also important for conversational and pseudoconversational transactions. This is where CICS stores information that is of possible use to the application program. For example, this is where a programmer can determine what PF key was pressed, the location of the cursor, and the size of the DFHCOMMAREA, among other things. We will discuss this in detail as needed.

The RETURN Command. Our RETURN command has grown somewhat in this example. The format is in Figure 2.16. This is a commonly used command, and you will frequently see it in CICS programs. Remember that, depending on what variables are coded, it will either return control to CICS, specifying the next transaction ID (the dialogue is not finished) or unconditionally (the dialogue is complete). Also, the TRANSID in the command may be for a different program than the one just ending (we'll see that in a menu example that follows).

```
EXEC CICS
        RETURN
        [TRANSID   (name)
        [COMMAREA  (dataname)
        [LENGTH    (data-value)]]]
END-EXEC

FUNCTION:   Return to CICS. When TRANSID is specified,
            that program will receive control when the
            user presses a function key. If COMMAREA
            is specified, that workarea will be made
            available to the program in its LINKAGE
            SECTION. LENGTH (of COMMAREA) is needed
            for VS/COBOL, but optional for COBOL II.
```

Figure 2.16. RETURN command syntax (basic).

The RETURN command, as shown in Figure 2.16, can be coded in several different formats, one to give control back to CICS and one to specify the next transaction to receive control when the terminal user finishes entering data.

Basics of pseudoconversational transaction structure. The new features of the RETURN command are going to allow us to develop a pseudoconversational transaction. This is because we can now relinquish control to CICS with the knowledge that, once the terminal user finishes entering data, CICS will give control back to our (or another) prespecified program.

All pseudoconversational transactions share some common structural components, primarily in having one leg of the structure for the initial entry and one leg for subsequent entries. This gives us a triangular structure with each "box" doing these or similar functions:

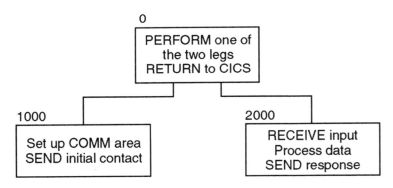

Top paragraph. Box 0 is (in well-structured programs) the first paragraph in the program, with all logic contained within that one paragraph. This paragraph must determine whether this is the first or a subsequent entry, give control to that processing path, and then return control to CICS. Also, depending on what processing decisions were made by the executed paths, this paragraph executes either a RETURN command (end of dialogue) or RETURN TRANSID command (dialogue not complete).

When transactions receive control directly from CICS, the most common technique to determine whether this is the first or a subsequent entry is to use the COMM area. This technique is possible because, on the first entry, there is no COMM area. Since one of the entries in the EIB (Execute Interface Block) contains the length of the

COMM area, this can be easily detected. The field is called EIBCALEN. To preserve this logic, it is important that the RETURN TRANSID command specify a COMM area. Doing so ensures that the length will be greater than 0 for subsequent entries. Therefore, one of the first instructions that you will see in a pseudoconversational transaction will be something like this:

```
IF  EIBCALEN  =  0
     PERFORM  1000-FIRST-ENTRY
ELSE
     PERFORM  2000-SUBSEQUENT-ENTRY
```

Our first program will use DFHCOMMAREA solely for this purpose, placing no values in it. That is why it is defined as just PIC X, ensuring it will have a non-zero length.

First entry paragraph(s). The processing leg for the first entry, shown as paragraph 1000 in the prior example, is usually used to initialize the COMM area (if needed), check any security issues (if any), and SEND any initial communication message. So far, the only SEND command you have seen is SEND TEXT, but the most common format is the SEND MAP, which we will cover shortly.

In our first example, this is a simple part of the transaction, but it will grow in size as our examples become more sophisticated. For our first program, we will leave it simple.

Subsequent entry paragraph(s). The subsequent entry logic path will be the most challenging to your structured programming skills. The goal is to RECEIVE the user's input, validate it, process it, format a reply on the screen, and SEND it back to the user. Also, this path usually determines if the transaction is logically complete, setting a flag for the highest-level paragraph (level 0 in the example) to either issue a RETURN or a RETURN TRANSID command. For our first example, all application processing logic is omitted so we can focus on the dialogue aspects.

First program. Our finished pseudoconversational program is in Figure 2.17. It's almost the same program as that shown in Figure 2.14, but it is capable of continuing the dialogue, responding to more than a request for a single employee SSN. Since most pseudoconversational transactions don't enter user data at inception (as our nonconversational transaction did by entering the SSN with the transaction ID), this transaction sends a request for each SSN. This improved version allows a terminal user to continue to enter more SSNs until the terminal user decides to terminate the dialogue by entering "Q" instead of a social security number. *Note*: Transactions should normally allow the terminal user to make the decision to terminate the dialogue, not the other way around. I could have chosen any code to signal a request to terminate.

```
IDENTIFICATION DIVISION.
PROGRAM-ID.   SAMPLE.
DATA DIVISION.
WORKING-STORAGE SECTION.

01 RESPONSE-AREA.
   05   FILLER    PIC X(21)   VALUE
        'SSN search results:   '.
   05   RESP-STATUS    PIC X(15).

01 INITIAL-MESSAGE.
   05   FILLER    PIC X(22)   VALUE
        'Please enter first SSN'.

01 WORK-AREA.
   05   FILLER           PIC XXX.
   05   SSN-AREA.
        10  SSN-1ST-BYTE    PIC  X.
        10  FILLER          PIC  X(11).

01 WORK-LENGTH        PIC S9(4)  COMP  VALUE  +15.

01 MY-COMMAREA    PIC X.

LINKAGE SECTION.
01 DFHCOMMAREA    PIC X.

PROCEDURE DIVISION.
1. IF EIBCALEN = 0
        PERFORM 100-SETUP-FIRST-ENTRY
   ELSE
        PERFORM 200-PROCESS-SUBSEQUENT.
   IF SSN-1ST-BYTE    NOT = 'Q'
        EXEC CICS
                RETURN
```

Figure 2.17. Sample of pseudoconversational approach to basic program.

```
                        TRANSID  ('A001')
                        COMMAREA (MY-COMMAREA)
                        LENGTH   (1)
            END-EXEC
      ELSE
            EXEC CICS RETURN
            END-EXEC.
      GOBACK.

100-SETUP-FIRST-ENTRY.
      EXEC CICS
                SEND TEXT
                FROM (INITIAL-MESSAGE)
                LENGTH (22)
                ERASE
      END-EXEC.

200-PROCESS-SUBSEQUENT.
      PERFORM 210-RECEIVE-DATA
      IF SSN-1ST-BYTE    NOT = 'Q'
           PERFORM 220-VALIDATE-DATA
           PERFORM 230-SEND-RESPONSE.

210-RECEIVE-DATA.
      EXEC CICS
                RECEIVE
                INTO (WORK-AREA)
                LENGTH (WORK-LENGTH)
      END-EXEC.

220-VALIDATE-DATA.
      PERFORM 221-CHECK-VALID-SSN            <== Not shown
      IF VALID-SSN                           <== Not shown
         MOVE 'Valid employee' TO RESP-STATUS
      ELSE
         MOVE 'Not an employee' TO RESP-STATUS.

230-SEND-RESPONSE.
      EXEC CICS
                SEND TEXT
                FROM (RESPONSE-AREA)
                LENGTH (36)
                ERASE
      END-EXEC.
```

Figure 2.17. (cont'd). Sample of pseudoconversational approach to basic program.

From Figure 2.17, you should see the three basic elements that I identified earlier: (1) the primary paragraph, (2) the first entry path, and (3) the subsequent path. This is *not* a program that you should model productional programs after. Yes, it works fine, but it requires some careful terminal manipulation. Since this is a technically incomplete transaction, you need to avoid creating any error conditions. This program requires that, prior to entering a SSN, you first home the cursor and press the EraseEOF key. Since this introductory transaction sends unformatted text to the screen (using the terminal similar to a typewriter terminal), there are some garbage bytes left within the terminal environment.

For example, notice how the input area, WORK-AREA, has a three-byte FILLER at the beginning of the record. This is because the terminal, not CICS, leaves some garbage in the buffer that is transmitted on the next RECEIVE. Pressing the CLEAR key would eliminate it, but it would also cause CICS to take control. Executing this simple transaction requires that you follow these steps:

1. Press the CLEAR key, followed by entering the TRANSID (in this example, 'A001'. That starts the transaction.

2. When it responds with a request for the first SSN, backspace the cursor to the beginning of the line, type in an SSN, followed by pressing the EraseEOF key. Then press Enter. I emphasize the EraseEOF key because you may otherwise cause your transaction to abend due to LENGERR (receiving more bytes of data than anticipated).

3. Terminate the transaction by entering 'Q', followed by pressing EraseEOF. The transaction ends but leaves the screen "dirty."

Okay, if this transaction is so clumsy, why did we do it? Because it is a simple way to gain some experience with CICS. If you enter more bytes of data than the RECEIVE is anticipating, the transaction will abend — so be careful. In future transactions, we will prevent such problems. For now, including the extra instructions to bulletproof the transaction would hide the structure from you.

For comparison, I have included a sample of the same program coded in COBOL II. (*Note*: The prior example would compile and execute just fine with COBOL II. When I reference COBOL II, I do so to demonstrate some features that are available to you that are *not* available with VS/COBOL.) Compare the code in Figure 2.18 with that from 2.17. These are small differences, but the importance will be more evident later.

```
TITLE  'Dave's example of COBOL II for this transaction'
ID DIVISION.
PROGRAM-ID.   SAMPLE.
DATA DIVISION.
WORKING-STORAGE SECTION.

01 RESPONSE-AREA.
   05          PIC X(21)    VALUE
        'SSN search results:   '.
   05   RESP-STATUS    PIC X(15).

01 INITIAL-MESSAGE.
   05          PIC X(22)    VALUE
        'Please enter first SSN'.

01 WORK-AREA.
   05                 PIC XXX.
   05   SSN-AREA      PIC X(12).

01 WORK-LENGTH      PIC S9(4)   COMP   VALUE   +15.

01 MY-COMMAREA    PIC X.

LINKAGE SECTION.
01 DFHCOMMAREA    PIC X.

PROCEDURE DIVISION.
1. IF EIBCALEN = 0
       PERFORM 100-SETUP-FIRST-ENTRY
   ELSE
       PERFORM 200-PROCESS-SUBSEQUENT
   END-IF
   IF SSN-AREA (1:1)    NOT = 'Q'
       EXEC CICS
               RETURN
               TRANSID  ('A001')
               COMMAREA MY-COMMAREA)
       END-EXEC
   ELSE
```

Figure 2.18. Sample of pseudoconversational approach to basic program in COBOL II.

```
            EXEC CICS RETURN
            END-EXEC.

100-SETUP-FIRST-ENTRY.
    EXEC CICS
            SEND TEXT
            FROM (INITIAL-MESSAGE)
            ERASE
    END-EXEC.

200-PROCESS-SUBSEQUENT.
    PERFORM 210-RECEIVE-DATA
    IF SSN-AREA (1:1) NOT = 'Q'
        PERFORM 220-VALIDATE-DATA
        PERFORM 230-SEND-RESPONSE.

210-RECEIVE-DATA.
    EXEC CICS
            RECEIVE
            INTO (WORK-AREA)
            LENGTH (WORK-LENGTH)
    END-EXEC.

220-VALIDATE-DATA.
    PERFORM 221-CHECK-VALID-SSN          <== Not shown
    IF VALID-SSN                         <== Not shown
        MOVE 'Valid employee' TO RESP-STATUS
    ELSE
        MOVE 'Not an employee' TO RESP-STATUS
    END-IF.

230-SEND-RESPONSE.
    EXEC CICS
            SEND TEXT
            FROM (RESPONSE-AREA)
            ERASE
    END-EXEC.
```

Figure 2.18. (cont'd). Sample of pseudoconversational approach to basic program in COBOL II.

In Figure 2.18, there are some COBOL II commands that may appear unfamiliar. One is the statement, TITLE. Haven't you frequently wanted to put a title on each page of a program listing? Well, each use of TITLE causes a page eject and a change of title. Neat stuff! Another new command is

```
IF SSN-AREA (1:1) NOT = 'Q'...
```

This is the *Reference Modification* feature of COBOL II, whereby you can reference specific bytes within a data area. In this example, I am referring to the first byte, for a length of one byte. With VS/COBOL, you achieve the same result by using the REDEFINES clause for SSN-AREA, such as the following:

```
05  SSN-AREA       PIC  X(11).
05  NEW-SSN-AREA  REDEFINES  SSN-AREA.
    10  SSN-1ST-BYTE        PIC  X.
    10  FILLER              PIC  X(10).
```

You might be thinking, "Why not just test SSN-AREA for a 'Q'?" Well, if this were a non-CICS application, I would agree that, since COBOL assumes remaining bytes are spaces, that would work fine. With CICS, however, only the data entered at the terminal is transmitted to the application with the RECEIVE command, with trailing bytes being filled with LOW-VALUES. This is an issue that you need to remember and will be discussed further in a later chapter. (*Note*: This is not true with MAPs, as data fields are formatted with RECEIVE MAP commands.)

You also spotted the END-IF clause, didn't you? I prefer this because it eliminates the need to use a period. Did you also notice that periods are scarce in both examples? That is because I try to keep the structure clear and simple. Surprisingly, COBOL sentences do more harm to a program's structure than almost any other thing you could do. This issue is covered in-depth in my Power Programming books, mentioned previously.

Did you notice that FILLER isn't used? That is one of those changes that should have been done years ago, isn't it? Did you notice the use of ID DIVISION? That option, using ID or IDENTIFICATION, may seem simple, but just how many six-syllable words do you know? I don't think I know any, except for IDENTIFICATION. Anything that reduces keystrokes or mental spelling improves my productivity.

Finally, you noticed the LENGTH parameter was omitted from CICS commands that send data outward. That is because COBOL II provides that information without your needing to code it. No magic, just a new addition to COBOL syntax that appears in the CICS-generated COBOL code. A comparison of the differences between code generated for VS/COBOL and for COBOL II is in Figure 2.19. This is caused by a PARM parameter passed to the CICS translator (covered later).

```
VS/COBOL-Generated Code:
*EXEC CICS
*          SEND TEXT
*          FROM (INITIAL-MESSAGE)
*          LENGTH (22)
*          ERASE
*END-EXEC.
      MOVE  '          00047       '  TO  DFHEIVO
      MOVE 22 TO DFHEIV11
      CALL 'DFHEI1' USING DFHEIVO DFHDUMMY INITIAL-MESSAGE
                    DFHEIV11.

VS/COBOL II-Generated Code:
*EXEC CICS
*          SEND TEXT
*          FROM (INITIAL-MESSAGE)
*          ERASE
*END-EXEC.
      MOVE  '          00043       '  TO  DFHEIVO
      MOVE LENGTH OF  INITIAL-MESSAGE  TO  DFHB0020
      CALL 'DFHEI1' USING DFHEIVO DFHDUMMY INITIAL-MESSAGE
                    DFHB0020.
```

Figure 2.19. Example of difference between generated code for COBOL II.

Again, no magic. COBOL II is capable of providing the length of any data element, so the LENGTH parameter isn't needed (but can be used, if desired, for compatibility with VS/COBOL). *Note:* The LENGTH keyword is still needed for RECEIVEd data, as CICS updates the field with the length of the data as received.

If you've been using COBOL II, none of this is new. If you haven't, I admit to teasing you a bit. Migrating to COBOL II is important for your career growth and for your company's technical expansion. I review some differences in a separate chapter, but I will try to demonstrate key features of it throughout the book. Wherever there are major differences in the coding logic (such as an END-IF in the middle of a paragraph), I will show the VS/COBOL approach or both approaches.

This first complete transaction is clumsy, not very user-friendly, and doesn't use the online terminal to advantage. Still, it has all the basics. The main problem it has with the environment is that it is subject to being abended by CICS, not because of any normal error, such as a divide by zero, but by not acknowledging CICS condition codes. This isn't the first time that I've mentioned that these early transactions are not "good" transactions. Their problem is that, because no code is imbedded to cope with error conditions, the programs are subject to abnormal termination. Yes, they work fine if you're careful, but the sample program will abend if the string of input characters for a SSN is too long. That isn't professionally acceptable. The next section will add some armor to the transactions you develop. After all, if your transaction abends, it is useless.

2.6.   TRAPPING CICS-ERRORS IN THE TRANSACTION

Earlier, I mentioned that these first programs were incomplete and useful only for helping you see the underlying structure. So far, the programs we've worked with would be unacceptable in any shop, primarily because they do not have any code to test for possible error conditions from CICS commands.

Almost all CICS commands are capable of encountering an error condition. This can range from a 'record not found' on a READ command to an 'invalid request' with any command (invalid request means the keywords were either incorrect or contained improper values). Obviously, the second error is truly an error, while the first one ('record not found') may be acceptable to the program's logic. Whether a condition encountered by a CICS command is truly an error, then, depends largely on your program. Unless you take control within your program, your program will be subject to default CICS treatment.

2.6.1. Condition Code Options

With each CICS command, certain condition codes are returned. If you do not elect to handle them, you defer to CICS to make the decisions for you. My advice is always to handle your own condition codes, as CICS may easily handle the situations in ways that are not to your liking. For example, your application may anticipate a "record not found" condition when attempting to read a record. That isn't an error, only an indicator of what action to take. Here are the options you face (and don't expect more experienced programmers to understand all of this — many don't):

1. *Let CICS handle the issue.* This is the default and you never, never, never want this to happen. This happens with simple programs such as those that you have coded so far. I mentioned earlier that these are not really acceptable for production for just this reason. You accomplish this by omitting any direction in your CICS commands.

2. *Tell CICS the names of paragraphs that will handle the issue.* Once upon a time, this was your only option to retaining control. No longer. When you identify what paragraphs will handle various condition codes, you force your application to use many GO TO statements to keep a semblance of control. (This is done by the HANDLE CONDITION command, one that I do *not* recommend. More on this later.)

3. *Take charge.* That's right, this is my recommendation. For each CICS command, you retain control of your options when you specify the keyword, NOHANDLE, on a CICS command and include the additional keyword, RESP (dataname). NOHANDLE indicates to CICS that all condition codes are to be ignored by CICS, letting the application handle them. RESP indicates that CICS should place the condition code (i.e., the RESPonse code) in a COBOL data area. These two keywords can be used with any CICS command. This is the only way I write CICS applications. It's cleaner, and I retain control of how the application is written.

   RESP must point to a full-word data item (PIC S9(8) COMP). This data item may then be compared to known CICS condition codes to make application logic decisions.

2.6.2. Condition Code Concepts

For every possible CICS command, there are certain possible results that CICS considers to be an error. If your application does not inform

CICS that you will handle it, then CICS may terminate the transaction. That's what you clearly do *not* want. The next step (in fact, the *only* step prior to CICS release 1.6) was to specify HANDLE CONDITION commands to specify what COBOL paragraph should receive control for identified conditions. This was similar to the COBOL "GO TO DEPENDING ON" statement. It wasn't a structured approach, but it got the job done. Programs written in this era are normally examples of the "spaghetti-structure program design" technique. See Figure 2.20 for an example of how the HANDLE CONDITION command might be used with our simple program.

```
200-PROCESS-SUBSEQUENT.
    PERFORM 210-RECEIVE-DATA THRU 210-EXIT
    IF ERROR-SWITCH = 'N'
        IF SSN-AREA (1:1) NOT = 'Q'
            PERFORM 220-VALIDATE-DATA
            PERFORM 230-SEND-RESPONSE.

210-RECEIVE-DATA.
    EXEC CICS
        HANDLE CONDITION
        EOC     (211-EOC-CONDITION)
        LENGERR (212-LENGERR-CONDITION)
    END-EXEC

    EXEC CICS
        RECEIVE
        INTO (WORK-AREA)
        LENGTH (WORK-LENGTH)
    END-EXEC

    GO TO 210-EXIT.

211-EOC-CONDITION.
    GO TO 210-EXIT.

212-LENGERR-CONDITION.
    MOVE 'Y' TO ERROR-SWITCH.

210-EXIT.
    EXIT.
```

Figure 2.20. Example of HANDLE CONDITION command.

In Figure 2.20, the HANDLE CONDITION command specifies what paragraphs should receive control on specific conditions (for future CICS commands, I will identify the common conditions to anticipate). You will find that CICS is well structured and that all conditions have consistent abbreviations (in other words I didn't just think up EOC or LENGERR). As you can see, using HANDLE CONDITION required the PERFORM THRU statement (a consistent trouble-maker for structured programs) and several GO TO statements (barf!). Furthermore, it made the program more clumsy. Notice how I do nothing in the paragraph named 211-EOC-CONDITION. I needed to name it, yet I knew it was not a problem.

Closely related to the HANDLE CONDITION command is its opposite, the IGNORE CONDITION command. I'm sure you can visualize the complexity of a program where part of it requests global control of certain conditions and, in other parts of the program, asks that those requests be ignored. In comparison, the hated ALTER verb from the early days of COBOL doesn't seem that bad. I won't review the IGNORE CONDITION command except to make you aware of its existence and that it negates previously issued HANDLE commands.

In criticizing this technique, I have no ill will toward the programmers who developed earlier CICS transactions. As I mentioned, until CICS 1.6, this was the cleanest technique available. While I do not encourage you to attempt to rewrite any current program that meets the business need, I do encourage that you restructure such programs with your management's approval.

In this book I show you the HANDLE CONDITION command and (later) the HANDLE AID command. Both of them are detrimental to your productivity and to the readability of your programs. Yes, they will be found in older programs and you need to be aware of their presence, but please don't use such programs as models for future development. (*Note*: I occasionally encounter companies that mandate programming techniques that use the PERFORM THRU and EXIT statements. This is an indication that those companies never really understood the whole concept of structured programming.)

On the error codes themselves, one (possibly the only) major problem was that many programmers deduced that the CICS error conditions were nonnegotiable, — the transaction was going to abend no matter what. That just isn't the case. What CICS does is identify potential problems and give you the opportunity to assume authority for each/every condition. For example, when CICS release 1.7 became available, a new feature was available. Now, programs could specify that CICS was to stay "hands off." How? Just add the keyword NOHANDLE to any CICS command and you're home free. To find out what condition actually occurred, include the RESP keyword to identify where CICS should store the condition code encountered. Simple? You bet. All it means is that you need to add two keywords to *any* CICS command where you anticipate possible problems. For example, our CICS RECEIVE command from the sample programs (the only one in the sample that is really capable of trashing the application) might look like this:

```
EXEC CICS
          RECEIVE
          INTO    (WORK-AREA)
          LENGTH  (WORK-LENGTH)
          NOHANDLE
          RESP    (MY-CICS-RESP-AREA)
END-EXEC
```

Reminder: Earlier I mentioned that the LENGTH keyword was not always needed for COBOL II programs. That was incomplete. It is still needed for any CICS command that receives new data into the environment. In this example, the dataname called MY-CICS-RESP-AREA will contain the value of any CICS-detected condition. Also, the data-area must be PIC S9(8) COMP.

Okay, so I've told you how to gain control (NOHANDLE) and how to have access to the information (RESP), but I never told you what the condition codes were, did I? Unless you know what a particular value of RESP means (for example, a value of 20 means ENDFILE), the RESP field is useless. As mentioned earlier, CICS has standardized the names of all condition codes and provides a facility for you to code the value symbolically in your program. That is done by coding DFHRESP(symbolic-value) wherever you would use the value.

Unlike other CICS commands that are converted to comment statements (* in column 7) and followed by the real instructions, the DFHRESP facility causes the CICS translator to directly replace the DFHRESP statement with a literal value. See Figure 2.21 for an example of how this looks.

The statement as coded:

```
210-RECEIVE-DATA.
     EXEC CICS
               RECEIVE
               INTO     (WORK-AREA)
               LENGTH   (WORK-LENGTH)
               NOHANDLE
               RESP     (RESP-VALUE)
     END-EXEC

     IF RESP-VALUE NOT = DFHRESP(EOC) AND
                   NOT = DFHRESP(NORMAL)
          MOVE 'Y' TO ERROR-FLAG.
```

The statement as translated:

```
210-RECEIVE-DATA.
*EXEC CICS
*          RECEIVE
*          INTO    (WORK-AREA)
*          LENGTH  (WORK-LENGTH)
*          NOHANDLE
*          RESP    (RESP-VALUE)
*END-EXEC
     MOVE '  { 00079      ' TO DFHEIVO
     CALL 'DFHEI1' USING DFHEIVO WORK-AREA WORK-LENGTH
     MOVE EIBRESP TO RESP-VALUE

     IF RESP-VALUE NOT =   6      AND
                   NOT =   0
          MOVE 'Y' TO ERROR-FLAG.
```

Figure 2.21. Example of DFHRESP interpretation.

As Figure 2.21 shows, the statement is meaningful as written but loses meaning after being converted as it appears in the COBOL listing. While this works fine, it is difficult to understand when reading a COBOL listing and trying to determine what condition codes were being tested. There is an easier (and better) way.

2.6.3.   Condition Code COPYbook

Since the objective is to provide readable source listings, my recommendation is to use 88 levels for all of the possibilities. That simplifies your coding and preserves the source statements through the translator and COBOL listings. This is simply done, since the RESP keyword causes the condition code value to be moved to your own data area.

Doing this requires only that your shop establish a COPYbook member that contains the condition codes commonly used at your shop. For an example, see Figure 2.22.

In Figure 2.22, I defined most of the condition codes you will encounter. If you have such a COPYbook, it should be COPYed into your WORKING STORAGE section and the 01-level name referenced in all RESP keywords. This allows you to directly use the 88-level names directly. While unorthodox, I use this technique exclusively and encourage you to use it. All examples in this book assume the presence of this COPYbook member, CICSRESP. Remember, you must code it, but you only need to do it once, and it will greatly improve documentation of your shop's CICS applications. You will find a brief explanation of most CICS condition codes in Appendix A.

Let's get a brief look at how our simple transaction from Figure 2.17 would look. Refer to Figure 2.23.

Figure 2.23 shows more realistic code than our earlier examples, in that it includes tests for error conditions following the RECEIVE command. (Actually, any CICS command could generate error conditions, especially if coded incorrectly.) For our situation, I am focusing only on the one command that could be beyond a programmer's control. This example uses the COPYbook member shown in Figure 2.22 (as will all future examples).

Notice also how the program is designed to let the decision to terminate (whether due to the user entering a "Q" or due to an error) be handled by the highest-level paragraph. I coded several CICS commands within the one paragraph, and having more than one RETURN in the same paragraph may violate your shop standards. If so, I encourage you to pursue getting your shop standards changed. Some people may say this is just a style issue. Yes, but it is more than that. I firmly believe that well-designed CICS transactions are entered and exited from the same paragraph. In this book, I will keep RETURN statements in the first paragraph (where they belong). (Yes, you will find me opinionated about how CICS programs should be structured.) One entry and one exit are well understood. These two properties *must* always be together. If the RETURN is not inside the highest-level paragraph, then that paragraph violates structured programming guidelines by being PERFORMed and not returning to the PERFORMing paragraph.

```
*  -  CICS  Response  Code  Values ─────────────
   01  CICS-RESP-CODE              PIC  S9(8)  COMP    VALUE  +0.
       88  CICS-NORMAL             VALUE  +0.
       88  CICS-ERROR              VALUE  +1.
       88  CICS-RDATT              VALUE  +2.
       88  CICS-WRBRK              VALUE  +3.
       88  CICS-EOF                VALUE  +4.
       88  CICS-EODS               VALUE  +5.
       88  CICS-EOC                VALUE  +6.
       88  CICS-INBFMH             VALUE  +7.
       88  CICS-ENDINPT            VALUE  +8.
       88  CICS-NONVAL             VALUE  +9.
       88  CICS-NOSTART            VALUE  +10.
       88  CICS-TERMIDERR          VALUE  +11.
       88  CICS-DSIDERR            VALUE  +12.
       88  CICS-NOTFND             VALUE  +13.
       88  CICS-DUPREC             VALUE  +14.
       88  CICS-DUPKEY             VALUE  +15.
       88  CICS-INVREQ             VALUE  +16.
       88  CICS-IOERR              VALUE  +17.
       88  CICS-NOSPACE            VALUE  +18.
       88  CICS-NOTOPEN            VALUE  +19.
       88  CICS-ENDFILE            VALUE  +20.
       88  CICS-ILLOGIC            VALUE  +21.
       88  CICS-LENGERR            VALUE  +22.
       88  CICS-QZERO              VALUE  +23.
       88  CICS-SIGNAL             VALUE  +24.
       88  CICS-QBUSY              VALUE  +25.
       88  CICS-ITEMERR            VALUE  +26.
       88  CICS-PGMIDERR           VALUE  +27.
       88  CICS-TRANSIDERR         VALUE  +28.
       88  CICS-ENDDATA            VALUE  +29.
       88  CICS-INVTSREQ           VALUE  +30.
       88  CICS-EXPIRED            VALUE  +31.
       88  CICS-RETPAGE            VALUE  +32.
       88  CICS-RTEFAIL            VALUE  +33.
       88  CICS-RTESOME            VALUE  +34.
       88  CICS-TSIOERR            VALUE  +35.
       88  CICS-MAPFAIL            VALUE  +36.
       88  CICS-QIDERR             VALUE  +44.
       88  CICS-SYSIDERR           VALUE  +53.
       88  CICS-ISCINVREQ          VALUE  +54.
       88  CICS-ENQBUSY            VALUE  +55.
       88  CICS-ENVDEFERR          VALUE  +56.
       88  CICS-INVPARTNSET        VALUE  +64.
       88  CICS-INVPARTN           VALUE  +65.
       88  CICS-PARTNFAIL          VALUE  +66.
       88  CICS-NOAUTH             VALUE  +70.
       88  CICS-DISABLED           VALUE  +84.
```

Figure 2.22. Example of condition code COPYbook member, CICSRESP.

```
IDENTIFICATION DIVISION.
PROGRAM-ID.   SAMPLE.
DATA DIVISION.
WORKING-STORAGE SECTION.

01 RESPONSE-AREA.
    05   FILLER     PIC X(21)   VALUE
            'SSN search results:   '.
    05   RESP-STATUS   PIC X(15).

01 INITIAL-MESSAGE.
    05   FILLER     PIC X(22)   VALUE
            'Please enter first SSN'.

01 ERROR-MESSAGE.
    05   FILLER     PIC X(24)   VALUE
            'Terminating due to error'.

01 WORK-AREA.
    05   FILLER        PIC XXX.
    05   SSN-AREA.
        10 SSN-1ST-BYTE PIC X.
        10 FILLER       PIC X(11).

01 MY-WORK-SPACE.
    05   WORK-LENGTH   PIC S9(4)   COMP  VALUE   +15.
    05   ERROR-FLAG    PIC X             VALUE   'N'.
        88   TIME-TO-QUIT                VALUE   'Y'.

01 MY-COMMAREA    PIC X.

    COPY CICSRESP.

LINKAGE SECTION.
01 DFHCOMMAREA    PIC X.

PROCEDURE DIVISION.
1. IF EIBCALEN = 0
        PERFORM 100-SETUP-FIRST-ENTRY
    ELSE
        PERFORM 200-PROCESS-SUBSEQUENT.
    IF TIME-TO-QUIT
        EXEC CICS
```

Figure 2.23. Example of program with code for condition codes.

```
                         SEND  TEXT
                         FROM  (ERROR-MESSAGE)
                         LENGTH  (24)
                         ERASE
            END-EXEC
            EXEC  CICS  RETURN
            END-EXEC.
     IF  SSN-1ST-BYTE      NOT  =  'Q'
            EXEC  CICS
                         RETURN
                         TRANSID    ('E420')
                         COMMAREA   (MY-COMMAREA)
                         LENGTH     (1)
            END-EXEC
     ELSE
            EXEC  CICS  RETURN
            END-EXEC.
     GOBACK.

100-SETUP-FIRST-ENTRY.
     EXEC  CICS
                  SEND  TEXT
                  FROM  (INITIAL-MESSAGE)
                  LENGTH  (22)
                  ERASE
     END-EXEC.

200-PROCESS-SUBSEQUENT.
     PERFORM  210-RECEIVE-DATA
     IF  NOT  TIME-TO-QUIT
         IF  SSN-1ST-BYTE      NOT  =  'Q'
              PERFORM  220-VALIDATE-DATA
              PERFORM  230-SEND-RESPONSE.

210-RECEIVE-DATA.
     EXEC  CICS
                  RECEIVE
                  INTO       (WORK-AREA)
                  LENGTH     (WORK-LENGTH)
                  NOHANDLE
                  RESP       (CICS-RESP-CODE)
     END-EXEC
```

Figure 2.23. (cont'd). Example of program with code for condition codes.

```
IF NOT CICS-EOC AND NOT CICS-NORMAL
    MOVE 'Y' TO ERROR-FLAG.  ✓
220-VALIDATE-DATA.
    PERFORM 221-CHECK-VALID-SSN       <=== Not shown
    IF VALID-SSN
        MOVE 'Valid employee' TO RESP-STATUS
    ELSE
        MOVE 'Not an employee' TO RESP-STATUS.

230-SEND-RESPONSE.
    EXEC CICS
            SEND TEXT
            FROM (RESPONSE-AREA)
            LENGTH (36)
            ERASE
    END-EXEC.
```

Figure 2.23. (cont'd). Example of program with code for condition codes.

SUMMARY

This was a major chapter, one where you got the opportunity to develop a complete CICS transaction. The program was simple, but it had all the basic elements to consider in designing a transaction. Dealing with condition codes, terminal response, and program structure is an issue that will either set you apart from the masses in program design or place you in the middle of mediocrity. You can decide your approach.

VOCABULARY REVIEW

This chapter covered an enormous number of new words. I won't test you on all of them, but here are some of the key words.

Pseudoconversational

Conversational

HANDLE

AID keys

Condition-codes

DFHRESP()

SEND TEXT

RECEIVE

RETURN

3

Building and
Using a MAP

This chapter will introduce you to the skills required to design and write CICS MAPs to use with full-screen transactions, rather than the simple, line-oriented examples we studied earlier. Almost all CICS transactions in use today are written for the IBM 3270 (or equivalent) family of terminals, and those terminals are the focus in this book. When I say "3270 terminal," I am not referring to a single specific terminal. The term *3270* refers to those terminals that use the IBM 3270 data format (called the "3270 data stream"). This began with the IBM 3278 and 3279 terminals, but almost all terminals attached to IBM mainframes belong to that family, even if the numeric identifier does not include 327. Also, there are a variety of 3270 terminal emulation software packages that allow a PC to be used instead of a 3270-type terminal. Some terminals are monochrome, some are color, some have extended features, and the keyboard layouts may vary significantly. We will focus on the common aspects in this book.

In this book, I commonly use the term screen when referring to the layout of a terminal screen. Some books refer to this as a panel. Where a MAP is used to define the content of one terminal screen (that's the norm), then a screen and a MAP have a one-to-one relationship.

3.1. USING A 3270 TERMINAL

Many programmers think of terminals as "dumb" if the terminal is connected to a mainframe. I agree that "glass typewriters" do exist in the computing industry, but the 3270 family isn't among them. A lot of technology exists between the keyboard and the mainframe application and you need to understand the basics to better appreciate the subject of building and using MAPs. (Incidentally, the process of conducting a dialogue between a terminal and a mainframe as done in this book has its own name. It is referred to as the LU 2.0 protocol, from IBM's System Network Architecture (SNA). I mention this because there is a new protocol being discussed today, the LU 6.2 protocol. Since LU 6.2 is newer, more complex, and not yet widely used, it is not discussed in depth in this book, although CICS is the vehicle to implement it.)

3.1.1. 3270 Terminal Concepts

First, the terminal is not directly attached to the mainframe. Instead, the terminal is attached to a controller that is attached to the mainframe. Providing a controller offloads many aspects of managing terminal hardware and may provide its own benefits.

Next, the terminal itself contains memory and logic, allowing it to format data on the terminal screen based on a predefined set of codes used by the mainframe software (CICS takes care of these codes based on the MAP, so we won't pursue them here.) In fact, the terminal can retain data on the screen from one transmission to the mainframe to the next. Knowing this can aid the programmer who wants to minimize the amount of data being transferred to/from the terminal. (Reducing the amount of data being transferred can reduce response time to the terminal user.)

The 3270 family of terminals comes in a variety of sizes. Since the most common terminal has a screen size of 80 columns by 24 rows, that is the one we will use in this book, although you will see in the book that it is not difficult to change this specification. With a screen of 80 × 24, there are 1,920 positions on the screen. That does *not* mean you can present that much data on the screen — nor should you want to. The best application screens are those that present only enough data for terminal users to make decisions and accomplish a business unit of work. (This guideline, by the way, is routinely violated, normally by users who feel they will reduce programming costs or transaction time by loading screens with as much data as possible.)

3.1.2. Using Attribute Bytes on the Screen

You may be wondering, "If there are 1,920 positions on the screen, why can't I use them?" Good question. Remember that in a prior paragraph I mentioned that the 3270 has the ability to format data on the screen. It does this by using "attribute bytes." An attribute byte is a byte of data that contains a special hexadecimal value to denote how the following positions (horizontally) on the terminal are to be treated. Since the attribute byte requires a position on the screen, each field to be presented on the screen reduces the number of positions available by one. Attribute bytes appear as blanks on the screen, so terminal users are not aware of their presence.

An attribute byte must be placed on the screen immediately preceding a field where the screen attributes will change. This is one of the functions performed by MAPs. When you build a MAP, you also specify what attributes the field is to have. Here are the more common possible attributes:

Protected: The field cannot be modified by the terminal user.

Unprotected: Data can be entered into this field.

Dark: The data is not visible (such as a password field).

Bright: The field is highlighted (such as for an error).

Numeric: Only numbers and decimal point are allowed.

Askip: The field is to be automatically skipped over (such as for a title on the screen).

Modified Data Tag: The field has been modified by the terminal user. This is normally set on whenever a terminal user enters data into an unprotected field. We'll see more on the implications of this later.

These attributes may be combined into the same attribute byte because each attribute is only a bit on or off. For example, a data field where a numeric password is to be entered might be defined as unprotected, dark, and numeric. Since the attributes need to be specified only when they change, you do not need to specify them for every line. Also, since a new attribute byte must be used every time the attribute must change, you will find more attribute bytes on the screen than you might at first imagine. See Figure 3.1.

Figure 3.1 is a simple screen for an application. Three of the fields are titles, explaining what is to be entered, for example, *Employee name:.* Each of these is preceded by an attribute byte (probably defined as askip so the terminal user can't modify them). The attribute byte following each title resets the screen attribute to allow data entry (unprotect).

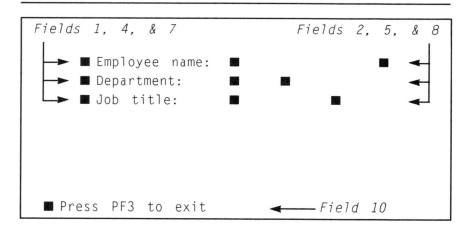

Figure 3.1. Example of 3270 screen.

Since we want to limit how many characters can be entered, notice that we must define an attribute at the end of each unprotected field to restore the screen to protect or askip mode. This causes the true screen format to contain "fields" that aren't part of the application, and are used only to restore basic screen attributes. The attribute bytes before *Department:* and *Job title:* aren't necessary since the screen is already protected at this point (from last attribute byte on prior line), but we usually code them when beginning a title field. (As you'll see later, it is easier this way.) The application logic is not affected by these extra fields, but you need to be sensitive to the concept when building MAPs, or the application will not act as you intended. The ninth field, for example, actually begins on the tenth row and continues to the beginning of the twenty-fourth row. It isn't used by the application except to keep the user from entering data there.

Sometimes, you will see attribute bytes serving double duty, ending an unprotected field and beginning a protected one. This is common on crowded screens. For example, you might see a screen with a line like this:

■Empl Id:■ ■Dept #:■ ■Job cd:■ ■Sal cat:■ ■Supvr:■ ■

It's messy, but it is often seen on transaction screens where a lot of data items are to be entered. Not only is the screen busy, but it usually forces applications to resort to codes because there isn't enough space to enter the actual data. In this example, the attribute bytes are alternately protect, then unprotect, then protect, then unprotect. By the way, with askip specified for the protected fields, the cursor on the terminal automatically moves to the next field when the terminal user types the maximum number of positions into the preceding unprotected field. Normally, you will want that, but there may be times when you don't. Designing a screen should be done with close involvement by the eventual user of the transaction.

There are several software products available that assist in doing screen design, but one of the best initial approaches, even if such software is available to you, is using pencil and paper. This technique, by being low technology, is less threatening to many users and can be done away from a computer terminal. There is a sample screen layout form in the back of this book that you may copy and use for this purpose. By having a true 80 × 24 layout, it is easier to demonstrate to a user that some things just won't work. This also lets you show where the attribute bytes are needed. (By the way, two attribute bytes cannot be coded back to back. There must always be at least one position between them.)

Earlier, I explained some of the basic attribute characteristics. Those will be the ones you will commonly use. Since many customer departments (and MIS departments) still use monochrome terminals, you need to know how attribute bytes affect the colors shown on screen. (Incidentally, many people prefer monochrome screens, including this author. Colorblindness is fairly common, so please don't assume that more color is always better.) When I referred earlier to the 3270 data stream, I avoided the fact that there is also an extended 3270 data stream. Most terminals use the standard data stream, which supports up to four colors. The extended data stream supports seven colors and also allows underscore, reverse color, and blinking (and combinations of those). We will limit our focus here to the standard data stream. Colors available are in Figure 3.2

A common practice in designing terminal screens is to define title fields as protected (blue), data entry fields as unprotected (green), and data entry fields in error as unprotected/bright (red). If the screen has a field for error messages, this is often defined as protected/bright (white). This approach ensures that, whether the user is using a color or monochrome terminal, errors are still distinguished from other text on the screen.

Attribute	Color Terminal	Monochrome Terminal
Protected	Blue	Normal intensity
Protected/bright	White	High intensity
Unprotected	Green	Normal intensity
Unprotected/bright	Red	High intensity

Figure 3.2. Color options with 3270 attribute bytes.

Normally, I suggest that the important thing in design is consistency. If the user is used to one format, then follow that. In screen design, however, I disagree. Very likely, most of the screens used by existing applications were designed years ago with little thought for how the person interacts with the terminal. Much has been learned about screen design in the past decade, and we, as an industry, should start somewhere to revamp some older transactions. One way is to start using some new formats. Maybe you'll get such an opportunity.

I reviewed some concepts of screen design in an earlier chapter, emphasizing that the screen should be separated into separate areas for easier use and that upper- and lower-case text helped. Placement of fields and use of colors and other attributes can also assist.

In the next topic, you will get the opportunity to put these concepts into practice, building a MAP for an application.

3.2. DEFINING A MAP

By now, you're familiar with the 3270 terminal concept, attribute byte functions, and screen size. Now you want to bring it all together. First, let's be sure we have eliminated any magic in the MAP-building process. A MAP is just a set of codes that is used by CICS to construct the 3270 data stream format to send/receive from the terminal. Since constructing the set of codes is tedious and complex, IBM provides a software approach to create MAPs (although your company may use a different tool for this). The IBM-provided tool consists of assembler commands for Basic Mapping Support (BMS), which we will review shortly. When you build a MAP, all you are doing is giving the software tool the information about how you want the fields to be defined, plus some information about the type of 3270 terminal that will be used.

The approach used in this book will be to build the MAP using the basic building blocks supplied by IBM. If your company uses an onscreen software package to define screens, by all means use it. For one thing, it will be faster. Still, I encourage you to develop a familiarity with the basic approach to defining MAPs, as you will benefit from seeing how the components are put together.

3.2.1.   COBOL Representation of a MAP

We think of a MAP as a layout for the screen itself. Actually, a MAP has two components, the MAP (which is used by CICS to communicate to/ from the terminal) and the program's data area (where CICS stores/ retrieves data for the application program's use). This second part is often confusing, even to experienced programmers. For COBOL programmers, this is an 01-level record description that is defined as a COPYbook and normally (but not always) placed in the WORKING-STORAGE SECTION. It is here that the program places data to be sent to the terminal and from here that it accesses data that was received from a terminal. This data area may also be used for additional communication between CICS and the application. For example, CICS stores the lengths of data fields here and it is here that the programmer may modify attribute bytes. We'll see more about that later.

Regardless of whether you use IBM's basic approach or a specialized software package to build your MAPs, the process is basically as follows:

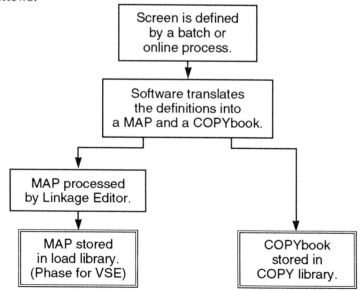

The importance of maintaining the MAP and its associated COPYbook is that each is dependent on the other for application integrity. If the MAP is changed to use an additional field or a different field length, the corresponding COPYbook must be replaced by a revised one and the COBOL program recompiled with the new COPYbook. The COPYbook member is sometimes referred to as a symbolic MAP or as a DSECT. Since DSECT is an assembler language term and does not relate to COBOL, I will use symbolic MAP in this book when referring to the data area for terminal I/O.

You should understand that the symbolic MAP is just what I mentioned earlier, an 01-level entry to allow the COBOL program to access data. There is nothing in the symbolic MAP that constructs the data stream. That is all done from the MAP by the BMS (Basic Mapping Services) component of CICS.

A symbolic MAP will have data fields for the length, the attribute byte, and the data component for each data field that was identified by the software as being a field the program must access. By that statement, I mean that there are usually fields (such as titles) that require no modification by the program. Such fields are not represented in a symbolic MAP. If you refer back to the sample screen in Figure 3.1, there were three data fields for data entry. Since the symbolic MAP contains three fields for each data field (one for the length, one for the attribute byte, and one for the data), the symbolic MAP for that screen would contain nine data fields. If the symbolic MAP is created by the basic IBM approach, it might look like the one shown in Figure 3.3.

I agree, the COBOL description in Figure 3.3 doesn't look too pretty at first glance. The names are too short, they seem meaningless, and why REDEFINE those one-byte fields, anyway? Since this is "just COBOL," you might feel that you would prefer to rewrite it into cleaner COBOL code, such as this:

```
01   EMPLOYEE-MAP.
     05   FILLER PIC X(12).
     05   EMPLOYEE-NAME-LENGTH   COMP   PIC   S9(4).
     05   EMPLOYEE-NAME-ATTR            PIC   X.
     05   EMPLOYEE-NAME-DATA            PIC   X(21).

     05   DEPT-NUMBER-LENGTH     COMP   PIC   S9(4).
     05   DEPT-NUMBER-ATTR              PIC   X.
     05   DEPT-NUMBER-DATA              PIC   X(7).

     05   JOB-TITLE-LENGTH       COMP   PIC   S9(4).
     05   JOB-TITLE-ATTR                PIC   X.
     05   JOB-TITLE-DATA                PIC   X(16).
```

```
01 EMPLIN1I.
   02   FILLER  PIC  X(12).
   02   EMPNAL       COMP   PIC    S9(4).
   02   EMPNAF       PICTURE  X.
   02   FILLER  REDEFINES  EMPNAF.
    03   EMPNAA       PICTURE  X.
   02   EMPNAI   PIC  X(21).
   02   DEPTNL       COMP   PIC    S9(4).
   02   DEPTNF       PICTURE  X.
   02   FILLER  REDEFINES  DEPTNF.
    03   DEPTNA       PICTURE  X.
   02   DEPTNI   PIC  X(7).
   02   JOBTITLL      COMP   PIC    S9(4).
   02   JOBTITLF      PICTURE  X.
   02   FILLER  REDEFINES  JOBTITLF.
    03   JOBTITLA      PICTURE  X.
   02   JOBTITLI   PIC  X(16).
01 EMPLIN1O  REDEFINES  EMPLIN1I.
   02   FILLER  PIC  X(12).
   02   FILLER  PICTURE  X(3).
   02   EMPNAO   PIC  X(21).
   02   FILLER  PICTURE  X(3).
   02   DEPTNO   PIC  X(7).
   02   FILLER  PICTURE  X(3).
   02   JOBTITLO   PIC  X(16).
```

Figure 3.3. Example of IBM-created symbolic MAP.

Looks better, doesn't it? Notice that each data field from the screen has three data fields. The first contains the number of bytes that were received by CICS. The second may contain an attribute byte or status code (more on that later), and the third field contains the actual data. Despite its cleaner look, I do not recommend writing your own symbolic MAPs (but your shop might insist on it, so check with them). If your shop uses a software package that prepares symbolic MAPs similar to this, great! Otherwise, I suggest that you stick with the messy one shown before. Why? Because screens sometimes must be frequently changed and most screens are not as simple as this one that has only three data entry fields.

Remember, any time the screen layout changes, either from additional titles, new fields, changes in field lengths, or placement of fields on the screen, the MAP must be reconstructed and the symbolic MAP must also be rebuilt and the application program recompiled with the new COPYbook. Usually, this occurs under pressure and a tight time frame. Having to manually recompute what the symbolic MAP must look like is time-consuming and also a bad gamble. After all, you might do it wrong and spend days debugging a transaction that doesn't seem to work correctly.

Okay, so if we're going to use the technique that generated the example in Figure 3.3, let's review it in more detail so we at least understand what is there. First, notice the FILLER with PIC X(12) at the beginning of the MAP. These 12 bytes are for CICS's use, so they must always be there. The rest of the symbolic MAP are entries for our application-specific data areas. There are five entries beginning with EMPNA, followed by five entries for DEPTN and five entries for JOBTITL. The sixth field appears after the REDEFINES statement. Let's review the fields that begin with EMPNA.

```
02  EMPNAL       COMP   PIC    S9(4).
02  EMPNAF       PICTURE  X.
02  FILLER  REDEFINES  EMPNAF.
   03  EMPNAA   PICTURE  X.
02  EMPNAI  PIC  X(21).
         .
         .
         .
02  EMPNAO  PIC  X(21).
```

Maybe, first, I'd better answer an unasked question: "Why are the names so short?" Well, the names are so short because the basic IBM software approach to create CICS screens is done by using some assembler language facilities (called macros). Since assembler language has a limit of eight characters per name, that restriction carries over to the generated COBOL entries. Since the facility adds a single character suffix to each name (L for length, F for flag, A for attribute, I for input data, and O for output data), you are restricted to coding only up to seven characters. You may not need both an input and an output description for the same data area, but the macros give you the opportunity in case your COBOL application wants to format output data with a different PIC than that used for input.

All five fields are created by the BMS macros whenever a name is specified for the field. The first field, EMPNAL, is used by CICS to store the length of the data entered by the terminal user. This field will be zero if no data was entered and is a simple way for a programmer to determine if a field contains data.

The second and third fields are actually the same one. The two names are used because some programmers like to reference each name for different purposes. This byte contains either the attribute byte for a field (hence the A suffix) or a flag denoting that the terminal user pressed the EraseEOF key for this field. There is rarely, if ever, any need to check the attributes of a field being received (at least, I know of no such reasons). (*Note*: CICS/ESA provides a new, optional function for the Flag field. See CURSLOC in the next topic.)

The fourth and fifth fields are, again, the same one. You may use either field or both. The BMS macros provide the opportunity to specify what COBOL PICTURE should be used for the data field on input and for output. Since CICS does *not* use this PICTURE clause, CICS doesn't care whether you reference the EMPNAO or the EMPNAI field. (CICS always moves fields as though they were PIC X).

To make the IBM macros useful, all you need to do is use seven character names for each field on the screen. That's easier than it may appear. Remember, these fields can be moved to other data areas in your program, letting you isolate the use of these names to just one or two paragraphs. You're right in thinking that they aren't as meaningful as longer names, but the tradeoff is improved productivity.

This was not intended to be a thorough review of the different ways that you can manipulate and detect data on the screen. There is much more we will cover. I added extra information to give you a flavor of some of the options available. Also, I indicated that the BMS macros provide five fields for each data field defined in the macros that is given a name by you. Well, there are more fields that could be generated in addition to the basic five. Since the additional fields are only for the extended data stream (color, highlighting, reverse color, blinking), I have avoided presenting them for this text. As you build experience in coding MAPs, you can specify those options yourself and see the differences.

3.2.2.   Macros for Building a MAP

In the previous section, I stated that IBM provided BMS assembler macros to create both MAPs and symbolic MAPs. That means that, although you might not think of it this way, you are actually writing, assembling, and link editing an assembler program when you create MAPs this way. That means you will be using JCL for the IBM assembler and, if you code any of the macros incorrectly, the errors will not necessarily be specific to CICS MAPs. If you make a serious coding error, you will receive assembler error messages. If that occurs, my advice is to look very carefully at what you coded. Normally, you won't need an assembler reference manual (although it does happen).

In this part of the book, I am not presenting all IBM macros, nor am I presenting all options. Instead, following the format already presented to you, I am including the options most commonly used. If you ever browse through the thousands of pages of IBM documentation for any given version of CICS, you will realize why I believe it is better to master a subset of any software product rather than be only vaguely aware of the complete set of options.

MACRO syntax. If you are used to assembler languages, then the term *macro* is not unknown to you. If the term is new to you, here is a brief explanation: A macro is an assembler statement that generates additional statements. Remember our discussion earlier where I stated that a MAP was just a set of codes to construct the data stream? Well, the macros that appear here are statements that, when processed by the assembler, cause those various codes to be generated into an object module. Normally, we do not want to see the generated code but only a listing of the macros themselves.

Assembler language has a set coding format so, when coding CICS macros, you need to follow the format rigidly. Here it is:

Column 1: Label (up to seven characters) if needed (you never need a label for a field unless your program modifies it)

Column 10: Macro name, followed by at least one space

Column 17–71: Optional keywords, each one separated by a comma with no intervening spaces. If more keywords are to be coded than will fit on one line, finish a complete keyword followed by a comma, code a nonblank in column 72, and continue with the next keyword in column 16 of the next line. (Yes, the columns are specific.)

For a comment, code an * in column 1.

Actually, the macro name doesn't have to start in column 10, nor do the keywords have to start in column 17. The rule is that there must be at least one space after the label and at least one space after the macro name. For example, your company may have standardized on using column 12 for the macro name. The columns that are explicit are column 1 for labels, column 72 for continuation, and column 16 for the beginning of the continued line.

We'll get a chance to review the syntax as we start coding macros.

Improving MAP documentation. These statements are not required, but they are very helpful in improving the documentation of your listings of assembled MAPs. The first is the TITLE statement. TITLE causes a heading to appear on each page of the assembled listing. (This is identical to the TITLE feature in COBOL II.) TITLE is coded as follows, beginning in column 10:

```
TITLE    'Your title goes here, up to column 71'
```

The next statement, more commonly used, is PRINT NOGEN. This statement tells the assembler that you do *not* want the generated code to appear on the listing (roughly equivalent to the NOLIST option of COBOL II or the NOPMAP option of VS/COBOL). Since the generated code will make no sense to you or me (and saves its share of paper), I suggest you always use PRINT NOGEN. Again, it appears beginning in column 10. So far, then, our first MAP has two lines, such as the following:

```
TITLE    ' My first MAP'
PRINT    NOGEN
```

Now, I encourage you to insert comments (using an * in column 1) so you and others can more easily understand what you did. If your shop has a standard that requires that you insert such comments in COBOL programs when they are changed, then your shop probably also has standards for documenting MAPs. As we end this bit on documentation, we have the following constructed:

```
     TITLE    ' My first MAP'
     PRINT    NOGEN
*    _____
*    MAP for first application, written on mm/dd/yy
*    Programmer: Your name here
*    _____
```

Now, let's do the rest of the MAP.

MAP module structure. There are three macros used to define a MAP:

- DFHMSD — coded twice, this defines a MAPSET

- DFHMDI — coded once for each MAP to be defined

- DFHMDF — coded for each attribute byte to be defined

Since the explanation of each macro comes next, you should first see how they are combined together into a MAPSET. Here is the format:

```
                TITLE              optional
                PRINT  NOGEN       optional
mapsetid        DFHMSD ...
mapname1        DFHMDI ...
fieldnamea      DFHMDF ...
fieldnameb      DFHMDF ...
fieldnamec      DFHMDF ...
                DFHMSD TYPE=FINAL
                END
```

Some of the macros have the same options. Where that happens, the lower-level macro overrides the higher level. For example, an option coded on a DFHMDF macro takes precedence over the same option coded on a DFHMDI macro, which in turn takes precedence over the same option coded on the DFHMSD macro. The END statement isn't documented elsewhere in this book, but, believe me, it's required. END should be coded after the last macro statement for your MAPSET.

So far, we've only discussed MAPs. So, what's a MAPSET? A MAPSET is a means provided by CICS for us to package all the MAPs that a given program might use. As you've probably concluded, MAPs are like programs themselves because they are processed by the Linkage Editor. Being programs, they must be predefined to CICS in the Processing Program Table (PPT). Actually, what we define in the PPT to CICS is the MAPSET. Then, if additional MAPs are needed for an application, we can just add more MAPs to the MAPSET. Usually, there is only one MAP to a MAPSET. (*Reminder*: You may have temporarily forgotten the various CICS tables that we discussed earlier in the book. Remember that every entity we use for CICS — whether a program, a transaction, a file, or a MAP — must be entered in one or more of CICS's tables.)

DFHMSD macro. The DFHMSD macro is used to define global information that applies to all MAPs within the MAPSET. At many shops, the options used with DFHMSD are standardized and used for all MAPSETs in the shop. I recommend that approach, as it eliminates the need to keep rediscovering the options.

There are two formats for the DFHMSD macro, one for the beginning of a MAPSET and one for the ending. The format for the first one is in Figure 3.4. Please remember that, while the syntax has a comma and continuation character in column 72 for each option, you may specify more than one option on each line and, more important, the last entered option should *not* contain either the comma or the nonblank character in column 72.

```
                                            column 72
name    DFHMSD  TYPE=&SYSPARM,                      X
                LANG=COBOL,                         X
                MODE=INOUT,                         X
                TERM=3270-2,                        X
                TIOAPFX=YES,                        X
                STORAGE=AUTOBASE=dataname,          X
                CTRL=(optiona,optionb...),          X
                CURSLOC=YES|NO, <==NEW with CICS/ESA X
Following options are for the 3270 extended
data stream only.
                EXTATT=YES|NO, <==Pre 1.7 support   X
                DSATTS=(type,type...),              X
                MAPATTS=(type,type...),             X
                COLOR=color,                        X
                HILIGHT=OFF|BLINK|REVERSE|UNDERLINE
```

Figure 3.4. DFHMSD macro.

As I mentioned previously, Figure 3.4 does not contain all possible options for the DFHMSD macro. Instead, I focused on the options that are more commonly used for CICS transactions that use 3270 terminals.

Naming the MAPSET. The name, coded in column 1, should be one to seven characters and should relate somewhat to the name of your application program. This is because this will be the name of the MAPSET that will be link edited into a load library (MVS) or phase (VSE) and will also be the name of the COPYbook that contains the symbolic MAP(s) in the MAPSET. It is good documentation to have the program and the MAPSET have something common in the names. This is a frequent problem at many shops, where the naming standard for application programs uses all eight characters and there is no provision for naming MAPSETs.

For example, if a program is named PAY25000, the MAPSET might be named PAY250M. Unfortunately, life isn't usually that simple. Before many shops ever realize they need some standards on this, there are already modules named PAY25000, PAY02500, PAY00250, and PAY00025. Creating MAPSET names that automatically document their relation to such program names is possible but difficult. Check with your shop's standards for information on selecting the MAPSET name. Remember, the MAPSET name must be defined in the PPT. Also, the TERM option for the DFHMSD macro can affect the name by causing a suffix to be appended.

The keywords. Also, some of the keywords in Figure 3.4 had other options available that weren't shown (e.g., LANG could have specified ASM, PLI, or C instead of COBOL). Here is a review of the keywords:

>   **TYPE=&SYSPARM | DSECT | MAP | FINAL** This defines to the assembler what type of MAP is to be created. DSECT specifies that the output should be a symbolic MAP, MAP specifies that a MAP should be generated, FINAL indicates the end of a MAPSET, and &SYSPARM specifies that the type will be handled in the JCL. &SYSPARM is most commonly used, as most shops use JCL procedures that invoke the assembler twice, one time to create the symbolic MAP and one time to create the MAP. By coding &SYSPARM, you don't need to be concerned. This also prevents you from getting into the bad habit of creating one type of MAP without creating the other. Remember, the two must be in sync.

>   **LANG=COBOL | ASM | PLI | C** If you are going to use the information in this book, always specify COBOL. This tells the assembler what type of symbolic MAP to generate.

>   **MODE=INOUT | IN | OUT** This specifies whether the MAP is used for input, output, or both input and output. Since there is no advantage of IN or OUT, I always use INOUT as that ensures I know what data fields are generated for the application's use.

>   **TERM=termtype | ALL** There are many possible terminal types that can be used here. I selected 3270-2 because that specifies to BMS that the terminal is a 3270 terminal with 80-column format, the type most people use and the type assumed in this book. Some programmers specify ALL or omit this keyword (omitting the option assumes ALL). I encourage

you always to use the terminal type that corresponds to the device being used as it will be more efficient. Before coding a MAP, I always confirm that the MAP will be used by 3270 terminals to be sure of coding this correctly. (If I'm ever told that the terminal will be some other type, I will have more to be concerned about than just this keyword.) **IMPORTANT NOTICE:** What you specify here affects the name of the load module (MVS) or phase (VSE) that BMS attempts to load into memory at run time. This is how BMS, at run time, selects the appropriate MAP for your application. For example, if the terminal type is 3270-2, BMS first looks for the MAPSET with the suffix "M." If ALL was specified, the suffix is a blank. If any MAPSET and appended suffix is *not* found, BMS will search for the MAPSET with no suffix (i.e., ALL assumed). This lets you assemble the same MAP for several different terminal types, if needed.

TIOAPFX=YES Don't ask, just code it as shown. Once upon a time, there were CICS programs that were written as macro programs not using the current approach (called *command level programming*). Remember that 12-byte FILLER shown at the beginning of the symbolic MAPs in the prior topic? Well, this tells CICS that EXEC CICS commands are being used, and is created by coding this parameter.

STORAGE=AUTO│BASE=dataname This is too complex for a full discussion of the pros and cons in this book. You may code one option or the other or neither. The issue being addressed is how much memory the symbolic MAP will require. Here are the basics:

STORAGE=AUTO specifies that, if there is more than one MAP in the MAPSET, they will be allocated contiguously. This option has no meaning if there is only one MAP in the MAPSET. If STORAGE=AUTO is not coded, the symbolic MAP will use the REDEFINES clause to overlay subsequent symbolic MAPs over the first. If one symbolic MAP is larger than others, it *must* be coded first in such an instance. If your application uses several MAPs, but only one per execution, then you can save memory by omitting this keyword.

BASE=dataname is used where there will be more than one MAPSET in an application, yet only one MAP will be used per execution. BMS generates the symbolic MAPSETs so that they REDEFINE dataname. There is no mystery here, just several 01-level entries REDEFINing a prior 01-level. For example, if two MAPSETs shared the same BASE name, they would be coded as follows and appear in the COBOL program as also shown:

```
MAPNUM1    DFHMSD  BASE=MAPAREA,...
MAPNUM2    DFHMSD  BASE=MAPAREA,...
.....................
01  MAPAREA       PIC  X(1920).
    COPY  MAPNUM1.
    COPY  MAPNUM2.
```

Normally, you won't have several MAPSETs in a single application, but, if you do, BASE= is a good option to control memory use.

In this topic, I've used the words *per execution*. By that, I mean from the time your program receives control from CICS until a RETURN command is executed. In most transactions, you will do this several times to complete a dialogue. In pseudoconversational processing, you would never SEND or RECEIVE multiple MAPs without relinquishing control back to CICS. Incidentally, the time your application has control up to a RETURN command is referred to as a *task* in CICS terminology.

CTRL=([FREEKB][,ALARM][,FRSET][,PRINT][,length])
You will always want to code one or more of these options. Here is what they mean:

FREEKB specifies that the keyboard is to be unlocked after a SEND command. This is a nice thing to do. Otherwise, the terminal user will have a locked keyboard and can't enter data. I'm sure there may be instances where you don't want the keyboard unlocked, such as if an application wants to send several MAPs to form a composite screen. You will normally use FREEKB on every MAP.

ALARM specifies that the terminal alarm is to sound when a MAP is sent. This option was intended for those situations where a special condition occurs and normal notification techniques (such as error messages) were inadequate to the situation. I don't recommend using this option. For one thing, many 3270-type terminals don't have an alarm (the keyboard locks, instead). For another, you will annoy the terminal user.

FRSET is complex, becoming intertwined with a broader subject on controlling data flow between the terminal and the mainframe. We'll review it more later, but I'll cover the concept here. Do you recall from a prior topic where I mentioned that the 3270 terminal had logic and remembered the screen contents? Do you also remember the concept of a modified data tag (MDT) in the attribute byte? (It is the attribute that is set when the terminal user enters data.) Well, FRSET specifies that, prior to a SEND MAP instruction, the MDT attribute flags at the terminal are to be reset. Otherwise, the MDT remains set for subsequent SENDs and RECEIVEs even though no data is entered. Since this won't be a concern for our first applications in this book, don't worry about it. When you are involved with large scale applications with high transaction traffic, it might become quite important.

PRINT is required if the SEND command is sending data to a 3270 printer. This causes the printer to print its buffer. This book does not focus on printers, but I include this information in case you work with a transaction that creates online printed output.

Length is required to indicate the line length on the printer (used with the PRINT option). Choices are L40, L64, L80. Each causes the printer to skip to a new line after printing 40, 64, or 80 lines. You can also specify HONEOM, causing the default printer line length to be used.

CURSLOC=YES\|NO New with CICS/ESA, this is a special technique that specifies that BMS is to use the Flag field to indicate if the cursor was in that field when the RECEIVE MAP command was processed. If your applications need to determine where the cursor was at the time the MAP was RECEIVEd (not uncommon), this is a great technique. There are other ways to do this, and we'll review both techniques.

DSATTS=([COLOR][,HILIGHT]) This specifies that the symbolic MAP should include entries for extended attributes. There are other options besides the two shown here, but even these may be more than you will encounter. You shouldn't use this option unless the terminals that will be using your application are terminals that support the 3270 extended data stream. Otherwise, you're wasting your time. All options specified in DSATTS must also be specified in MAPATTS.

COLOR indicates that the program wants the ability to control color on a field-by-field basis. This is beyond that shown in Figure 3.2, where combinations of other attribute bytes created a color. This relates to the COLOR keyword.

HILIGHT indicates that the program wants the ability to control field highlighting. This relates to the HILIGHT keyword.

MAPATTS=([COLOR][,HILIGHT])   This has the same meaning as the DSATT options, but it applies only to the actual MAP, not the symbolic MAP. Normally, you should specify the same ones for both.

EXTATT=YES I NO I MAPONLY   This is a keyword that is carried over from earlier releases of CICS. For that reason, I do not encourage you to use it. This option specified whether extended attribute descriptions should be included in the symbolic MAP.

NO indicates the equivalent of not coding DSATTS and MAPATTS.

YES is the equivalent of coding DSATTS=(COLOR,HILIGHT) and MAPATTS=(COLOR,HILIGHT).

MAPONLY is the equivalent of coding MAPATTS=(COLOR, HILIGHT).

COLOR=DEFAULT I color   This is used to define the color for the screen. The assumption is COLOR=DEFAULT. Normally, this keyword is not coded here but on the DFHMDF macro (the one that specifies attributes for a single field). Possible colors are BLUE, RED, PINK, GREEN, TURQuoise, YELLOW, and WHITE. COLOR must be specified in DSATTS and MAPATTS options.

HILIGHT=OFF I BLINK I REVERSE I UNDERLINE   This is used to specify the default highlighting for fields. As with COLOR, this is usually defined at the field level with the DFHMDF macro (covered later). These attributes should be used with caution and discretion. While a screen with several different colors, some in reverse color and some blinking, may be interesting to look at, a terminal user would get headaches quickly.

Coding a DFHMSD macro. Now that we have covered the most popular options (and some that aren't), let's review a typical definition.

```
PAY2500      DFHMSD TYPE=&SYSPARM,               X
                    MODE=INOUT,                   X
                    LANG=COBOL,                   X
                    TERM=3270-2,                  X
                    TIOAPFX=YES,                  X
                    CTRL=(FREEKB)
```

In the above example, the MAPSET name will be PAY2500 and the load module or phase will be PAY2500M. Despite all of the options defined for the DFHMSD macro, the above are what I use for most MAPs. If you are using CICS/ESA, then you will eventually want to also include the CURSLOC=YES keyword.

I mentioned that there were two formats for the DFHMSD macro. The second one is used at the end of the MAPSET, after all other macros have been coded. It is simply

```
DFHMSD TYPE=FINAL
```

The DFHMSD macro defined the basic MAPSET and any defaults that should apply to all MAPs. We will next discuss the BMS macro that defines a MAP.

DFHMDI macro. The DFHMDI macro defines the basic attributes of a single MAP. Many of the keyword options on the DFHMSD macro may be used here, and they should be when they apply specifically to this MAP. (That is one reason why I always code very little on the DFHMSD macro.) In Figure 3.5 are many of the same keywords from Figure 3.4. In all cases, they have the same meaning. Where you have several MAPs in a MAPSET and each has different attributes, then the DFHMDI macro is a good place to code them. Figure 3.5 shows some common options for the DFHMDI macro.

Naming the MAP. As with the DFHMSD macro, the name is important. With the DFHMSD macro, it became an external name that needed to be defined in the PPT. The MAP name must also not exceed seven characters, but the MAP name isn't used outside of the application. The

MAP name specified on the DFHMDI is also what the name of the 01-level symbolic MAP will be, followed by "I" or "O." I usually try to use a name that is derived from the MAPSET name, but your shop may have its own standards. Never name the MAP and the MAPSET the same, as that will confuse BMS.

```
                                                   column 72
   name     DFHMDI  TYPE=&SYSPARM,                       X
               LANG=COBOL,                               X
               MODE=INOUT,                               X
               TERM=3270-2,                              X
               TIOAPFX=YES,                              X
               STORAGE=AUTO|BASE=dataname,               X
               CTRL=(optiona,optionb...),                X
               CURSLOC=YES|NO, <==NEW with CICS/ESA      X
   Following options are specific to DFHMDI.
               SIZE=(line,column),                       X
               LINE=number,                              X
               COLUMN=number,                            X
   Following options are for the 3270 extended
   data stream only.
               EXTATT=YES|NO, <==Pre 1.7 support         X
               DSATTS=(type,type...),                    X
               MAPATTS=(type,type...),                   X
               COLOR=color,                              X
               HILIGHT=OFF|BLINK|REVERSE|UNDERLINE
```

Figure 3.5. DFHMDI macro.

Since there are only three new keywords, let's just review those. The documentation for the others mirrors that already defined for the DFHMSD macro.

The keywords. The keywords here are specific to screen size and placement of the MAP on the screen. That's right, you don't have to always place a MAP over the entire screen of the terminal.

    SIZE=(line,column)   This specifies how much of the screen is to be covered by the MAP. Normally, this will be all of it.

For all of a 3270 terminal, specify SIZE=(24,80) for 24 lines and 80 columns.

LINE=number   This specifies on what line the MAP is to be mapped to the receiving terminal. The default is LINE=1.

COLUMN=number   This specifies on what column the MAP is to be mapped to the receiving terminal. The default is COLUMN=1.

Coding a DFHMCI macro. As with the DFHMSD macro, despite the options, most applications use as few options as possible. Here is an example

```
PAY2501   DFHMDI  SIZE=(24,80),CURSLOC=YES
```

Not complicated, is it? As you probably guess, this DFHMDI can be used with almost any 3270 MAP. In this example, the MAP that I reference when SENDing or RECEIVing data will be PAY2501. CURSLOC should not be used unless your shop has CICS/ESA *and* your application needs to determine the cursor location.

DFHMDF macro. So far, the BMS macro examples we have used have used few of the available options. That changes with the DFHMDF macro, as it is used for each field. Since fields vary considerably, the DFHMDF macro will use many of its options. Figure 3.6 shows the most frequently used options, although there are many more.

```
                                         column 72
name      DFHMDF  POS=(line,column),                 X
                  LENGTH=number,                      X
                  INITIAL='literal',                  X
                  ATTRB=(optiona,optionb...),         X
                  JUSTIFY=(LEFT|RIGHT[,BLANK|ZERO]),  X
                  PICIN='COBOL PIC value',            X
                  PICOUT='COBOL PIC value',           X
Following options are for the 3270 extended
data stream only.
                  COLOR=color,                        X
                  HILIGHT=OFF|BLINK|REVERSE|UNDERLINE
```

Figure 3.6. DFHMDF macro.

Since the DFHMDF macro defines an attribute byte, you will need two of them to define a data field. If this confuses you, then you may want to review the prior topic on attribute bytes.

Naming a data field. The name on the DFHMDF macro is optional and should *not* be coded unless this is for a field that the application program will need to access. This is because any time a field is named, BMS inserts the field into the symbolic MAP. Fields such as titles or instructions should normally not be named.

The name should be one to seven characters long. From the discussion in a prior topic on attribute bytes, you know that the name you select will have a character appended to it for each of the five possible field names. For example, if you identify a DFHMDF macro with the name EMPNAME, the resulting entries in the COBOL COPYbook will be EMPNAMEL for the length, EMPNAMEF for the flag, EMPNAMEA for the attribute byte, EMPNAMEI for the input data field, and EMPNAMEO for the output data field. You may recall that the fields ending in F and A both define the same area, and the fields ending in I and O both define the same area, also.

The keywords. While you may never remember the keywords for the DFHMSD and DFHMDI macros, you will soon memorize the more commonly used keywords for the DFHMDF macro. It's simple. You will use them more often. The only ones you need to code are POS and LENGTH, but you will frequently want some of the others. For information on COLOR and HILIGHT, see information on DFHMSD.

POS=(line,column)   This defines where the attribute byte is defined (the field BEGINS with the NEXT position).

LENGTH=number   This defines the number of bytes for the field. This value must not include any attribute bytes. This is not required if PICIN or PICOUT is coded.

INITIAL='literal'   If you want the field to contain an initial value, this is how you do it. Otherwise, the field will contain LOW-VALUES. This is normally used only for title fields to display on the screen, or to assist a user in understanding a data field format. For example, I have seen screens where the field for DATE was initialized to 'mmddyy' to assist the user in keying in month, day, and year in that order. How you use this is up to you, but you have lots of flexibility. You should remember that if you use this for a data entry field, some of the initial data may still be there when CICS presents the RECEIVEd data to you. We'll see some of that later.

**ATTRB=([ASKIP I PROT I UNPROT][,BRT I DRK I NORM][,NUM]
[,FSET][,IC])** This option specifies the attribute(s) for the
screen, beginning with this attribute byte. All specified options will be in effect until the next attribute byte is encountered (by coding another DFHMDF macro). If this keyword is
not coded, ASKIP and NORM are assumed. If this keyword is
coded, UNPROT and NORM are assumed unless mutually
exclusive options are coded. There are two sets of mutually
exclusive options: ASKIP, PROT, and UNPROT; and BRT,
DRK, and NORM.

ASKIP specifies that the field is both protected from data
entry *and* the cursor is to be automatically skipped over the
field. This is usually desirable for title fields or other protected fields.

PROT specifies only that the field is protected from data
entry. At first glance, you might think that ASKIP or PROT
fields never need a dataname because the COBOL program
probably never accesses them. Not true. You will often find
there are fields, such as date or time-of-day, that you want
the program to be able to send to the screen but don't want
the terminal user to modify.

UNPROT is for data entry fields, specifying that the field
should allow data entry. When specifying such fields, you
will normally also assign a name to the macro so your
COBOL program can access it.

BRT specifies that the field should be displayed in high-
intensity. On a color terminal, this translates to white if the
field is ASKIP or PROT and to red if the field is UNPROT.

DRK specifies that the field should not be displayed (or
printed, if the MAP is for a printer). This is usually used for
security fields, where data is not to be seen.

NORM is rarely coded as it is the default for all situations.
This specifies that the field should be displayed in normal
intensity.

NUM specifies that the terminal should allow only numeric
characters to be entered. Any other key, except a period,
will lock the keyboard. An additional process that this
triggers (only when coded on the MAP) is that BMS right
justifies the field, filling high-order positions with zeros when
the field is stored in the symbolic MAP. See JUSTIFY, below, for more information.

FSET specifies that the modified data tag (MDT) should be turned on in the attribute byte. This flags the data field so that on subsequent RECEIVEs from the terminal, this field will always be sent from the terminal to the mainframe. I always specify at least one field with this attribute, which I will explain later.

IC specifies that the cursor should be positioned on this field after a SEND command. This is not commonly used, as there are more flexible ways to control the cursor from within the program. If coded, this should be on only one field. My recommendation is not to code it.

JUSTIFY=(LEFT | RIGHT[,BLANK | ZERO]) This keyword is used in combination with the NUM attribute. The keyword determines whether, on a RECEIVE command, fields are left or right justified and whether they are padded with spaces or zeros. The default is left justified, space filled, assuming the receiving field is alphanumeric (i.e., will be the equivalent of the COBOL PIC X). If NUM is specified, then the default is right justified, zero fill. Normally, then, you don't need to code this. You need to specify it only when, for whatever reason, the normal justification process for alphanumeric or numeric data should not be followed. *Note*: This process only occurs if the data field contains only what was entered by the terminal user. For example, if an INITIAL value was coded, parts of the INITIAL value may still be present.

PICIN='COBOL PIC value' PICIN and PICOUT are two of the most misunderstood options in this macro. BMS provides them for use by the application only. *BMS does not use them to format data.* Also, BMS does not verify that the PIC clause entered is what you really want. The PIC clause you enter on PICIN will be placed in the symbolic MAP data field that ends in "I." The default is PIC X, so if the LENGTH parameter was 7, for example, the picture clause would be PIC X(7). To explain my earlier point, if you specify PICIN='999V99', BMS does not do any decimal point validation but simply places whatever was entered into the field. The data is right justified if NUM (or the appropriate JUSTIFY option) is specified, but that's it. Editing the data is up to the application.

PICOUT='COBOL PIC value' What I said about PICIN applies here, too. You normally code a PICOUT value when you want to format output to the terminal in a different format than the field was received. I encourage caution in doing this, as the characters sent to the terminal may come back to haunt your application on the next RECEIVE command. Consider this scenario:

You specify a field as

```
LENGTH=7,PICIN='99999V99',PICOUT='$$$9.99', and NUM.
```

The user enters 2715. BMS right-justifies the data on the next RECEIVE as 0002715. Your program retrieves the data from the input field, verifies it, and moves the data to the output field definition. The field now contains $$27.15. After the next SEND command, the user, by moving the cursor, changes the 7 to an 8, leaving all other data as is. On the next RECEIVE, the field contains $$28.15, not 0002815. If your program attempts to use the same instructions to process it, your application will abend. (COBOL II allows a numeric-edit field to be MOVEd to a numeric field, but, even with this capability, your program must determine which field to reference.)

Coding a DFHMDF macro. As I mentioned, you will normally code two of these for a data entry field and one for other fields. That is because the attributes specified continue until changed. Let's assume you want a title to appear on line 1, column 30. This might be the company name, for example. Here is how we code it.

```
DFHMDF   POS=(1,29),LENGTH=29,                          X
         INITIAL='Ajax Software and Brewery Co.'
```

That's it. The data will be displayed in normal intensity, have the ASKIP and PROT attributes, and will not be in the symbolic MAP (because no name was provided). If the field were to be displayed in high intensity (something too many programmers overdo), I would need to specify not just ATTRB=BRT but ATTRB=(ASKIP,BRT). This is because the default attributes change once you specify the ATTRB parameter. This is a little-known fact, so you may want to reread the information on ATTRB. By the way, I specified column 29 in the POS keyword because I want the data to appear in column 30. Remember, the first byte assigned to the screen will be the attribute byte.

Now, let's assume we want to specify a data entry field on the same MAP. Since most data entry fields are preceded by a descriptive title, we'll need to code both the descriptive title and the data entry field *and* a follow-on attribute byte to cause the cursor to stop at the end of the field. Here goes:

```
         DFHMDF POS=(6,10),LENGTH=7,INITIAL='Salary:'
SALARY   DFHMDF POS=(6,18),LENGTH=5,ATTRB=(UNPROT,NUM),      X
            PICOUT='ZZ9V99'
         DFHMDF  POS=(6,24),LENGTH=1
```

There is much information in that simple example, so let's review it carefully. First, notice the POS values. I had to keep the attribute bytes in mind as I computed the locations (you will receive a warning message if the fields overlap). The title "Salary:" will appear in positions 11 through 17, the beginning of the data entry field is in column 19 (I used only the attribute byte to separate the title from the data entry field), and the attribute byte that terminates the field is in position 24, restoring the screen to ASKIP and NORM. (Attribute bytes that are inserted only to terminate a data entry field are often called "stopper bytes" or "stopper fields.")

You may be wondering why I didn't use PICIN='999V99' and PICOUT='ZZ9.99' so a decimal point would be displayed. Well, for one thing, that would require that the LENGTH be changed to 6 and, more important to me, makes my program have to work harder. For example, if the user enters nothing in this field, I would be having to cope with a numeric picture and the possibility of an 0C7 ABEND (invalid data format). As it is, I have a PIC X(5) for the input field. It's much easier to deal with this if data is not what I expected.

On the output side, by using ZZ9V99, I avoid having to deal with a possible decimal point on a subsequent RECEIVE command. Yes, these issues can be addressed in a variety of ways, but it does increase program complexity. You will find that the cleanest, most user-friendly transactions spend a lot of the program logic on issues such as these. If your project has the time, then by all means spend the extra time to make the application easier to use. On the other hand, if the target date is right around the corner, do it the easy way.

Coding a simple MAP. Do you recall that sample screen we reviewed in Figure 3.1 and its symbolic MAP in Figure 3.3? Here is the code that would create that screen:

```
          TITLE   ' Employee Inquiry MAP'
          PRINT   NOGEN
*  _____
*  MAP for Simple Employee Inquiry, written  on  mm/dd/yy
*  Programmer: Your  name  here
*  _____
EMPLINQ DFHMSD TYPE=&SYSPARM,                                X
               MODE=INOUT,                                   X
               LANG=COBOL,                                   X
               TERM=3270-2,                                  X
               TIOAPFX=YES,                                  X
               CTRL=(FREEKB)
*
EMPLIN1 DFHMDI SIZE=(24,80)
*
        DFHMDF POS-(6,14),LENGTH=15,                         X
               INITIAL='Employee name:  '
EMPNA   DFHMDF POS=(6,30),LENGTH=21,ATTRB=(UNPROT)
        DFHMDF POS=(6,52),LENGTH=1
        DFHMDF POS=(8,14),LENGTH=15,                         X
               INITIAL='Department:       '
DEPTN   DFHMDF POS=(8,30),LENGTH=7,ATTRB=(UNPROT,NUM)
        DFHMDF POS=(8,38),LENGTH=1
        DFHMDF POS-(10,14),LENGTH=15,                        X
               INITIAL='Job Title:       '
JOBTITL DFHMDF POS=(6,30),LENGTH=16,ATTRB=(UNPROT)
        DFHMDF POS=(6,47),LENGTH=1
        DFHMDF POS=(24,5),LENGTH=17,                         X
               INITIAL='Press PF3 to exit'
        DFHMSD TYPE=FINAL
        END
```

You may have done this differently, especially if you prefer a different color scheme on the terminal. You may have preferred to receive department number with a PIC 9(7). I personally prefer PIC X(7). Also, since that is the default, it simplifies my coding.

If you're thinking, "Gee, the BMS process of building MAPs certainly seems messy," I agree with you. If your shop has software that does this for you, I encourage you to use it. Even with such software, however, I still like to know all the options. Sometimes a programmer wants a particular set of options for a MAP or a data field. When all else fails, come back to these BMS macros. They may seem dirty, but they can do everything that can be done.

One of the many software products on the market that auto-mates the process of creating CICS screens is IBM's Screen Definition Facility (SDF). This is a separate software product and is not part of the base CICS product. An advantage of SDF (and others like it) is that SDF generates the BMS macros for you. Then, if you already know BMS, you can tweak the generated macros, if desired.

It took a lot of code, didn't it, to create such a simple screen? Bear that in mind when you encounter a MAP for a screen with lots of data fields. The listing of such a MAP may go on for several pages and appear intimidating. More than likely, 40 percent of the MAP will be DFHMDF stopper bytes, 40 percent of the MAP will be DFHMDF data entry fields, and the remainder DFHMDF title fields.

This part of the book bears rereading after you get some exposure to writing MAPs. This is not the type of material that you should expect yourself to memorize. Life is much easier if you just know what it can do and where you last placed this book.

MAP coding assignment. For now, photocopy the screen layout sheet at the back of this book, lay out the screen shown in Figure 3.7, and then code the BMS macros for the screen. Place the fields wherever you feel they look neat, but please keep them in the same order. My suggestion is to place PAYR2500 on line 1 at the far left; place the MSG field somewhere between rows 20 and 23; and place the bottom comment ("Press PF3 to terminate") on line 24.

The only data entry field is Employee number. This needs to be three separate fields to allow for the "-" between the digits. The Employee number title field, the variable fields (shown as either x's, $'s or 9's), plus the message field near the bottom of the screen should be in high intensity. The variable fields all need names because they will be modified by the program, but they should not be accessible by the terminal user. A sample solution appears at the end of this chapter. This is a good place to stop, review some of the BMS macros covered here, and make a few starts on the MAP. Once you get started, you'll find that, while it's tedious, it's not brain surgery either.

```
PAYR2500                                                   .

              Employee Number:    999 - 99 - 9999

Last Name: xxxxxxxxxxxxxxxx 1st Name: xxxxxxxxxx Education: xx

Dept #  : xxx
Job Code : xx
Salary  : $$$,$$9.99




xxxxxxxxxxxxxxxxxxxxxxxxxxxxxxxxxxxxxxxxxxxxxxxxxxxxxxxxxxx
Press PF3 to terminate
```

Figure 3.7. Sample screen to code.

3.3. ASSEMBLING A MAP

Compared to the prior topic, this is a snap. We've already covered most of what you need to do here. I apologize to the VSE reader as, while the steps are the same, I don't have a JCL example to show you. Please check with your supervisor, coach, or team member for JCL to use at your shop. For that matter, I encourage MVS readers to do the same, as I'm sure the sample JCL that I will show you does not match your shop's procedure. In a previous topic, we reviewed some of this, primarily that both the physical MAP and the symbolic MAP need to be created at the same time to ensure that they match each other. Here we will see all the steps as they are done.

3.3.1. The Logic Flow

Since there are two outputs, a physical MAP and a symbolic MAP, you will see that we must invoke the assembler software twice, once for each of the outputs. Here is an overview of the steps:

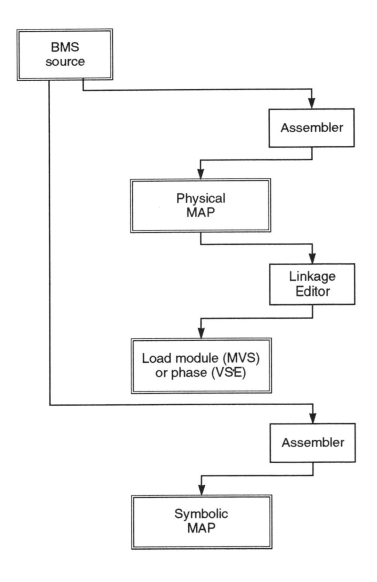

The output should be carefully understood, depending on the standards at your shop. The symbolic MAP should be stored in your shop's designated library for COBOL COPYbooks, and the linkage editor's output needs to be in a designated library that is assigned to your CICS environment. (Remember, since this is for an online environment, the designated library is preassigned by your systems programmers). Don't forget to recompile your COBOL program to use the new COPYbook!!! That may sound obvious, but often when we are involved with the design and coding of a MAP, we sometimes forget to reassemble the COBOL program. This is especially true when a programmer feels the change in the MAP was "insignificant."

3.3.2. The JCL for Assembling a MAP

In Figure 3.8 is a sample MVS PROC to assemble a MAP. If you follow it, you will see that it has the same steps in it that are shown in the previous flowchart. The JCL used at your shop is undoubtedly different, but only in the details. This PROC uses symbolic parameters to identify the BMS source library and the output libraries. This PROC also stores the symbolic MAP with a suffix of "C." Your shop may follow similar practices. This technique lets me know that, if I code a MAP called PAY2500, the symbolic MAP will be named PAY2500C.

In this PROC, the physical MAP is named to match the name of the BMS source by combining the NAME and SUF keywords. If you remember the DFHMSD macro and its TERM keyword, you realize the possibilities of using this option. For example, if you are using the same BMS source to create MAPs for a variety of terminals (not just 3270's), you might want to specify the appropriate suffix for that terminal type (e.g., a standard, 80-column 3270 is a suffix of M). If I were assembling a MAP named PAY2500 from a default source library but, because it contains TERM=3270-2, I might code the EXEC statement as

```
//ASMBL    EXEC  DFHMAPS,NAME=PAY2500,SUF=M
```

Naturally, if this is done, the PPT needs to reflect the PAY2500M name, not the normal PAY2500. This in itself does not improve performance, whether for MVS or VSE. The performance improvement comes from specifying the proper terminal on the TERM option. This JCL technique is only so, where there might be several terminal types being accessed (and you have modified the TERM= parameter and separately assembled separate MAPs for each), BMS can automatically find the correct MAP for the given terminal.

```
//DFHMAPS PROC  OUT='*',
//              LIB='your.source.lib',       TARGET FOR MAP
//              LOAD='your.cics.loadlib',    TARGET FOR DSECT
//              NAME=,                        NAME OF MAPSET
//              SUF=,                         SUFFIX OF MAPSET
//              A=,                           USE A FOR ALIGNED MAP
//              OUT='*'                       SYSOUT CLASS
//ASMMAP   EXEC  PGM=IEV90,
//              PARM='SYSPARM(&A.MAP),DECK,NOLOAD'
//SYSPRINT DD   SYSOUT=&OUT
//SYSLIB   DD   DSN=CICS.MACLIB,DISP=SHR
//         DD   DSN=SYS1.MACLIB,DISP=SHR
//SYSUT1   DD   UNIT=SYSDA,SPACE=(CYL,(5,5)),DCB=BLKSIZE=32760
//SYSUT2   DD   UNIT=SYSDA,SPACE=(CYL,(5,5)),DCB=BLKSIZE=32760
//SYSUT3   DD   UNIT=SYSDA,SPACE=(CYL,(5,5)),DCB=BLKSIZE=32760
//SYSPUNCH DD   DSN=&&MAP,UNIT=SYSDA,
//              DCB=(RECFM=FB,LRECL=80,BLKSIZE=3200,NCP=5),
//              SPACE=(400,(50,50)),DISP=(,PASS)
//SYSIN    DD   DSN=&LIB.(&NAME),DISP=SHR
//LINK     EXEC  PGM=IEWL,COND=(0,LT),
//              PARM='LIST,LET,XREF,SIZE=(2000K,900K)'
//SYSPRINT DD   SYSOUT=&OUT
//SYSLMOD  DD   DSN=&LOAD.(&NAME&SUF),DISP=SHR
//SYSUT1   DD   UNIT=SYSDA,SPACE=(CYL,(3,2))
//SYSLIN   DD   DSN=&&MAP,DISP=(OLD,DELETE)
//ASMDSCT  EXEC  PGM=IEV90,COND=(0,LT),
//              PARM='SYSPARM(&A.DSECT),DECK,NOLOAD'
//SYSPRINT DD   SYSOUT=&OUT
//SYSLIB   DD   DSN=CICS.MACLIB,DISP=SHR
//         DD   DSN=SYS1.MACLIB,DISP=SHR
//SYSUT1   DD   UNIT=SYSDA,SPACE=(CYL,(5,5)),DCB=BLKSIZE=32760
//SYSUT2   DD   UNIT=SYSDA,SPACE=(CYL,(5,5)),DCB=BLKSIZE=32760
//SYSUT3   DD   UNIT=SYSDA,SPACE=(CYL,(5,5)),DCB=BLKSIZE=32760
//SYSPUNCH DD   DSN=&LIB.(&NAME.C),DISP=SHR
//SYSIN    DD   DSN=&LIB.(&NAME),DISP=SHR
```

Figure 3.8. Sample MVS PROCedure for assembling a MAP.

SUMMARY

Back a few pages, you were asked to code a sample MAP from Figure 3.7. A sample solution appears in Figure 3.9. I'm sure that yours is different because the specifications that I gave were intentionally vague. I'm also sure we were different in our use of stopper bytes. For example, they weren't required after protected, variable fields (such as JOBCODE) because there was no need to protect the terminal user from entering too much data.

So why did I include the stopper bytes? Because I usually find that a MAP used for only inquiry purposes is often used for data entry, too. Since the attribute bytes can be modified by the program, I always try to set up MAPs so that they can be used for more than one function. That usually means the same MAP might be used for inquiry, updates, and additions. My purpose in this exercise, other than giving you an opportunity to practice BMS macros, was also to reinforce that MAPs will usually appear similar for any given screen but will still have differences.

Near the bottom of the MAP in Figure 3.9 is a field that I named XTRAFLD. It isn't required, but I inserted it anyway. I'll explain why I do this on my MAPs in the next chapter.

This was a major chapter and, although the emphasis was on 3270 terminals, much of it applies to other terminals, too. Plus, I hope you got some insight on BMS and how it works. Now that you've got some experience with a simple CICS program and understand MAPs, we will pursue developing applications that use full-screen MAPs, the type of program that is most likely used at your shop.

There are many books that breeze through the BMS macros in a page or two. That is great for a person who just wants to code a simple MAP for a classroom exercise. I made this chapter bigger because I remember, when I was coding my second or third MAP, I began to discover that I needed more knowledge of the options and of the process.

You may, depending on the people in your shop, hear folktales about what works and what doesn't. If it contradicts what you read here, look for proof. I, too, suffered from hearing others describe processes that supposedly occur between CICS, the MAP, and the COBOL program. If you can't understand it or demonstrate it, be suspicious.

```
            TITLE 'MAPSET PAYR250 for coding practice'
            PRINT NOGEN
*****************************************************************
** This is a sample solution to figure 3.7.
*****************************************************************
PAYR250   DFHMSD TYPE=&SYSPARM,                                    X
            MODE=INOUT,                                            X
            LANG=COBOL,                                            X
            TIOAPFX=YES,                                           X
            CTRL=(FREEKB)
PAY2501   DFHMDI SIZE=(24,80)
          DFHMDF POS=(01,01),LENGTH=08,                           X
            INITIAL='PAYR2500'
          DFHMDF POS=(05,19),LENGTH=17,ATTRB=(BRT,ASKIP),         X
            INITIAL='Employee Number: '
EMPNUM1   DFHMDF POS=(05,37),ATTRB=(UNPROT,NUM),LENGTH=3
          DFHMDF POS=(05,41),ATTRB=(BRT,ASKIP),LENGTH=1
EMPNUM2   DFHMDF POS=(05,43),ATTRB=(UNPROT,NUM),LENGTH=2
          DFHMDF POS=(05,46),ATTRB=(BRT,ASKIP),LENGTH=1
EMPNUM3   DFHMDF POS=(05,48),ATTRB=(UNPROT,NUM),LENGTH=4
          DFHMDF POS=(05,53),ATTRB=(BRT,ASKIP),LENGTH=1
          DFHMDF POS=(07,06),LENGTH=10,                           X
            INITIAL='Last Name:'
LASTN     DFHMDF POS=(07,17),LENGTH=15,ATTRB=(PROT,BRT)
          DFHMDF POS=(07,34),LENGTH=14,INITIAL='   1st Name:'
FIRSTN    DFHMDF POS=(07,49),LENGTH=10,ATTRB=(PROT,BRT)
          DFHMDF POS=(07,60),LENGTH=15,INITIAL='   Education:'
EDUCAT    DFHMDF POS=(07,76),LENGTH=02,ATTRB=(PROT,BRT)
          DFHMDF POS=(07,79),LENGTH=1
          DFHMDF POS=(10,06),LENGTH=9,                            X
            INITIAL='Dept #   :'
DEPTNO    DFHMDF POS=(10,16),LENGTH=03,ATTRB=(PROT,BRT)
          DFHMDF POS=(10,20),LENGTH=1
          DFHMDF POS=(11,06),LENGTH=9,                            X
            INITIAL='Job Code:'
JOBCODE   DFHMDF POS=(11,16),LENGTH=04,ATTRB=(PROT,BRT)
          DFHMDF POS=(11,21),LENGTH=1
          DFHMDF POS=(12,06),LENGTH=9,                            X
            INITIAL='Salary   :'                                  .
SALARY    DFHMDF POS=(12,16),LENGTH=10,ATTRB=(PROT,BRT),          X
            PICOUT='$$$,$$9.99'
          DFHMDF POS=(12,27),LENGTH=1
MSG1      DFHMDF POS=(22,01),LENGTH=79,INITIAL=' ',               X
            ATTRB=(BRT,PROT)
          DFHMDF POS=(24,1),LENGTH=22,                            X
            INITIAL='Press PF3 to terminate'
XTRAFLD   DFHMDF POS=(24,78),LENGTH=1,INITIAL=' ',                X
            ATTRB=(PROT,FSET)
          DFHMSD TYPE=FINAL
          END
```

Figure 3.9. Sample solution to Figure 3.7.

VOCABULARY REVIEW

Your vocabulary grew quite a bit here, didn't it? You were introduced to the concept of a task, the 3270 terminal, BMS, and many attributes of MAPs. Test yourself on these questions:

Write the names of the three macros.

Write at least three keywords and their options for the three macros.

What are the default attribute byte options for a field if nothing is specified?

A good practice exercise would be to review some MAPs of screens already in use at your shop. Some of them won't make sense until you have more experience, but you may also discover that some aren't well done. That occurs because much of the skill in building MAPs is passed down from one programmer to another with little use of textbooks. When people are in a hurry, it is not unusual to borrow what someone else has done just to meet the target date. I've done it, and you may have, too. With practice, experienced CICS programmers do many things with MAPs. So practice, practice, practice. Whenever time allows, write your MAPs from scratch. You will learn new tricks each time.

4

Developing Expanded Transactions

This chapter will take you through two applications, one that uses a single MAP and one that uses a menu approach. The logic will be simple, as I don't think you (or I) want to wade through a massive real-life application with thousands of lines of code. What I have found from working with CICS and watching others learn CICS (or learn other computer skills) is that most programmers just need a few pointers and examples and can then pick up the rest themselves.

4.1. INTERACTING WITH A TERMINAL USING A MAP

Right now, other than the specifics of the SEND MAP and RECEIVE MAP commands, you have all the skills needed to write an application using MAPs. Just review back over the first application we did using the SEND TEXT and RECEIVE TEXT commands, and I'm sure you will see that you could probably salvage 9/10 of that program. That would be a workable program but not a good one. That's why I want first to introduce you to some additional information on the dialogue itself and some techniques that can improve the quality and user-friendliness of your applications.

One issue that is little understood is the basic set of steps that occur between the terminal and the mainframe and how BMS is involved. Despite our discussion earlier that the 3270 terminal is not a "glass typewriter," I have seen many programmers who assume that it is. By that, I mean that they assume that everything sent from the application goes to the terminal, never to return. They also assume that everything on the screen is returned to them. It is more complex than that. Here are the basics, presented as they can be logically perceived, not as the actual mechanics are processed.

Logical steps that occur during a SEND MAP to a terminal:

1. CICS constructs the data stream using MAP. Data fields containing LOW-VALUES are *not* included.

2. Attribute bytes from symbolic MAP replace those in the MAP if the attribute byte fields in symbolic MAP are *not* LOW-VALUES.

3. The first length field in the symbolic MAP that is -1 becomes the cursor position, overriding any specified in MAP.

4. Using options in the SEND MAP command, the data stream is sent to the terminal.

Logical steps that occur for a RECEIVE MAP in pseudoconversation processing:

1. CICS RECEIVES the terminal input when user presses an AID key.

2. CICS updates the EIB (Executive Information Block) and then initiates the transaction identified for this terminal from the previous RETURN TRANSID command.

3. When the application issues a RECEIVE MAP command, CICS formats the data into the symbolic MAP identified in the RECEIVE command.

This may seem irrelevant now, but, when you are reviewing how best to use the SEND MAP command and some programmer-oriented features that let you override MAP attributes, this may assist you. Also, knowing that these are the basic steps will help you determine the desired order of processing steps to take when executing a RECEIVE MAP command.

For example, this chapter will demonstrate how you can override attributes specified in the MAP and how to control what data fields are sent/received. The comments in this topic about LOW-VALUES are critical to that process. CICS combines the symbolic and physical MAPs by overlaying the symbolic MAP over the physical MAP. If any field in the symbolic MAP is not LOW-VALUES, that field (whether it is an attribute field, a length field, or a data field) overrides the physical MAP, and may create unexpected results.

Recently, I assisted a programmer who was having difficulty getting his program to work properly. The program seemed to be written well, and it was puzzling to many programmers. The problem? He had the statement, MOVE SPACES to mapname, immediately preceding the first SEND MAP command, causing all the attributes to be set to hex '40'. When he changed his MOVE statement to 'MOVE LOW-VALUES to mapname', the program worked.

4.1.1. The SEND MAP Command

The SEND MAP command appears similar to the SEND TEXT command, but, because it interacts with BMS and with the terminal, there are additional considerations. The options shown in Figure 4.1 are the most commonly used features.

```
FUNCTION: Sends MAP to terminal

EXEC CICS SEND MAP(mapname)
          [[ FROM(dataname) ] [ DATAONLY ] | MAPONLY ]
          [ MAPSET(mapsetname) ]
          [ CURSOR(value) ]
          [ FREEKB ]
          [ ALARM ]
          [ ERASE | ERASEAUP ]
          [ FRSET ]
          [ HANDLE | NOHANDLE [ RESP(dataname) ] ] ]
END-EXEC

Most probable error condition: INVMPSZ
```

Figure 4.1. SEND MAP basic syntax.

The SEND TEXT command was rather plebeian. This one ain't. While your first programs may use a simple set of options for the SEND MAP command, you will find that good CICS programmers use the options judiciously, as they affect data traffic to and from the host. While it's okay for a small, infrequently used application to send lots of data back and forth, it's another matter when there are hundreds of users accessing the system. In those situations, your goal will be to send as few bytes as possible. It is for this reason that you may see several different SEND MAP commands in a program. For now, don't worry too much about it, but you will see some opportunities as we go. Also, you will discover that choices in the BMS macros can be combined with choices in the SEND MAP command for optimum results.

The keywords are pretty straightforward, and some may remind you of some BMS options. They should, since they are an alternate way of providing the function.

MAP(mapname) This specifies the name of the MAP that is to be sent. This can be either a literal or a dataname containing the literal. If MAPSET is not coded also, BMS assumes that this is the MAPSET name and that there is only one MAP in the MAPSET. This is the only mandatory keyword to code.

FROM(dataname) This specifies the 01-level dataname from your symbolic MAP. You created this name when you coded the DFHMDI command. BMS appends an "I" to it. Do not specify if MAPONLY is specified.

DATAONLY|MAPONLY This can affect data traffic. If neither is specified, BMS sends the physical MAP (this contains all the title and comment fields) and the symbolic MAP (this contains the variable data fields that you identified by assigning names when you coded the DFHMDF macros). Certainly there are times when you want to send everything, possibly the first SEND MAP command. But on subsequent SENDs, you may determine that some of that information is already glowing brightly on the terminal and need not be resent. Good examples of this are the title fields and other fixed information that are on the screen. If the only fields that have changed are the data entry fields, you could specify DATAONLY and only the symbolic MAP contents are sent. Likewise, there will be times, such as when no data has been entered, that MAPONLY is appropriate. You can get some good advice here by discussing this with some of the better programmers at your shop. In this book, we won't attempt to tweak this too much. Your supervisor or coach can also advise you on how important this is for your applications. At some shops, the only important issue is getting the application up and functioning.

MAPSET(mapsetname) This specifies the name of the MAPSET. This isn't needed if there is only one MAP in the MAPSET. Still, I prefer to code it, as I am protected if, for some reason, an additional MAP is defined to the MAPSET later. As with MAP, this may be either a literal or the dataname containing the literal. This will be the name you coded on the DFHMSD macro.

CURSOR(value) This may be used to specify where the cursor should be placed on the screen. You may recall that this could also be controlled on the DFHMDF macro. I don't recommend the DFHMDF approach as you normally want more flexibility. Even if you did code it on a DFHMDF macro, this option will override it. There are two approaches to using CURSOR. One is to code a numeric value following CURSOR, such as CURSOR(175) or reference a data field (PIC S9(4) COMP) that contains the value. That would place the cursor on position 175, relative to 0, on the screen. That's messy, because it requires that you first figure out where that is. So don't do it. Instead, just code CURSOR without a following value. That indicates that the cursor location is programmatically controlled. We will cover all of that shortly. For now, just code CURSOR and have faith.

FREEKB, ALARM, and FRSET These all have exactly the same meaning as they did in the BMS macros. If you coded them on the macros, you don't need to code them here. If you code them here, they do the same thing. If you review programs at your shop, you will probably find that they are often coded on both the macros and in the SEND MAPs. There's no reason for this, other than habit. (I often find myself doing it, too.)

ERASE I ERASEAUP This specifies the degree, if any, that the screen should be erased prior to formatting the MAP onto the screen. If you are sending a new MAP, you will want to specify ERASE as, otherwise, any data already on the screen and not overwritten will remain. Your use of this option should also be considered when specifying DATAONLY or MAPONLY. For example, specifying DATAONLY and ERASE would cause all the titles to be erased, leaving nothing but the data fields — not a desired result.

ERASEAUP serves a special need. This specifies that *only* the unprotected fields are to be erased, leaving all the protected fields. This can be advantageous if your application has just finished processing one unit of work and is not sending back a fresh screen for the terminal user to resume with the next business unit (such as inquiring on a person's loan status). When this approach is used, it should be combined with DATAONLY. This would be similar to specifying MAPONLY and ERASE. Which is more appropriate depends on the amount of fixed and variable data on your screens.

HANDLE I NOHANDLE [RESP (dataname)] We reviewed this back in Chapter 2 when I covered the need to handle CICS error conditions. This can be coded on any CICS command where a possibility of an error may occur and you want to handle it yourself. The default is HANDLE, so, if you code nothing, the CICS default will apply. If you code NOHANDLE, CICS will defer to you on what to do. Normally, that is my recommendation. When you code NOHANDLE, you should also code RESP and the name of a PIC S9(8) COMP field to store the condition code. In Chapter 2, I gave you two options, either using my sample COPYbook, CICSRESP, or the DFHRESP function in a COBOL statement. Examples in this book will generally use the CICSRESP COPYbook because it's cleaner.

If we had a MAPSET named PAY2500 and a MAP named PAY2501, here are some examples, assuming that I specified FREEKB in the BMS macros:

```
EXEC CICS SEND MAP ('PAY2501')     This sends the
               MAPSET ('PAY2500')   physical and
               FROM   (PAY2501I)    symbolic MAP
               CURSOR
               ERASE
END-EXEC

EXEC CICS SEND MAP ('PAY2501')     This sends only
               MAPSET ('PAY2500')   data fields
               FROM   (PAY2501I)
               DATAONLY
               CURSOR
END-EXEC
```

```
EXEC CICS SEND MAP (MAP-NAME)       This can send
               MAPSET (MAPSET-NAME) any MAP
               FROM   (SYM-MAP-AREA)
               ERASE
               CURSOR
END-EXEC
```

The third example is often used if a program sends more than one MAP. By first moving the MAP name to the field called MAP-NAME, the MAPSET name to the field called MAPSET-NAME, and the entire symbolic MAP to the 01-area called SYM-MAP-AREA. This might be something like this:

```
   05  MAP-NAME      PIC   X(8).
   05  MAPSET-NAME   PIC   X(8).
01 SYM-MAP-AREA      PIC   X(1920).
```

The advantage of this approach is that a program has only one SEND MAP command for several possible MAPs. There are cases where this is advantageous, such as where there may be ten or more MAPs that are to be sent with the same options, but the complexity and overhead of the additional logic and data movement should also be considered. This also may increase the memory used by the application.

Incidentally, I defined SYM-MAP-AREA as PIC X(1920) only because, as an area that must be as large as the largest symbolic MAP, I used the size of the largest possible screen on a 24 X 80 screen. In reality, the largest screen for an application would be much less.

In Figure 4.1, I included reference to the most probable error condition. I will include such information on other commands from here on. If you recall our discussion of error conditions in CICS (in Chapter 2), you are responsible for trapping them or deferring to CICS to handle them. This condition, INVMPSZ (which is short for INVALID MAP SIZE), is so rare that it's not even included in my sample COPybook, CICSRESP. Since I am dealing with 3270 terminals and I always specify SIZE=(24,80) on the DFHMDI macro, I don't worry about it. This is a case where the possible error is such that I couldn't recover programmatically anyway, so I don't test the RESP code after SEND MAP commands. That contradicts my earlier pronouncement that you should always test for possible errors after a CICS command, but I meant it as a guideline and I wanted to sensitize you to the issue. If I wanted to test for this condition, and

because that condition isn't in the CICSRESP COPYbook, here is how
it could be coded, if desired:

```
EXEC CICS SEND MAP     ('PAY2501')
               MAPSET  ('PAY2500')
               FROM    (PAY2501I)
               CURSOR
               ERASE
               NOHANDLE
               RESP    (CICS-RESP-CODE)
END-EXEC

IF CICS-RESP-CODE = DFHRESP(INVMPSZ)
   code to handle error condition goes here
END-IF
```

The problem, of course, is figuring out what action to take. Any
time you can't figure out what to do, let CICS handle it. If your shop
has a standard program to CALL to Abend in such situations, that
might be an alternative. In this situation, it might be feasible to use
a SEND TEXT command to the terminal, explaining that their terminal is inconsistent with your assumptions and to call some helpdesk
for assistance.

Now that you have a grasp of the SEND MAP command, you
may want to review the first topic in this chapter to see the implications. For example, that topic states that fields with LOW-VALUES
in the symbolic MAP are not sent to the terminal. That becomes
another tool in your toolbox on how to control what data is/is not sent
to a terminal. For example, by moving LOW-VALUES to the 01-level
symbolic MAP prior to a SEND MAP command causes no data to be
sent. Likewise, moving a space to a data field causes whatever was
on the terminal screen to be removed.

4.1.2. The RECEIVE MAP Command

Unlike the SEND MAP command with all of its technical considerations, the RECEIVE MAP (Figure 4.2) is much simpler. However, it
is also more susceptible to encountering errors than the SEND MAP
and, also unlike the SEND MAP, these are errors that you can usually recover from.

```
FUNCTION: Receives MAP from a terminal
EXEC CICS   RECEIVE MAP(mapname)
          [ SET(pointer) | INTO(dataname) ]
          [ MAPSET(mapsetname) ]
          [ HANDLE | NOHANDLE [ RESP() ] ]
END-EXEC

Most probable error conditions: INVMPSZ, MAPFAIL
```

Figure 4.2. RECEIVE MAP basic syntax.

First, remember that this is not the equivalent of a READ command, although it sometimes seems like one. Instead, since we are doing pseudoconversation programming, CICS has *already* read the data from the terminal and now, upon your request, CICS formats the data (if any) into your symbolic MAP.

MAP, MAPSET, and the HANDLE These options are the same as in SEND MAP. Also, while I will continue to show the HANDLE options on other commands, I won't make further reference to them.

SET(pointer) This is used when the program is requesting that CICS dynamically allocate a data area in the LINKAGE SECTION to store the MAP. Since this is a little tricky, let's postpone it for awhile. In fact, your shop may never use it. This is one of the techniques programmers use to manage the memory required by their application. In a batch application, this type of technique would never be a consideration.

INTO(dataname) This is the equivalent of the FROM option in SEND MAP. This names the symbolic MAP 01-level area where the MAP is to be stored. It is not uncommon for programs to SEND and RECEIVE into the same area.

As you see, this is much simpler than the SEND MAP. Here is an example of the RECEIVE MAP command, using the CICSRESP COPYbook. (As a reminder, CICS-RESP-CODE is a dataname in that COPYbook. It is defined as PIC S9(8) COMP.):

```
EXEC CICS RECEIVE MAP    ('PAY2501')
                  MAPSET ('PAY2500')
                  INTO   (PAY2501I)
                  NOHANDLE
                  RESP   (CICS-RESP-CODE)
END-EXEC
```

Earlier, I stated that the RECEIVE MAP command may encounter errors. This is because you have no control over what the terminal user does. You tried to design an easy-to-use transaction, but the terminal user has a lot of keys to press; some of them you may prefer they never used.

For example, the user may have pressed the Enter key when nothing had been entered. When that happens, there is no data for BMS to process, as it only processes unprotected fields with the MDT set. When no data has the MDT set, that causes the MAPFAIL error to occur, and, if you don't take charge, CICS considers this error sufficient to abend the transaction. Naturally, you don't want that to happen every time a terminal user presses the Enter key without having entered data. This particular situation can be prevented by always defining an extra field on the MAP that always contains data and is always RECEIVEd. This could be done in the MAP with something such as this:

```
XTRAFLD DFHMDF POS=(24,78),LENGTH=1,INITIAL=' ',   X
               ATTRB=(PROT,FSET)
```

This extra field, which could be coded anywhere on the MAP, ensures that, if the user enters no data, at least this one-byte field will be returned with a RECEIVE MAP command. The field will appear in your symbolic MAP COPYbook, but you should just ignore it. This is why I inserted an extra field in the MAP back in Figure 3.9. This frees me from worrying, in the application, about whether any data was entered.

However, that macro trick only protects against one possibility. The other common possibility is that the user might press the CLEAR key. This resets the 3270 terminal to its base state, causes an interrupt to the controller (which treats it as a signal to the host transaction) which then sets the interrupt for the operating system to notify CICS that the terminal wants attention. Whew! Anyway, by the time CICS gives control to your program, not only did no data get transferred, but the screen is now blank so there is nothing at all on the terminal screen.

Solving the CLEAR key problem is clearly not as controllable as the other situation was. Now that NOHANDLE feature gets useful. Using the previous sample RECEIVE MAP, I would follow the command with something like this:

```
If using the CICSRESP COPYbook:
    IF CICS-MAPFAIL
        insert logic here to ensure no data process-
        ing occurs and that a SEND MAP is reinitiated
        to establish the titles and data fields
If not using the CICSRESP COPYbook:
    IF CICS-RESP-CODE = DFHRESP(MAPFAIL)
        same logic as the previous example
```

The complexity of what must be done is dependent on your application. If you used the DFHMDF approach to protect against the transmission of no data, then you know the CLEAR key must have been pressed. Knowing that everything is gone from the terminal screen can be a major problem for some transactions, and a simple process to correct for others. It will depend on the use of various SEND MAP options and on whether there was data on the screen that needs to be constructed, such as rereading data from a file. (*Reminder*: In older programs, you may see the HANDLE CONDITION command being used for MAPFAIL.)

4.2. DETERMINING WHAT AID KEY WAS PRESSED

In discussing the RECEIVE MAP command, we saw that a person could press the CLEAR key and cause a problem to occur, one that we could fix, but one where we weren't sure what happened. Well, there is help. CICS has the ability to tell us what key the user pressed. You may recall that one of the data areas used by CICS to communicate with the application is the EIB (Executive Interface Block).

You read in the first topic of this chapter that CICS updates the EIB just before it gives control to the application. The EIB contains lots of fields, some of which we will encounter later. For now, we are concerned with the field named EIBAID. This is a one-byte field that contains a value representing which of the AID keys was pressed. You can test the value of EIBAID with an IF statement. The question is "What values do I use?" To answer this, IBM provides a COPYbook that you can COPY into your WORKING STORAGE SECTION. This

COPYbook is named DFHAID and contains a field for each of the values that could be in EIBAID. A listing of DFHAID is in Appendix A of this book.

This changes our view of the previous MAPFAIL problem. Since the EIB is updated before the RECEIVE MAP is issued (*Reminder*: true only for pseudoconversational transactions), we can test for the CLEAR key before issuing the RECEIVE MAP if we want to. This can make the logic easier to follow. For example, one of the first instructions in our program might be:

```
IF EIBAID = DFHCLEAR

    perform logic that sends initial MAP
    and return control via RETURN TRANSID
```

This also gives us application power. For example, when you coded that MAP assignment, one of the titles on the screen was 'Press PF3 to terminate'. Now you know how we can determine that. That could be done by something such as:

```
IF EIBAID = DFHPF3
    EXEC CICS RETURN END-EXEC
END-IF
```

Your company probably has some standards on PF key use, so check with them for which ones you should use. I personally like to use the PF key assignments that IBM uses for its ISPF software. From your user community perspective, the important thing is that all transactions should use the same keys for the same function. I also recommend that all PFkeys that may be used by an application be listed at the bottom of the screen. This helps users to use the application more effectively.

In an earlier topic, we discussed the HANDLE CONDITION command, a command that was the only way to intercept error conditions prior to CICS 1.7. I recommended that you not use it, relying on the NOHANDLE approach within CICS commands. There was (still is) another command that was used to determine which AID key was pressed. That command, HANDLE AID, is similar to the HANDLE CONDITION command. You may see this technique in older programs. The command was normally issued prior to the RECEIVE MAP command. The code was something like this:

```
EXEC CICS HANDLE AID
          PF3     (paragraph-name-a)
          CLEAR   (paragraph-name-b)
          ANYKEY  (paragraph-name-c)
END-EXEC

EXEC CICS RECEIVE MAP
    .
    .
    .
```

As with the HANDLE CONDITION command, this caused CICS to transfer control to the named paragraph if, when processing the RECEIVE MAP command, CICS determined that the named AID key was pressed. This caused programs to have many GO TO statements and PERFORM THRU statements in an attempt to maintain control of the program logic. Worse, the HANDLE command, whether for CONDITION or AID, stays in effect for the remainder of the task, possibly being invoked when your program did not expect it. So, my recommendation for new programs is *don't use the handle commands.* Instead, test for AID keys through the EIBAID entry in the EIB and for error conditions through the RESP option. Also, always specify NOHANDLE on CICS commands.

4.3.   CONTROLLING THE CURSOR

We've seen that one key factor to a clean application is being able to control the cursor on SEND commands and detect where the cursor is on RECEIVE commands. We will review the approach to each separately.

4.3.1.   Controlling the Cursor on SEND MAP Commands

So far, we've identified several ways to control the cursor. One was to do it with the DFHMDF macro. The downside of that approach is that it limits you to using the same field all the time on SEND commands. Most applications prefer to place the cursor where the terminal user's attention is desired, such as a field in error.

The alternate approach we saw was to use the CURSOR(datavalue) option on the SEND MAP command. That works, but it requires that the application keep a table of values (manually computed) of where each affected field is written on the screen. *That* works, but it's messy, and, if the screen is rearranged, the values are all wrong.

Since neither of those two approaches gives the flexibility you need, you're still waiting for me to give a solution. Here's all you have to do. Remember those five fields defined in the MAP for each data field? Do you recall that the first field was the length field and its name was constructed by using the one- to seven-character name you entered appended with an "L"? That field is documented as being a field that contains the number of characters entered into the field for use after a RECEIVE MAP command. Well, it has another, possibly more important, function. If you move a -1 to the field prior to a SEND MAP command, BMS will position the cursor at that field location. (Don't forget to include the word CURSOR on the SEND MAP command.) If you move -1 to more than one field, BMS sets the cursor at the upper leftmost field on the screen. This works even if the fields are rearranged later. What I like about this technique is that it lets the program focus on the application logic and not on what row and column of the screen contains the data.

As an example, if I had defined a field as DEPTNO and wanted the SEND MAP to position the cursor at that field, I would code

```
MOVE    -1   TO DEPTNOL
SEND MAP  ...
     CURSOR
     •
     •
```

You will usually find the technique used in that part of the application logic where the application is checking if data was entered correctly or where required data is missing.

4.3.2.   Controlling the Cursor on RECEIVE MAP Commands

On a RECEIVE MAP command, your need is to know where the cursor was. This is less often a requirement than controlling a cursor on the SEND MAP command, but it is often needed.

Some applications are designed to take action depending on what row or what field the cursor is on. For example, if a screen contains a list of ten or so employees, the terminal user may need to see (or modify) additional information for a particular employee from the list. A common technique is to designate a PF key for the function and to use the cursor position to determine which employee's record to read and display on screen.

Doing this is a little more work than we saw in controlling the cursor for the SEND MAP. First, there is a field in the EIB that contains the location, relative to zero, where the cursor was when the AID key was pressed. This field is named EIBCPOSN. After you execute the RECEIVE MAP command, you can test the value to determine if it is within the bounds of a particular row or field. If you're thinking that this is just as clumsy as using the CURSOR(datavalue) on the SEND MAP command, I agree. Unfortunately, until CICS/ESA, there was/is no other choice. CICS/ESA gave us the CURSLOC keyword on the DFHMDI and DFHMSD macros that will help us identify a field, and we'll review that in a moment. It still didn't address the need to identify the cursor over a larger area, such as a row on the screen.

Determining field location from the EIB value. This is a major issue where that screen layout sheet can assist you in figuring out screen locations. You can also do it by referencing the DFHMDF macro for the particular field. Let's work through one, assuming the following macro was in our MAP:

```
EMPNAME    DFHMDF    POS=(15,12),LENGTH=15,...
```

We know the attribute byte begins on row 15, column 12, and the data field is in row 15, columns 13 through 27. Now we need to figure what value might be in EIBCPOSN if the cursor were anywhere in that range. First, remember that the value is relative to zero, not to 1. That means that the cursor position values for the first row are 0 through 79, not 1 through 80. My technique is to use this formula, although you may have an easier way. Since you know COBOL, I'll demonstrate it with a pseudo COMPUTE statement:

```
Compute cursor-position = (row - 1) * 80 + column-position - 1
```

So, for our example, that translates to (15 -1) * 80 + 12 -1 = 1131 for the leftmost position and (15 - 1) * 80 +27 -1 = 1146 for the rightmost position. After executing the RECEIVE MAP command, we are reduced to traditional COBOL code to determine if the cursor was over the field called EMPNAME. That would simply be

```
IF EIBCPOSN > 1130 AND < 1147
    logic for desired action goes here
```

Determining rows from the EIB value. I agree it's dirty, but my goal is to help you learn CICS basics and be able to understand CICS programs. You may see such statements in your shop's programs. At least you will now know what the purpose is. To identify rows, some shops have set up COPYbooks for general use with entries something like the following:

```
01  CICS-CURSOR-POS   PIC   S9(4)   COMP.
    88  ROW-ONE        VALUE    0 THRU    79.
    88  ROW-TWO        VALUE   80 THRU   159.
    88  ROW-THREE      VALUE  160 THRU   239.
    88  ROW-FOUR       VALUE  240 THRU   319.
        .
        .
        .
```

This works, but it overlooks the cumbersome code required to determine that the cursor was in a range of rows, so I don't recommend it. As an example, assuming the program will take action if the cursor is in rows 5 through 15 (possibly those are the rows where a list of names is displayed), this is not atypical code. The repetitive nature indicates a simpler method must exist.

```
MOVE EIBCPOSN TO CICS-CURSOR-POS
EVALUATE TRUE
    WHEN ROW-ONE    MOVE 1 TO ROW-USED
    WHEN ROW-TWO    MOVE 2 TO ROW-USED
    WHEN ROW-THREE  MOVE 3 TO ROW-USED
        .
        .
        .
```

If that's the goal, I would prefer to just use this calculation:

```
05 ROW-USED     PIC S9(4) COMP.

COMPUTE ROW-USED = EIBCPOSN / 80 + 1
IF ROW-USED > 4 AND < 16
    PERFORM 2000-LOCATE-RECORD
ELSE
    PERFORM 2010-SEND-ERROR-MSG.

          or, with COBOL II:

EVALUATE EIBCPOSN / 80 + 1
```

```
WHEN 5 THRU 15.99
      PERFORM 2000-LOCATE-RECORD
WHEN OTHER
      PERFORM 2010-SEND-ERROR-MSG
END-EVALUATE
```

As you see, there are no easy solutions, just your normal COBOL code to solve the issue. The downside of my calculation is that less experienced programmers won't know what I'm doing. Anyway, you have choices on this. Now, let's investigate the new CURSLOC feature provided with CICS/ESA.

Using CURSLOC feature for CICS/ESA. Back when we coded the BMS macros, CURSLOC was an option at the MAPSET level (DFHMSD macro) or the MAP level (DFHMDI). I don't recommend that you specify CURSLOC=YES routinely, but only when the application needs it. Why? Anytime you ask for a special service, always expect it to require code to accomplish the service. If you don't need it, don't ask for it. That's one of my (many) mottos. Assuming we wanted to check to see if the cursor was over a field called JOBTITL, we remember that one of the five fields defined by the DFHMDF macro was JOBTITLF (for flag). We would, of course, specify CURSLOC=YES on either the DFHMSD or the DFHMDI macro. Then, we would need to use another IBM COPYbook, DFHBMSCA (documented in Appendix A). DFHBMSCA contains values for most attributes and flags (they are the same field) that can occur in BMS. We'll see more use of that COPYbook in the next topic. For now, we would do this code:

```
MOVE JOBTITLF TO DFHBFLG
IF DFHCURSR
    logic to proceed when cursor is over this
    field goes here
```

DFHCURSR is a new 88-level with CICS/ESA and does not appear in prior versions of the COPYbook. This IF statement will be true even if the user presses EraseEOF (clears data) for the field. Many companies do not use IBM's DFHBMSCA COPYbook, although most companies use the others mentioned in this book. The reason is that the names in the DFHBMSCA COPYbook are difficult to remember and DFHBMSCA doesn't have some of the screen attribute combinations that the shops want. For that reason, I have an example of a COPYbook in Figure 4.3. The important issue, of course, is to use what your company uses. Ask first, because they may not be using, or not want you to use, DFHBMSCA.

If your shop is using CICS/ESA, there is an additional consideration, that of downward compatibility. Most programmers check for the EraseEOF key by comparing the flag field for the data item to a value of hex '80'. In VS/COBOL, this required that you establish a data element in WORKING STORAGE with the hex value. In COBOL II, you can simply code the following:

```
IF JOBTITLF = X'80'
```

The problem is that, if you add CURSLOC=YES to your MAP specification, the possibilities for EraseEOF become either X'80' or X'82'. This will require that you change those programs that just check for X'80'.

4.4. OVERRIDING ATTRIBUTES ON THE SCREEN

This is the final item we will review for screen management. We covered the AID keys and the cursor. Now we will investigate how you can manage the attributes of fields from within your program. You will use this technique routinely.

Back when you were coding BMS macros, you may have gotten the impression that attributes (protected, bright, numeric) were fixed for any given field. Not true. In most applications there is a need to modify them as the application progresses. As an example, consider a data entry application where a field has been verified as good. A way to prevent the operator from overtyping what has already been verified is to change the field from UNPROT to PROT. On the same note, if a field is incorrect, you may want to change the attribute from UNPROT to UNPROT,BRT to draw attention to it. *Note*: When changing the attribute of a field, remember that you must not just specify the attribute to change; you must specify all attributes that apply to the field. This is because attributes are bit combinations that are prepackaged in the DFHBMSCA COPYbook.

Examine the entries in Figure 4.3, then look at the datanames in DFHBMSCA in Appendix A. I think you'll agree that my example in Figure 4.3 is easier to understand and provides better documentation within the application.

If your shop doesn't have such a COPYbook, you can copy and rename DFHBMSCA and just change the titles. That's the easy way. Don't accidentally change the VALUEs, however. Many of them are bit-combinations that may appear onscreen as a known character when, in fact, they are something different. If you use a text editor such as IBM's ISPF, set HEX ON while viewing the COPYbook and you will see what I mean. The other way is to build one from scratch. This is harder because you have to figure out all the possible hexadecimal values for each attribute combination. That's not easy. The codes in Figure 4.3 are exactly as shown.

```
01  CICS-ATTRIBUTES.
    05  CICS-UNPROT                     PIC  X(01)  VALUE  SPACE.
    05  CICS-UNPROT-MDT                 PIC  X(01)  VALUE  'A'.
    05  CICS-UNPROT-BRT                 PIC  X(01)  VALUE  'H'.
    05  CICS-UNPROT-BRT-MDT             PIC  X(01)  VALUE  'I'.
    05  CICS-UNPROT-DARK                PIC  X(01)  VALUE  '<'.
    05  CICS-UNPROT-DARK-MDT            PIC  X(01)  VALUE  '('.
    05  CICS-UNPROT-NUM                 PIC  X(01)  VALUE  '&'.
    05  CICS-UNPROT-NUM-MDT             PIC  X(01)  VALUE  'J'.
    05  CICS-UNPROT-NUM-BRT             PIC  X(01)  VALUE  'Q'.
    05  CICS-UNPROT-NUM-BRT-MDT         PIC  X(01)  VALUE  'R'.
    05  CICS-UNPROT-NUM-DARK            PIC  X(01)  VALUE  '*'.
    05  CICS-UNPROT-NUM-DARK-MDT        PIC  X(01)  VALUE  ')'.
    05  CICS-PROT                       PIC  X(01)  VALUE  '-'.
    05  CICS-PROT-MDT                   PIC  X(01)  VALUE  '/'.
    05  CICS-PROT-BRT                   PIC  X(01)  VALUE  'Y'.
    05  CICS-PROT-BRT-MDT               PIC  X(01)  VALUE  'Z'.
    05  CICS-PROT-DARK                  PIC  X(01)  VALUE  '%'.
    05  CICS-PROT-DARK-MDT              PIC  X(01)  VALUE  '_'.
    05  CICS-ASKIP                      PIC  X(01)  VALUE  '0'.
    05  CICS-ASKIP-MDT                  PIC  X(01)  VALUE  '1'.
    05  CICS-ASKIP-BRT                  PIC  X(01)  VALUE  '8'.
    05  CICS-ASKIP-BRT-MDT              PIC  X(01)  VALUE  '9'.
    05  CICS-ASKIP-DARK                 PIC  X(01)  VALUE  '@'.
    05  CICS-ASKIP-DARK-MDT             PIC  X(01)  VALUE  QUOTE.
    05  CICS-CURSOR-FLAG                PIC  X(01).
CICS/ESA  &->  88  CICS-CURSOR-ERASE    VALUE  X'80', X'82'.
COBOL II   ->  88  CICS-CURSOR-SELECT   VALUE  X'02', X'82'.
```

Figure 4.3. Example of CICSATTR COPYbook.

If you're wondering why there are no combinations of PROT and NUM in the COPYbook, it is because NUM and PROT share the same bit in the attribute byte. Besides, if a field is protected, NUM is irrelevant.

While this may seem an esoteric note, I want to remind you that specifying an attribute byte from within the program has no effect on the coded or default JUSTIFY option (DFHMDF macro) for that field. Normally, this isn't a concern, as you don't normally change a numeric field to a nonnumeric field. Still, if you do, don't expect the field's justification to change. That feature is within the physical MAP and cannot be changed.

4.5. A SIMPLE TRANSACTION WITH A MAP

The program we will do here will use the MAP developed at the end of Chapter 3. As a reminder, several CICS tables must be updated prior to attempting to run the program. For the example as coded, the PPT would need to be updated to contain both the program name (EMPY0250) and the MAPSET name (PAYR250 or PAYR250M). The PCT would need to reflect that transID P250 relates to program EMPY0250. Finally, the FCT would need an entry for the file called EMPLPAYR.

This program includes a READ command that we haven't covered yet, but I wanted a complete example for you. File I/O is covered in a later chapter. In the example program, the READ command is used to read a record from a VSAM file, using the employee number as a search key. If the record is found, the employee number is valid. If there is no matching record, then the employee number is assumed to be invalid.

This is a simple application, used here only to demonstrate how you tie the various CICS techniques discussed so far into a program. In none of the programs in this book will you encounter extensive application logic. That's not why you're reading this book.

This program is for inquiry only, although it could be modified to allow update using other VSAM I/O commands (or DB2 or SQL or DL/I if that is what your shop uses). The terminal user is expected to enter a full employee number. If the number is numeric, the program will attempt to locate a matching employee record. If the user enters invalid or incomplete data, an error message is produced.

I included a few techniques that aren't necessary but add to the quality of the application. Your shop may not want to use such techniques. Also, for serious error conditions, I just send a message and terminate. In a productional environment, that isn't usually sufficient. Your shop may have standards on what action to take (e.g., abend), so don't assume that the actions I take are necessarily good or proper for error conditions. The basic structure chart follows:

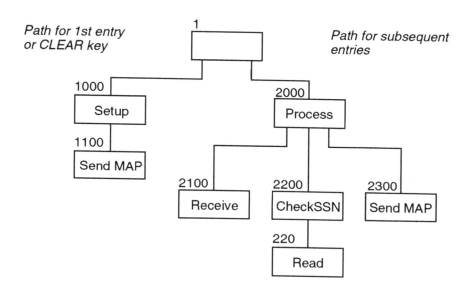

For now, review the program in Figure 4.4 and we'll pick up on it after you've walked through it. Notice that the structure chart is similar to the pseudoconversational program we did earlier that didn't use MAPs. All (most?) pseudoconversational programs resemble each other, at least in the basic structure.

Let's walk through the program from the beginning, starting with WORKING STORAGE. (Your shop may require an entry for ENVIRONMENT DEVISION, but it isn't needed.) I created a field to hold a hex '80' field (done by specifying HEX ON in ISPF). With COBOL II, this isn't needed. This field is here because I want to check whether the user pressed the EraseEOF key, a common practice for users to erase a field. (*Note*: If I had specified CURSLOC=YES on the MAP, I would also need to check for hex '82'.)

```
IDENTIFICATION DIVISION.
PROGRAM-ID.   EMPY0250.
*AUTHOR.   David Shelby Kirk.
DATA DIVISION.
WORKING-STORAGE SECTION.
01 LOCAL-WORK-AREAS.
    05  HEX-80        PIC X      VALUE   ' '.
    05  TERM-SW       PIC X      VALUE   ' '.
    05  TERM-MSG      PIC X(24) VALUE
        ' Transaction terminated.'.
    05  COMPILE-DATE-INFO.
        10 COMPILE-DATE     PIC X(8).
        10 TIME-COMPILED    PIC X(8).

01 INIT-MSG.
    05  FILLER   PIC X(54)    VALUE
    'Employee Inquiry Transaction EMPY0250 - Version 2.1 '.
    05  MESSAGE-DATE          PIC X(12).

01 MY-COMM-AREA      PIC X.
    COPY  CICSRESP.
    COPY  CICSATTR.
    COPY  DFHAID.
    COPY  PAY250C.

01 WS-FILE-DATA.
    05  WS-EMP-FILE    PIC X(8)    VALUE 'EMPLPAYR'.
    05  WS-EMP-LEN     PIC S9(4)   COMP   VALUE +60.
    05  WS-SEARCH-KEY  PIC X(11).
    05  WS-KEY-LEN     PIC S9(4)   COMP   VALUE +11.

01 WS-EMPLOYEE-RECORD.
    05  PAY-SSN         PIC X(11).
    05  PAY-LAST-NAME   PIC X(15).
    05  PAY-FIRST-NAME  PIC X(10).
    05  PAY-EDUCATION   PIC XX.
    05  PAY-DEPT        PIC X(4).
    05  PAY-JOBCODE     PIC X(4).
    05  PAY-SALARY      PIC S9(5)V99    COMP-3.
    05  FILLER          PIC X(10).
```

Figure 4.4. Example of program using MAP.

```
LINKAGE SECTION.
01 DFHCOMMAREA          PIC X.

PROCEDURE DIVISION.
1.  IF EIBCALEN = 0 OR EIBAID = DFHCLEAR
        PERFORM 1000-SETUP
    ELSE
        PERFORM 2000-RETRIEVE-RESP.
    IF TERM-SW = 'Y'
        EXEC CICS SEND TEXT
            FROM    (TERM-MSG)
            LENGTH (24)
            ERASE
            NOHANDLE
            RESP    (CICS-RESP-CODE)
        END-EXEC

        EXEC CICS RETURN
        END-EXEC
    ELSE
        EXEC CICS RETURN
                  TRANSID   ('P250')
                  COMMAREA (MY-COMM-AREA)
                  LENGTH    (1)
        END-EXEC.
    GOBACK.

1000-SETUP.
    MOVE LOW-VALUES TO PAY2501I
    MOVE WHEN-COMPILED TO COMPILE-DATE-INFO
    MOVE COMPILE-DATE TO MESSAGE-DATE
    MOVE INIT-MSG TO MSG10
    PERFORM 1100-SEND-MAP1.

1100-SEND-MAP1.
    MOVE -1  TO EMPNUM1L
    EXEC CICS
         SEND MAP   ('PAY2501')
              MAPSET ('PAYR250')
```

Figure 4.4. (cont'd). Example of program using MAP.

```
                       FROM    (PAY2501I)
                       ERASE
                       FREEKB
                       CURSOR
                       NOHANDLE
                       RESP    (CICS-RESP-CODE)
        END-EXEC.

2000-RETRIEVE-RESP.
    MOVE DFHCOMMAREA TO MY-COMM-AREA
    PERFORM 2100-RECEIVE-MAP
    IF TERM-SW NOT = 'Y'
        PERFORM 2200-CHECK-SSN
        PERFORM 2300-SEND-MAP.

2100-RECEIVE-MAP.
    EXEC CICS RECEIVE MAP('PAY2501')
                      MAPSET    ('PAYR250')
                      INTO      (PAY2501I)
                      NOHANDLE
                      RESP      (CICS-RESP-CODE)
    END-EXEC

    IF EIBAID = DFHPF3
        MOVE 'Y' TO TERM-SW
    ELSE
        IF CICS-MAPFAIL
            MOVE 'Y' TO TERM-SW
            MOVE 'ERROR - MAPFAIL occurred' TO TERM-MSG.

2200-CHECK-SSN.
    MOVE CICS-UNPROT-NUM-BRT  TO EMPNUM1A EMPNUM2A EMPNUM3A
    MOVE CICS-PROT-BRT TO MSG1A
    MOVE -1   TO EMPNUM1L
    IF (EMPNUM1L = 0   OR
        EMPNUM2L = 0      OR
        EMPNUM3L = 0)     OR
       (HEX-80 = EMPNUM1A OR EMPNUM2A OR EMPNUM3A)
        MOVE 'Please enter a complete SSN' TO MSG10
    ELSE
```

Figure 4.4. (cont'd). Example of program using MAP.

```
       IF  EMPNUM1I  NUMERIC  AND
           EMPNUM2I  NUMERIC  AND
           EMPNUM3I  NUMERIC
              PERFORM  2210-READ-FILE
         ELSE
              MOVE 'SSN is not numeric as entered' TO MSG1O.

2210-READ-FILE.
    STRING EMPNUM1I EMPNUM2I EMPNUM3I DELIMITED BY SIZE
       INTO  WS-SEARCH-KEY
    EXEC  CICS  READ
                FILE       (WS-EMP-FILE)
                INTO       (WS-EMPLOYEE-RECORD)
                LENGTH     (WS-EMP-LEN)
                RIDFLD     (WS-SEARCH-KEY)
                KEYLENGTH (WS-KEY-LEN)
                EQUAL
                NOHANDLE
                RESP       (CICS-RESP-CODE)
    END-EXEC

    IF  CICS-NOTFND
        MOVE 'No  record  found  for  that  SSN' TO MSG1O
    ELSE
        IF  CICS-NORMAL
            MOVE  PAY-LAST-NAME  TO  LASTNO
            MOVE  PAY-FIRST-NAME  TO  FIRSTNO
            MOVE  PAY-EDUCATION  TO  EDUCATO
            MOVE  PAY-DEPT  TO  DEPTNOO
            MOVE  PAY-JOBCODE  TO  JOBCODEO
            MOVE  PAY-SALARY  TO  SALARYO
            MOVE  ' '  TO  MSG1O
            MOVE  CICS-UNPROT-NUM  TO  EMPNUM1A EMPNUM2A
                                          EMPNUM3A
            MOVE  CICS-PROT        TO  MSG1A.

2300-SEND-MAP.
    EXEC  CICS
            SEND MAP    ('PAY2501')
                MAPSET  ('PAYR250')
```

Figure 4.4. (cont'd). Example of program using MAP.

```
                    FROM      (PAY2501I)
                    DATAONLY
                    FREEKB
                    CURSOR
                    NOHANDLE
                    RESP      (CICS-RESP-CODE)
     END-EXEC.
```

Figure 4.4. (cont'd). Example of program using MAP.

The TERM-MSG and INIT-MSG aren't needed. They are style
issues. I inserted them as a suggested way to communicate with the
user. Many transactions simply 'quit' with no terminating message.
The SEND TEXT command for TERM-MSG could be removed if the
TERM-MSG isn't desired. *Note*: This use of WHEN-COMPILED is not
compatible with VS/COBOL. With VS/COBOL, the time data precedes
the date data and the date data is 12 bytes, not 8. The format shown
is for COBOL II.

I have logic in the program for INIT-MSG, as this is a little-used
but desirable way to notify users of the release level or other information about the transaction. As with TERM-MSG, this logic could be
removed with no loss of basic function. This type of message is especially useful if the user knows there are new features included in
the new version but doesn't know if the new program version is active. This can also be useful for users to reference when reporting
problems. If you check the references to the MSG10 field in the MAP,
you will see that this message appears only once. From then on, the
message field is either initialized with a space or an error message.

This program doesn't use the COMM area except to determine
if this is the first or a subsequent transaction. That is why it is only
one byte. The COPY statements are important, ensuring that the
necessary reference items are in the program. CICSRESP frees me
from coding DFHRESP entries, CICSATTR provides the attribute bytes
needed to override the MAP (DFHBMSCA would also provide these),
DFHAID has the values for AID keys, and PAY250C is my symbolic
MAP. You won't see reference to PAY250C in the program, however.
Remember, the 01-level gets its name from the DFHMDI macro. Since
I named it PAY2501, the 01-level name is PAY2501I from the BMS
assembly.

The two 01-level entries are fields for the file I/O, so we won't review them in detail here. The fields in WS-FILE-DATA are items that CICS needs to access a file: the file's eight-byte name for the FCT, the record length, the search key, and the search key length. (COBOL II does not require a LENGTH except for variable-length records.)

The first statement in the PROCEDURE DIVISION is not recommended for all programs. I combined the test of EIBCALEN and the test for the CLEAR key here because, for this program, the necessary process to recover is the same. I do this because, if the CLEAR key was pressed, all data is removed from the screen and the physical MAP must be resent. If the program didn't test for it here, the subsequent processing path could execute the SEND MAP command in paragraph 2300. Since that SEND MAP command specifies DATAONLY, the terminal would receive data, but all headings would be lost.

The 1000-SETUP paragraph sets up the initial message and initializes the symbolic MAP to low-values. Although the initial message is optional, initializing the symbolic MAP to low-values is not. The SEND MAP specifies ERASE and, since neither DATAONLY or MAPONLY is specified, the full MAP is sent. FREEKB is not needed, since it was also specified on the MAP, but I sometimes code what isn't needed from habit. I included this unnecessary option because you will frequently see unnecessary options coded.

The 2000-RETRIEVE-RESP paragraph processes all responses from the terminal, except if the CLEAR key is pressed. This logic path also sets the TERM-SW so the first paragraph can determine whether to continue the dialogue or terminate. The first statement, MOVE DFHCOMMAREA TO MY-COMM-AREA, isn't needed in this program. I include it because, for most programs that use the COMM area, it is important to save the data for future use.

The RECEIVE MAP paragraph is straightforward, including a test for PF3 and a test for MAPFAIL. The MAPFAIL test could also have been coded as

```
IF CICS-RESP-CODE = DFHRESP(MAPFAIL)
```

if you did not have the CICSRESP COPYbook. In that case, you would have needed to specify a WORKING STORAGE entry for the field named CICS-RESP-CODE (or other name) with PIC S9(8) COMP.

The first interesting paragraph (my opinion) is 2200-CHECK-SSN. Here I change the attributes of the three entry fields to UNPROT,

NUM, and BRT. (Remember, the attribute field for each data element always ends in "A.") These data fields were defined in the MAP as UNPROT, NUM. Adding an attribute always requires that you specify all attributes — you can't change just one. My approach in this program is initially to assume the fields are entered in error by setting the attribute to bright. Later in the program logic (paragraph 2210-READ-FILE, following the CICS-NORMAL condition), I reset them to their proper attributes. If the program logic does not successfully retrieve a record, or if the fields are missing or not numeric, the attributes will already have been set for errors. This technique saves me from specifying the attributes for each error. The same technique was used for the message field, so any error message would also be highlighted.

This program does not extensively use the cursor control facility as, whether the data was entered correctly or incorrectly, I always want the cursor positioned at the first field. This is because, for this application, all three fields are really one item. If we wanted to check each field separately, we could have by writing that logic something like this:

```
IF EMPNUM1L = 0 OR EMPNUM1A = X'80' OR EMPNUM1 NOT NUMERIC
    MOVE -1 TO EMPNUM1L
END-IF
IF EMPNUM2L = 0 OR EMPNUM2A = X'80' OR EMPNUM2 NOT NUMERIC
    MOVE -1 TO EMPNUM2L
END-IF
IF EMPNUM3L = 0 OR EMPNUM3A = X'80' OR EMPNUM3 NOT NUMERIC
    MOVE -1 TO EMPNUM3L
END-IF
IF -1 = EMPNUM1L OR EMPNUM2L OR EMPNUM3L
        MOVE 'SSN is not numeric as entered' TO MSG10
ELSE
      PERFORM 2210-READ-FILE.
```

The STRING statement in paragraph 2210-READ-FILE is not allowed in a CICS program that is written in VS/COBOL. The later topic on COBOL II and VS/COBOL will review this and other differences.

This program has some flaws, primarily in how the user sees the screen. Correcting the issues is possible, but it would have made the program larger. After understanding the flaws, you may want to write the additional logic that could prevent it. Here is an explanation of the basic flaw.

Notice that the program resets the attributes of the entry fields and never resets the contents for fields retrieved from the file. Let's review what that means. If a user enters one employee number, gets a valid response, and then presses PF3 (a typical, but incomplete unit test done by some programmers), the error does not appear.

The error occurs after the user has entered a valid employee number and then wishes to enter another. The screen contains all the information for the last valid employee but none of the fields have the MDT attribute set. So, if the user presses the Enter key, none of the data values are transmitted, even though they are appearing on the screen. That will cause the program logic to state that the fields on the screen are invalid, even though they are valid. That can confuse the user.

Another error is that, if the user enters an incorrect employee number for other than the first inquiry, the error message will be produced, but the data fields from the file for the last valid employee are still on screen. Remember, since they do not have MDT set, they are not returned with a RECEIVE MAP command, so the values stored in the symbolic MAP on the RECEIVE MAP will be LOW-VALUES. Since LOW-VALUES are not sent with a SEND MAP command, the fields on the screen are not overwritten. (This applies to both attribute fields and to data fields.)

These errors don't prevent the program from functioning, but they can confuse users. There are many ways to solve the issues. One way to prevent the data fields from the file from continuing to be presented would be to move spaces to all output fields when an error message is sent. The three entry fields could always be retrieved by setting the MDT when modifying the attribute bytes (the entry in CICSATTR is CICS-UNPROT-NUM-MDT). That would ensure that these three fields would always be retrieved, even if nothing were entered.

I purposely omitted these techniques from the program because I wanted you first to understand the program and then cope with these screen management issues. Becoming a good CICS programmer demands that you cope with such concerns. There has been much written on the tradeoffs, but most of it is self-evident. Anything you can do to minimize the data traffic will improve performance (for high-volume transactions), but the tradeoff is that your program logic becomes more involved. The difficulty (to me) is that you must also cope with the fact that data already sent to the terminal remains there until erased or new data is sent.

4.6. DEVELOPING A SIMPLE MENU TRANSACTION

The previous CICS program was a stand-alone application. By that, I mean that the one program handled the entire dialogue with the user. Many times you will find that, although the user may not know it, the transaction invoked by the user does only part of the process, using other programs to handle parts of it. The programs can, if properly designed, continue to interact throughout the dialogue. An example of this is a menu-driven application.

Menu transactions are quite popular, primarily because they allow the user to narrow the scope of transaction requirements. It's possible, of course, for a stand-alone program to use a menu approach by juggling more than one MAP to the user. The advantage of separate programs for each process is that the application can be more flexible. Since menu transactions usually exist where there are processing options, let's assume some processing requirements. Our transaction is to allow a terminal user to administer a file of employee information. For example, let's assume the following for our sample transaction:

- New employees can be added to the file.

- Current employee data can be modified.

- Data for terminated employees can be removed.

I agree, it's simple, but it is difficult to understand the ramifications of the logic. In the above example, what do you do if attempting to add a new employee when the employee number already exists? What data can be modified? When can data for terminated employees be removed? All these situations should be documented. (Every time I make assumptions about user requirements, I am usually only partly right.)

For our theoretical situation, let's assume the following transaction structure:

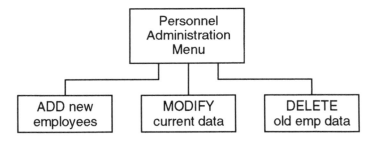

In each situation, there are several general steps:

First, the application must use a SEND MAP to show the menu to the user. This is usually a screen that presents the choices that are available.

Next, the transaction must RECEIVE the request and validate it.

Third, the initial program must transfer control to another program that will handle the request. There are several ways to do this, depending on program structure, as we'll see.

The next program to receive control is automatically attached to the same terminal, so there is continuity from the user's perspective. This program might be given some information from the menu program (via the COMM area) on the processing required, or it might issue its own SEND MAP command to collect the data. This program continues to interact with the terminal user in much the same way as our earlier program.

Finally, when this program is finished, it does not usually issue a RETURN command, although it could if desired. Instead, because it is part of the menu application, the program will transfer control back to the menu program. The menu program can then represent the menu to the user, so the user can pick another selection or request termination.

In doing menu transactions, you should always remember that the structure of menus allows you to gather data selectively as needed by providing different screens for different concerns. This allows the transaction to keep data that may be important if a decision is eventually reached by the transaction. (*Reminder*: In conducting a dialogue, avoid the temptation to update records before all information is available. If it becomes necessary to terminate a dialogue for an error condition, you don't want to be wondering if any file updates/additions were done that must now be undone.)

Before you can write a menu application, you need to learn some more about CICS, plus learn a few more commands.

4.6.1. CICS Architecture Components for Menu Applications

There are several elements of CICS that contribute to effective dialogues with the computer. Understanding the basics will help you develop more sophisticated transactions.

The Terminal Connection. When a terminal user enters a transaction identifier at the terminal, CICS establishes an environment that is dedicated to this particular terminal. That means that every program that is given control as a result of the initial dialogue is automatically attached to this one terminal. I mention this here because I want you to understand that, regardless of how many different programs are invoked in a dialogue, they all are connected automatically to the original terminal. This feature will grow in importance as you develop applications that transfer control from program to program to satisfy a particular user request. (*Exception*: The START command, briefly described in this chapter, requires that the terminal resource be specified. This has special uses.)

The Task Concept. To CICS, a task is any program sequence that retains control for a given interaction with a terminal user. For example, a transaction that receives a request and sends a response is one task, while a transaction that receives the subsequent response and handles it is a different task. In summary, a task ends whenever a program issues a RETURN command, whether conversational, nonconversational, or pseudoconversational. Since the task number will change every time the terminal user presses an AID key, the task number is primarily a local control for CICS and is not something that the application should use throughout the dialogue. (If required, the task number is available in the EIB in the field named EIBTASKN.) Since I use the word task frequently, you may want to reread this paragraph to be sure that you understand that a task is not a transaction or a program. A task is all the activity that occurs from the time CICS gives control to the transaction until some form of the RETURN command is issued.

The Level Concept. In CICS, there are various levels of processing, similar to that found in any hierarchical structure. CICS allows program modules to interact at various levels (similar to the COBOL CALL statement), producing the basic concept of program structure as shown in Figure 4.5. While not complete, this demonstrates the basics of CICS program structure.

Programs at the highest level are those that can be directly invoked by a terminal user and that, when executing a RETURN command, return control directly to CICS. When the dialogue is incomplete, these are the programs that use the RETURN TRANSID command to identify the next program to receive control. All such programs must be defined in both the PPT and the PCT. (*Note*:

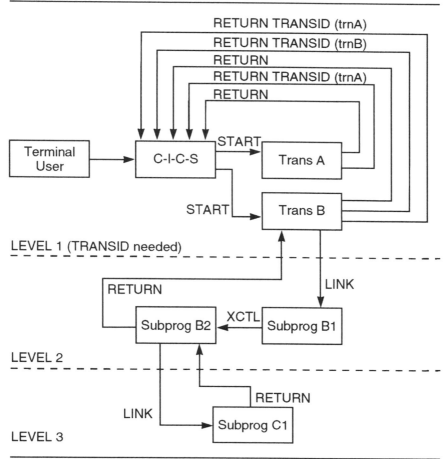

Figure 4.5. CICS transaction structure.

Figure 4.5 indicates that CICS is at level 1. Technically, CICS is really at level 0. I depict it at level 1 because CICS, logically, interacts with level 1 programs as though an XCTL command had been issued. The difference is that CICS actually starts a new task (not the START command), not relinquishing its control within the region.)

Programs at lower levels function similar to a traditional CALL statement, in that they RETURN control not to CICS but to the invoking program. These programs need only be defined to the PPT.

4.6.2. The Structure of Program-to-Program Communications

The structure demonstrated in Figure 4.5 shows many possibilities within the CICS framework. Several major CICS verbs are shown, including XCTL and RETURN. You already have a grasp for RETURN, so let's summarize the differences between RETURN and XCTL and LINK. Since these three commands are the prime movers in any CICS architecture, you need to understand them well. This is also where you will normally see the COMM area used extensively, because each program normally needs to provide some information to the new program. Here are the fundamentals:

RETURN As stated previously, this command returns control to CICS. If TRANSID is also coded, that transid will receive control when the designated terminal enters data.

XCTL If we were discussing football, I would call this a lateral pass. Control (the ball) is passed to a colleague with the option of having the ball passed back again, if needed. This is different from the traditional CALL verb, where the CALLed program *always* returns control to the CALLer. With the XCTL command, control has been transferred, removing the originating program from the command chain. The program issuing the XCTL command is essentially removed from the action (much as a quarterback is out of the action once the football has been thrown). Since a program that receives control via the XCTL command assumes the same level of control as the originating program, XCTL is commonly used to maintain control of the terminal dialogue. These programs must be defined in PCT if they are at the top level and if they may be invoked by a RETURN TRANSID command.

LINK This is similar to the familiar COBOL CALL statement, where the program always returns control to the program that initiated it. Since LINK is always subordinate to the originating program, the LINKed program must always return control to its originator. This means that programs that are invoked by the LINK command need only be defined in the PPT, not the PCT.

START This is a command that you will rarely need. START is a command that starts a new task within the region. The START command is not used in our example, but you will occasionally see it used. When an application issues a START command, the affected terminal MUST be specified. This command is often used when a transaction needs access to a resource other than the designated terminal, such as a dedicated printer.

In Figure 4.5, CICS gives control to either transaction A or B, depending on the input from the terminal user. (Therefore, these two programs must be defined in both the PPT and the PCT). These two programs may either (or both) give temporary control to subprograms with the LINK command or request to CICS that a specified program (normally the same one) be given control after the terminal user enters data. No level below the first level may directly receive control from CICS. (*Note:* It is only at this level that XCTL may be used to give control to another program that will execute a RETURN TRANSID command.

FUNCTION: Pass control to a subprogram at next lower level

```
EXEC  CICS  LINK
          PROGRAM(program-name)
        [ COMMAREA(dataname) [ LENGTH(datavalue) ] ]
        [ HANDLE | NOHANDLE [ RESP() ] ]
END-EXEC
```

Most probable error conditions: NOTAUTH, PGMIDERR

Figure 4.6. LINK command.

For the LINK command (Figure 4.6), the COMMAREA parameter need not be the same COMM area used by the LINKing program. The LINK command used to be (before COBOL II) the only way to transfer control to a lower-level subprogram. With COBOL II, this can be done with the CALL dataname statement. I'll review that in the next section. By now, you know that the LENGTH keyword is not required for COBOL II programs.

The NOTAUTH condition is raised if your shop has established security control for programs and your terminal is not authorized to access the program. The PGMIDERR condition is raised if the program is not in the PPT or, for whatever reason, is not available. (Elsewhere in this book is information on CICS commands, such as CEMT and CEDC, that give information on such issues.) You will often want to

include code in your programs to check for PGMIDERR, so you will have
the option of another action (or a controlled termination).

FUNCTION: Transfer unconditional control to another program

```
EXEC CICS  XCTL
           PROGRAM(program-name)
         [ COMMAREA(dataname) [ LENGTH(datavalue) ] ]
         [ HANDLE | NOHANDLE [ RESP() ] ]
END-EXEC
```

Most probable error conditions: NOTAUTH, PGMIDERR

Figure 4.7. XCTL command.

As you see, the options for both LINK and XCTL (Figure 4.7) are
similar, with several keywords being identical to the RETURN TRANSID
command. In this case, even the common error conditions are the same.

FUNCTION: Start a new task in the CICS region

```
EXEC CICS  START
           TRANSID(transaction-id)
         [ FROM(dataname) [ LENGTH(datavalue) ] ]
         [ TERMID(terminal-id) ]
         [ HANDLE | NOHANDLE [ RESP() ] ]
END-EXEC
```

Most probable error conditions: INVREQ, NOTAUTH, TERMIDERR
                                TRANSIDERR

Figure 4.8. START command — basics.

Fully exploring the START command (Figure 4.8) is beyond the
scope of this book. There will be times when an application needs to
have multiple tasks active concurrently. An example would be where
one transaction has created a report to be printed at an online terminal,
so it uses the START command to start another task that is attached

to the printer. Remember, your transaction is automatically attached to
the terminal that invoked the transaction. This cannot be changed.
Accessing other terminals requires that another task be STARTed.

   I won't review the START command in detail, as the names are
fairly self-explanatory. I do include an example of the START command in the menu program, where I use it to logoff the application
if a specified AID key (PF2 in the example) is pressed. Your shop may
have other approaches to do this or may not allow this technique.

4.6.3.   The Menu Structure

Traditional menu structures are designed to simplify the coding required for a user to accomplish a basic unit of work. This is done with
CICS by decomposing the business work units into menu components
that operate as parallel computer work units (i.e., they use the XCTL
command to transfer control between like components). As the example in Figure 4.9 demonstrates, menu programs are quite
straightforward in that they transfer control to other programs, depending on the value entered by the user. This decomposition of the
processing logic simplifies the overall system design, even though it
may require additional programs to be developed.

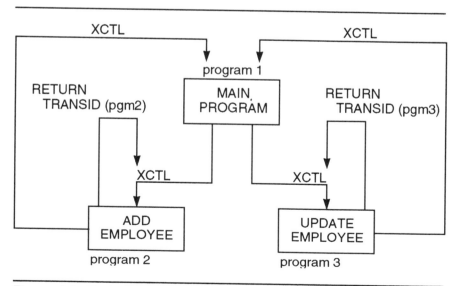

Figure 4.9. Typical pseudoconversational structure for menus.

As Figure 4.9 demonstrates, the menu process works similarly to a tag-team; each transaction relinquishes control of the region to a parallel task (e.g., PGM2 is given control if there is a need to add a new employee). After processing the logic to add a new employee to the company data files, the PGM2 transaction transfers control back to the main menu program. This type of structure is highly successful but requires that all programs be aware of the structure and use it appropriately.

4.6.4.   A Sample Menu Program

Using the program developed in the previous chapter, we will modify it somewhat to be part of a menu application. For our example, the menu program will provide a choice of add, update, or delete a record, appearing basically as the example in Figure 4.9 demonstrates. While that is a process that might be handled without a menu approach, it does demonstrate the technique. Our example will include the menu program and just one of the possible programs that it invokes. For this example, I will show only the program for the delete function, as all programs in a menu structure use the same techniques.

The MAPs. Our basic menu program is shown in Figure 4.10. This is simple, and most menu applications you will see at your shop will involve many more programs. The structure and building blocks, however, are the same.

```
        Employee  Payroll  Administration  Menu

               FUNCTIONS  AVAILABLE:
               Code:   Function:
               A       ADD data for new employee
               U       UPDATE data for employee
               D       DELETE data for employee
          Enter function code ==>   _

    ENTER   F1=Help F2=Logoff F3=Exit
```

Figure 4.10. Sample menu screen.

Usually, a menu program does some type of validation, either of the terminal user's authority within the system or of some additional fields being entered. In our example, we will restrict it to entering a single field.

To add some additional CICS interaction, I also provided a help screen. Surprisingly, most CICS applications provide no help facility. My approach is simple, although the concept could easily be expanded. In this application, if the user presses PF1, a single screen of information is presented. While that isn't much information, it can be helpful to new users. Also, developing help screens is so simple that I'm surprised they aren't part of more applications. A sample help screen is in Figure 4.11. I've found that this goes over big with users because I let them develop all the text, specifying what fields to highlight, so I can convert the text into a MAP. In this example, I have placed the menu MAP *and* the help MAP in the same MAPSET.

```
PAYR0250                Employee  Payroll  Administration

Basic  structure  of  this  transaction:
There are 3 modes:  ADD,     data for new employees are added
                    UPDATE, employee  data  is  modified
                    DELETE, data  on  former  employees  is
                            removed

To  ADD:  You  need  a  signed  HR  form  264-1,  showing
employee  position  number,  job  position  code,  with  all
information  in  box  B  completed.

To  UPDATE:  All  updates  are  processed  on  the  second
Tuesday AM  of  each month.   You may  still  enter  changes
at  other  times  (e.g.,  a  change  in  salary).

To  DELETE: Deletions  may  be  made  only  by  supervisory
personnel. HR Form 420 must be signed by the HR department
manager  prior  to  this  action.

See  chapter  3  of  HR  Manual.   IF  ALL  ELSE  FAILS,
CALL  (XXX)  XXX-XXXX  FOR  ASSISTANCE

Press  Enter  key  to  return  to  menu  screen.
```

Figure 4.11. Sample help screen.

Figure 4.11 indicates that only the Enter key will cause the menu to be redisplayed. Actually, no matter what AID key is pressed, the application will return to the menu. This is not intended to confuse the user. Just the opposite. Most users will do what is documented and don't care that there are almost 30 different keys that will work.

For the application program that is invoked from the menu, I will use the same MAP that we used in our prior application (Figure 3.9). The MAP for our menu and help MAP is in Figure 4.12.

Okay, so I didn't fill in all of the help MAP. The entire MAP is pure text, so I decided not to inundate you with all of those DFHMDF macros. As a reminder, when entering pure text that exceeds a coding line, code up to column 71, place a nonblank character in column 72, and continue coding on the next line, beginning in column 16. I encourage you to finish the MAP. It's tedious, but practice goes a long way toward learning CICS.

Notice that I specified FSET for the field called PROCESS. Since this is a one-byte field, I decided to set the MDT on it permanently, thus ensuring that it was always returned with a RECEIVE MAP command, preventing a MAPFAIL condition. To ensure this happens, I will need to keep this in mind in the program, including the MDT attribute when setting/resetting the field.

The programs. The programs will appear similar to the prior program. The differences are important, though. For one thing, programs that work interactively can't just test EIBCALEN for a nonzero value to determine a logic path. For example, the menu program might be invoked by the terminal user or by an XCTL from the application program. Also, the menu program may have issued a RETURN TRANSID command after sending a help MAP or after sending a menu MAP. The menu program needs to be able to determine all of these possibilities.

You will see the COMM area used not only by the menu program to determine the above conditions, but the application program that receives control from the menu program also receives information from the menu program from the passed data area. Up to now, we have used the COMM area only for yes/no type information.

The CICS tables would need several entries for these two programs to function. The PPT would need to have entries for MENUPGM and DELETPGM because both programs are invoked. The PPT would also need entries for my two MAPSETS, MENUAPP and PAYR250. (We defined PAYR250 in our previous example.) Since the help MAP is part

```
          TITLE 'MAPSET MENUAPP for Menu application'
          PRINT NOGEN
*****************************************************
**        Menu for sample application                 column
*****************************************************   72
MENUAPP   DFHMSD TYPE=&SYSPARM,                              X
          MODE=INOUT,                                       X
          LANG=COBOL,                                       X
          TIOAPFX=YES,                                      X
          CTRL=(FREEKB)
MENUMAP   DFHMDI SIZE=(24,80)
          DFHMDF POS=(01,25),LENGTH=36,                     X
          INITIAL='Employee Payroll Administration Menu'
          DFHMDF POS=(7,29),LENGTH=20,                      X
          INITIAL='FUNCTIONS AVAILABLE:'
          DFHMDF POS=(9,29),LENGTH=18,                      X
          INITIAL='Code:   Function:'
          DFHMDF POS=(11,30),LENGTH=33,                     X
          INITIAL='A        ADD data for new employee'
          DFHMDF POS=(13,30),LENGTH=32,                     X
          INITIAL='U        UPDATE data for employee'
          DFHMDF POS=(15,30),LENGTH=32,                     X
          INITIAL='D        DELETE data for employee'
          DFHMDF POS=(18,30),LENGTH=24,                     X
          INITIAL='Enter function code ==> '
PROCESS   DFHMDF POS=(18,55),LENGTH=1,ATTRB=(UNPROT,FSET), X
          INITIAL=' '
          DFHMDF POS=(18,57),LENGTH=1
MSG1      DFHMDF POS=(22,01),LENGTH=79,INITIAL=' ',         X
          ATTRB=(BRT,PROT)
          DFHMDF POS=(24,01),LENGTH=32,                     X
          INITIAL='ENTER  F1=Help F2=Logoff F3=Exit'
HELPMAP   DFHMDI SIZE=(24,80)
          DFHMDF POS=(1,1),LENGTH=8,INITIAL='PAYR0250'
          DFHMDF POS=(01,25),LENGTH=31,                     X
          INITIAL='Employee Payroll Administration'
          DFHMDF POS=(03,01),LENGTH=35,                     X
          INITIAL='Basic structure of this transaction'
                              .
                              .
                              .
          DFHMSD TYPE=FINAL
          END
```

Figure 4.12. Sample MAP for menu and help screens.

of the MAPSET, it does not require a separate entry. The FCT entry would be the same as the previous example, since it is the same file. The PCT would need entries for MENUPGM and transID M401, and for DELETPGM and transID D401. By the way, once an entry is made in a CICS table, you do not need to make new entries just because the program, MAPSET, or file will be accessed in a new program structure.

The menu program has the following structure. Remember, you must also review the second program before you can fully see how they communicate with each other.

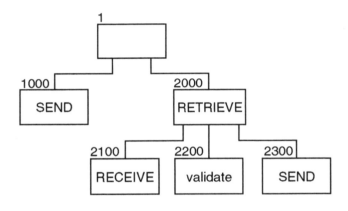

```
        IDENTIFICATION DIVISION.
PROGRAM-ID.   MENUPGM.
*AUTHOR.   David Shelby Kirk.
DATA DIVISION.
WORKING-STORAGE SECTION.
01   LOCAL-WORK-AREAS.
        05   STATUS-FLAG     PIC X          VALUE    ' '.
                88   INPUT-ERROR      VALUE 'E'.
                88   TIME-TO-QUIT     VALUE 'Q'.
                88   TIME-TO-LOGOFF   VALUE 'L'.
                88   TRANSFER-NEEDED  VALUE 'A', 'U', 'D'.
                88   HELP-WANTED      VALUE 'H'.
        05   MAP-NAME          PIC X(8) VALUE 'MENUMAP '.
        05   XCTL-NAME         PIC X(8).
```

Figure 4.13. Example of menu program.

```
01    MAP-AREA              PIC  X(1920)  VALUE  LOW-VALUES.

01    MY-COMM-AREA.
      05    COMM-LAST-MAP     PIC  X(4)      VALUE  'MENU'.
      05    COMM-PRIOR-PGM    PIC  X(8)      VALUE  'MENUPGM '.
      05    COMM-ACTION-FLAG  PIC  X         VALUE  ' '.

      COPY  CICSRESP.

      COPY  CICSATTR.

      COPY  DFHAID.

      COPY  MENUAPPC.

LINKAGE  SECTION.
01    DFHCOMMAREA.
      05    LINK-LAST-MAP   PIC  XXXX.
      05    LINK-PRIOR-PGM  PIC  X(8).
      05    FILLER          PIC  X.

PROCEDURE  DIVISION.
1.  IF  EIBCALEN  <  13  OR  EIBAID  =  DFHCLEAR
        OR  LINK-PRIOR-PGM  NOT  =  'MENUPGM '
        OR  LINK-LAST-MAP  =  'HELP'
           PERFORM  1000-SETUP
      ELSE
           PERFORM  2000-RETRIEVE-RESP
      END-IF
      EVALUATE  TRUE
        WHEN  TIME-TO-QUIT
          EXEC  CICS  RETURN  END-EXEC
        WHEN  TIME-TO-LOGOFF
          EXEC  CICS  START  TRANSID  ('CSSF')
                             TERMID   (EIBTRMID)
          END-EXEC
          EXEC  CICS  RETURN  END-EXEC
        WHEN  TRANSFER-NEEDED
          EXEC  CICS  XCTL
                      PROGRAM    (XCTL-NAME)
                      COMMAREA   (MY-COMM-AREA)
                      LENGTH     (13)
                      NOHANDLE
```

Figure 4.13. (cont'd). Example of menu program.

```
                       RESP        (CICS-RESP-CODE)
           END-EXEC
           IF  CICS-PGMIDERR
                EXEC  CICS  ABEND
                             ABCODE('1234')
                             NODUMP
                END-EXEC
           END-IF
       END-EVALUATE
       EXEC CICS RETURN
                TRANSID  ('M401')
                COMMAREA (MY-COMM-AREA)
                LENGTH   (13)
       END-EXEC
       GOBACK.

1000-SETUP.
    MOVE  LOW-VALUES  TO  MENUMAPI
    MOVE  -1    TO  PROCESSL
    EXEC  CICS
            SEND  MAP      ('MENUMAP')
                  MAPSET   ('MENUAPP')
                  FROM     (MENUMAPI)
                  ERASE
                  CURSOR
    END-EXEC.

2000-RETRIEVE-RESP.
    PERFORM  2100-RECEIVE-MAP
    IF  STATUS-FLAG  NOT = 'Q'  AND  NOT = 'L'
        PERFORM  2200-CHECK-DATA
        IF  STATUS-FLAG = 'H'  OR  'E'
            PERFORM  2300-SEND-MAP.

2100-RECEIVE-MAP.
    EXEC  CICS  RECEIVE  MAP   ('MENUMAP')
                         MAPSET   ('MENUAPP')
                         INTO     (MENUMAPI)
                         NOHANDLE
                         RESP     (CICS-RESP-CODE)
    END-EXEC
```

Figure 4.13. (cont'd). Example of menu program.

```
    IF  EIBAID  =  DFHPF3
        MOVE  'Q'  TO  STATUS-FLAG
    ELSE
        IF  EIBAID  =  DFHPF2
            MOVE  'L'  TO  STATUS-FLAG
        ELSE
            IF  CICS-MAPFAIL
                MOVE  'Q'  TO  STATUS-FLAG.

2200-CHECK-DATA.
    IF  EIBAID  =  DFHPF1
        MOVE  'HELP'  TO  COMM-LAST-MAP
        MOVE  LOW-VALUES  TO  HELPMAPO
        MOVE  HELPMAPO  TO  MAP-AREA
        MOVE  'HELPMAP'  TO  MAP-NAME
        MOVE  'H'  TO  STATUS-FLAG
    ELSE
        IF  PROCESSI  =  'A'  OR  'U'  OR  'D'
            MOVE  PROCESSI  TO  STATUS-FLAG
                                COMM-ACTION-FLAG
            EVALUATE  PROCESSI
              WHEN  'A'  MOVE  'ADDPGM'  TO  XCTL-NAME
              WHEN  'D'  MOVE  'DELETPGM'  TO  XCTL-NAME
              WHEN  'U'  MOVE  'UPDATPGM'  TO  XCTL-NAME
            END-EVALUATE
        ELSE
            MOVE  'E'            TO  STATUS-FLAG
            MOVE  CICS-UNPROT-BRT-MDT  TO  PROCESSA
            MOVE  CICS-PROT-BRT  TO  MSG1A
            MOVE  -1  TO  PROCESSL
            MOVE  'Please enter a valid code '  TO  MSG1O
            MOVE  MENUMAPO  TO  MAP-AREA.

2300-SEND-MAP.
    EXEC  CICS
            SEND MAP      (MAP-NAME)
                 MAPSET   ('MENUAPP')
                 FROM     (MAP-AREA)
                 CURSOR
    END-EXEC.
```

Figure 4.13. (cont'd). Example of menu program.

The menu program. Figure 4.13 contains the menu program. The field, STATUS-FLAG, can contain many values, although several aren't used. I do that only to help me in any potential debugging efforts. The COMM area is set up to save three pieces of information for the two programs: the name of the last MAP sent (needed by the menu program), the name of the last program invoked (so each program can determine if the SETUP path should be executed), and an action flag (so the program receiving control from the menu program knows what action was requested). This will become more evident as you read through the program.

Notice how the program begins. This is a major departure from a stand-alone application. Where the stand-alone application only needed to check EIBCALEN, the menu program needs to check for several possibilities. Let's review each:

- EIBCALEN < 13 will be true if the program is invoked for the first time

- EIBAID = DFHCLEAR will be true if the CLEAR key is pressed. With our simple application, we just restart the process.

- LINK-PRIOR-PGM NOT = 'MENUPGM' will be true if the menu program is receiving control (via XCTL) from another program. This, of course, assumes that both programs follow this communication protocol. You will see similar logic in the second program.

- LAST-LINK-MAP = 'HELP' will be true if the menu program's last MAP sent was the help MAP. Since our program had no need to retain information about the application, the SETUP path will be followed to ensure the proper MAP is sent.

If you're not familiar with the EVALUATE statement (COBOL II only), remember that it's just a cleaner way to handle nested IF logic.

In 2200-RETRIEVE-RESP you see that the second SEND MAP is not issued unless an error occurred or the help MAP is to be sent. This is a departure from a stand-alone program because menu programs do *not* send the MAP when all entries are correct, but only when incorrect. When the data on the received MAP is correct, the menu program transfers control to the appropriate program, and it is that program that will issue a SEND MAP to the terminal.

In 2200-CHECK-DATA you see that, if PF1 is pressed, the program moves all appropriate information (MAP name, symbolic MAP) to a common area and also updates the COMM area so the menu program will be able to determine this when it begins again after executing a RETURN TRANSID command. I move LOW-VALUES to the symbolic MAP to ensure the proper attribute bytes are sent to the terminal.

2200-CHECK-DATA points out another aspect of this menu program that is different from stand-alone programs. You will recall that our earlier program would set and reset the attribute bytes for data fields. Since this MAP is never sent when data is good, I only need logic in it to highlight errors. When the data is entered correctly, I will not send the MAP, so there is no need to reset any attribute bytes. If this confuses you, take a few minutes (and pencil and paper) and walk through the dialogue. Developing the ability to visualize the entire dialogue will help you envision future problems and programming requirements.

2300-SEND-MAP sends a prespecified MAP. Since the only modification would be the help MAP, there is no need to move the menu MAP to MAP-AREA since, if a RECEIVE MAP was executed, the MAP was received there anyway (see paragraph 2100-RECEIVE-MAP).

I didn't mention it, but you may be wondering why I don't issue a RECEIVE MAP command for the help MAP. Well, some programmers think that all MAPs that are sent must be received. Not true. For one thing, it contained no data and I set no MDT attributes in the MAP, so a MAPFAIL condition is pretty definite (although I could prevent it by including an extra, dummy field). The main reason I don't receive the help MAP is that it contains no information for the program. All the program needed to know was that the last MAP sent was the help MAP. This information was in the COMM area, signalling that the menu MAP must be sent again. Although this is a simple program, I hope you see that the logic to include a help screen is negligible.

Admittedly, I sneaked a new CICS command into the program, the ABEND command. It's pretty simple, so I didn't bother to explain it. Your shop probably has its own standards or programs to use instead of this command. I inserted the ABEND command to demonstrate that you normally need to take some action if a serious error condition occurs. Incidentally, the NODUMP option is only allowed with CICS/ESA and CICS/VSE.

I'll just briefly explain the START command used to logoff. The normal CICS transaction is CSSF, so I start that transaction, specifying the same terminal ID (from the EIB) that the program is already using. Since CICS only allocates one task to a resource, the CSSF transaction doesn't take effect until my task ends. That is why, immediately following the START command, there is a RETURN command. You will often see some form of this technique used in major menu applications to allow users to logoff without knowing the command or just for simplicity.

All programs contain flaws, including this one. A major one that you may want to solve is including appropriate code to document the MAPFAIL condition. This is a condition that may never occur (I protected against no data by setting a field with the MDT attribute in the MAP and also checked for the CLEAR key), but, if the condition ever happened, the transaction would simply terminate. The program would be cleaner if the error were recorded.

```
IDENTIFICATION DIVISION.
PROGRAM-ID.   DELETPGM.
*AUTHOR.   David Shelby Kirk.
DATA DIVISION.
WORKING-STORAGE SECTION.
01   LOCAL-WORK-AREAS.
     05   HEX-80          PIC X      VALUE   ' '.
     05   TERM-SW         PIC X      VALUE   ' '.
     05   COMPILE-DATE-INFO.
          10   COMPILE-DATE     PIC X(8).
          10   TIME-COMPILED    PIC X(8).

01   INIT-MSG.
     05   FILLER     PIC X(54)   VALUE
     'Employee Delete Transaction EMPY0250 - Version 2.1 '.
     05   MESSAGE-DATE          PIC X(12).

     COPY CICSRESP.

     COPY CICSATTR.

     COPY DFHAID.
```

Figure 4.14. Example of program invoked via XCTL from menu.

```
      COPY  PAY250C.

01   WS-FILE-DATA.
     05   WS-EMP-FILE       PIC  X(8)    VALUE  'EMPLPAYR'.
     05   WS-SEARCH-KEY     PIC  X(11).

LINKAGE  SECTION.
01   DFHCOMMAREA.
     05   LINK-LAST-MAP   PIC  XXXX.
     05   LINK-PRIOR-PGM  PIC  X(8).
     05   ACTION-FLAG     PIC  X.

PROCEDURE  DIVISION.
1.  IF  EIBCALEN  <  13  OR
      (LINK-PRIOR-PGM  NOT  =  'MENUPGM'  AND
       LINK-PRIOR-PGM  NOT  =  'DELETPGM')
          EXEC  CICS  RETURN  END-EXEC.
      IF  LINK-PRIOR-PGM  =  'MENUPGM'  OR
       EIBAID  =  DFHCLEAR
          PERFORM  1000-SETUP
      ELSE
          PERFORM  2000-RETRIEVE-RESP.
      IF  TERM-SW  =  'Y'
          EXEC  CICS  XCTL
                      PROGRAM   ('MENUPGM')
                      COMMAREA  (DFHCOMMAREA)
                      LENGTH    (13)
          END-EXEC
      ELSE
          EXEC  CICS  RETURN
                      TRANSID   ('P401')
                      COMMAREA  (DFHCOMMAREA)
                      LENGTH    (13)
          END-EXEC
      GOBACK.

1000-SETUP.
    MOVE  'DELETPGM'  TO  LINK-PRIOR-PGM
    MOVE  LOW-VALUES  TO  PAY2501I
    MOVE  WHEN-COMPILED  TO  COMPILE-DATE-INFO
    MOVE  COMPILE-DATE  TO  MESSAGE-DATE
    MOVE  INIT-MSG  TO  MSG10
    PERFORM  1100-SEND-MAP1.
```

Figure 4.14. Example of program invoked via XCTL from menu. (cont'd)

```
1100-SEND-MAP1.
   MOVE -1   TO  EMPNUM1L
   EXEC CICS
            SEND  MAP    ('PAY2501')
                  MAPSET ('PAYR250')
                  FROM   (PAY2501I)
                  ERASE
                  FREEKB
                  CURSOR
                  NOHANDLE
                  RESP   (CICS-RESP-CODE)
   END-EXEC.

2000-RETRIEVE-RESP.
   PERFORM 2100-RECEIVE-MAP
   IF  TERM-SW  NOT = 'Y'
       PERFORM 2200-CHECK-SSN
       PERFORM 2300-SEND-MAP.

2100-RECEIVE-MAP.
   EXEC CICS RECEIVE MAP    ('PAY2501')
                     MAPSET ('PAYR250')
                     INTO   (PAY2501I)
                     NOHANDLE
                     RESP   (CICS-RESP-CODE)
   END-EXEC

   IF  EIBAID = DFHPF3
       MOVE 'Y' TO TERM-SW
   ELSE
       IF  CICS-MAPFAIL
           EXEC CICS  ABEND
                      ABCODE('2345')
                      NODUMP
           END-EXEC.

2200-CHECK-SSN.
   MOVE CICS-UNPROT-NUM-BRT  TO EMPNUM1A EMPNUM2A EMPNUM3A
   MOVE CICS-PROT-BRT      TO MSG1A
   MOVE -1   TO EMPNUM1L
   IF (EMPNUM1L = 0    OR
       EMPNUM2L = 0    OR
       EMPNUM3L = 0)   OR
      (HEX-80 = EMPNUM1A OR  EMPNUM2A OR  EMPNUM3A)
```

Figure 4.14. (cont'd). Example of program invoked via XCTL from menu.

```
      MOVE 'Please enter a complete SSN' TO MSG10
  ELSE
      IF EMPNUM1I NUMERIC AND
         EMPNUM2I NUMERIC AND
         EMPNUM3I NUMERIC
            PERFORM 2210-PROCESS-REQUEST
      ELSE
            MOVE 'SSN is not numeric as entered' TO MSG10.

2210-PROCESS-REQUEST.
    STRING EMPNUM1I EMPNUM2I EMPNUM3I DELIMITED BY SIZE
    INTO WS-SEARCH-KEY
    EXEC CICS DELETE
              FILE    (WS-EMP-FILE)
              RIDFLD  (WS-SEARCH-KEY)
              NOHANDLE
              RESP    (CICS-RESP-CODE)
    END-EXEC

    IF CICS-NOTFND
        MOVE 'No record found for that SSN' TO MSG10
    ELSE
        IF CICS-NORMAL
            MOVE 'Record successfully deleted' TO MSG10
            MOVE CICS-UNPROT-NUM  TO EMPNUM1A EMPNUM2A
                                     EMPNUM3A
        ELSE
            EXEC CICS ABEND
                      ABCODE('2345')
                      NODUMP
            END-EXEC.

2300-SEND-MAP.
    EXEC CICS
            SEND MAP    ('PAY2501')
                 MAPSET ('PAYR250')
                 FROM   (PAY2501I)
                 DATAONLY
                 CURSOR
                 NOHANDLE
                 RESP  (CICS-RESP-CODE)
    END-EXEC.
```

Figure 4.14. (cont'd). Example of program invoked via XCTL from menu.

The application program. Figure 4.14 contains the program that receives control from the menu program. The logic structure is similar to the earlier, stand-alone application, but there are some differences. For one, the earlier program used the SEND TEXT command to issue error information as well as an end-of-dialogue message. Since this program will not terminate the dialogue, such a message is not appropriate.

That last sentence is important. In a menu application, the program invoked by XCTL will usually terminate by executing an XCTL command back to the menu program and will not have a RETURN command (other than a RETURN TRANSID command). The two programs must act together so the terminal user is unaware of the technical processes involved.

Now, on to the program. First, review how the program begins. Where all previous programs accepted a value of zero in EIBCALEN as valid, using it as a trigger to PERFORM the SETUP path, this program refuses to continue. This is because it is dependent on receiving a valid COMM area that must have been set up by either the menu program or by this program. Since any other use of the program would cause it to fail, it shuts down immediately. Your shop may have standards or other processes to handle a situation where a transaction has been improperly invoked, but, in this book, I just use a RETURN command. Therefore, even though the program and transID are defined in the PCT, the program itself refuses to run if certain conditions are not met. The menu program could be invoked from a terminal by entering its transID of M401. Entering this program's transID of P401 would cause nothing to appear to happen.

The SETUP path also is different in that the program stores its name, DELETPGM, in the COMM area. This is the trigger it will use the next time the program is entered to determine what path to execute. After this program terminates by executing an XCTL command back to the menu program, the menu program will use this information to trigger executing its SETUP path.

There is a new command, DELETE. I'll cover that in a later chapter, along with READ and some other I/O commands. I think you can figure out what it is doing and that's one reason that, even though this book does not explore all CICS commands in depth, I still believe this book format is all you need to survive in a CICS world. The DELETE command deletes the record with the specified key. If the condition raised is NORMAL, then a record was deleted. If the NOTFND condition is raised, the record doesn't exist. For this example, I assume any other condition is a technical error from which I can't recover. I can't emphasize enough how important it is for you to check with your shop's procedures for handling errors. If this were a major application, just issuing an ABEND would be intolerable, as it doesn't provide any information other than the fact that an error occurred.

In reviewing the menu example, there is a major issue that you will not usually encounter. I divided the logic between the two programs so that I could emphasize the control and interaction aspects of the programs. Normally, the division of application logic would be different. In menu applications, you will usually find that the options let the user pick more complete business units (such as Payroll Administration or Insurance Claim Inquiry). The menu program will usually require additional information to validate that the terminal user has authority to access the other program(s) and may even ask for some data fields to be filled in.

SUMMARY

This chapter bears occasional rereading until you are comfortable with the commands and processes. You may have gotten the impression from this chapter that every possible error condition needs to be trapped and all possible idiosyncrasies in screen presentation need to be resolved. Realistically, that isn't true. I encourage you to expend the extra energy when designing a program to control those error conditions that are most likely to happen (such as a NOTFND condition). Otherwise, it becomes a time and cost tradeoff. If a transaction is used only occasionally, there will be little demand to spend the time polishing it when that same time could be spent on projects with better payback.

Although you do not know many CICS commands, after finishing this chapter, I believe you are now able to work with real transactions at your shop. Practice in compiling, modifying, and testing will work wonders on your skills. Most of the commands to be addressed in the next chapter relate to application issues. The commands that set the pseudoconversational structure of CICS transactions have all been covered, as well as the means to create screens. If you read no further in this book, you could survive in a maintenance world by having this book and the appropriate IBM application programmer reference for your shop's CICS system. (IBM books are listed in the last chapter in the book.)

VOCABULARY REVIEW

In this chapter, we covered terms such as XCTL, LINK, START, READ, DELETE, task, and terminal ID. Some error conditions were NOTAUTH, PGMIDERR, NOTFND, NORMAL. The level number concept of managing modules was presented. You should feel comfortable on these issues:

- Describing the difference between XCTL and LINK and when to use them.

- Describing differences between RETURN and RETURN TRANSID, explaining how each is used in pseudoconversational programs.

- Identifying what data will be on a screen after any given option of the SEND MAP command.

- Identifying what data, if any, is placed in your symbolic MAP by a RECEIVE MAP command.

This is a good time to practice what you've read, possibly by locating programs at your shop that are of similar size and structure and reviewing them, not to compare with my style, but to understand what they are doing. If you can read and understand the programs, you're doing fine.

Part 2

CICS Techniques

5

COBOL/370, COBOL II, and VS/COBOL

Your choice of what COBOL language statements to use in a CICS/ COBOL application are not just dependent on how many COBOL commands that you know. It is also contingent on which COBOL compiler that you are using and which version of CICS is applicable at your shop. Read on.

When IBM introduced COBOL II in 1984, the application opportunities increased significantly. No longer were COBOL applications denied use of extended memory management or access to high-performance I/O facilities. Most important, COBOL II allowed COBOL programmers to use true structured program development techniques.

Then, in late 1991, when IBM introduced COBOL/370, all the features of COBOL II were incorporated, plus many enhancements that extend COBOL to the programmer workstation. This places COBOL/370 as part of IBM's program development environment called AD/Cycle. Although COBOL/370 provides many new features, since they aren't particular to CICS, they are not part of this book. Also, COBOL/370 is available *only* with MVS and only then with CICS/ ESA version 3.2.1 or later.

Additionally, COBOL/370 requires that the IBM product, Language Environment/370 (LE/370) be present on the computer. This is because COBOL/370 does not have its own specific subroutine library as did all prior IBM COBOL compilers. Instead, COBOL/370 uses a shared library of runtime subroutines that provide extended compatibility with other languages that use LE/370. Again, that is too large a topic for a text on CICS.

For a simplified overview of the various CICS versions, the required operating system, and what versions of COBOL will function in the specific environment, see Figure 5.1. Please do not infer from Figure 5.1 that the different versions of COBOL can be in the same run unit. To mix multiple programs together in one executable unit, use the same compiler for all affected programs. I admit that this oversimplifies the situation, as there are a few ways to get programs from different compilers to "talk" to each other, but such techniques are beyond our objective here. To keep your life simple (and your home phone from ringing at midnight because of problems with your code), keep all code with the same compiler.

	CICS/ESA 3.2.1	CICS/ESA 3.1.1	CICS/MVS 2.1	CICS/VSE 2.1	CICS/VS 1.7
MVS	X	X	X		X
VSE			X	X	
LE/370	X				
COBOL/370	X				
COBOL II	X	X	X	X	X
OS/VS/COBOL	X	X	X		X
DOS/VS COBOL			X	X	

Figure 5.1. Comparison of COBOL and CICS versions.

Naturally, whether you use COBOL/370, COBOL II, or VS/COBOL is a matter of which compiler your employer supplies. Even if COBOL II or COBOL/370 is available, you may find yourself supporting older transactions that were written for VS/COBOL. No problem. Over time, you will find that these older applications can be converted to newer technologies. It just takes a little longer.

I have consciously avoided using only COBOL/370 and COBOL II features in this book, because you might not be familiar with them. There are some COBOL II facilities in almost every example, but I would have written them somewhat differently if I assumed you knew COBOL II well.

Also, as COBOL II and COBOL/370 are the compilers of choice for high-performance applications, new versions of CICS have provided more support for them.

5.1.   NEW FEATURES OF COBOL II AND COBOL/370

More than likely, if your company migrated to COBOL II or COBOL/ 370, it was for some immediate performance payback. Unfortunately, one of these compilers' strengths are that they provide management with some performance improvements without investing any time in the application programmer to learn new features. For example, programs compiled with COBOL II or COBOL/370 can address memory that VS/COBOL programs cannot. That relieves contention for existing memory space and improves application throughput. Regrettably, it also bypasses the programmer's yearning to learn a new environment and to master it. A review of COBOL II and COBOL/370 is beyond the scope of this book, but I encourage you to learn them and all the features that ANSI 85 bring to your professional skills. Here is a brief summary of some of the major differences that affect CICS programs:

- Extended memory addressability, whether in MVS or VSE environments

- Significantly improved debugging techniques, both for batch and for CICS

- Improved efficiency of the generated object code

- Simpler coding requirements for memory management techniques in COBOL

- Full access to the ANSI 85 standards, allowing true structured programming

There are some of the newer COBOL statements in some of the programs, but I didn't use many of the new facilities because they didn't improve the program examples, especially if you aren't familiar with COBOL II or COBOL/370.

5.2.   DIFFERENCES/RESTRICTIONS FOR CICS APPLICATIONS

First, we will examine the restrictions that apply to your use of COBOL. Then, we will examine some basic changes in COBOL application program design that apply with COBOL II.

5.2.1.   General COBOL Restrictions

Some of these restrictions may seem obvious by now, but I wanted to summarize them for you for easy reference.

Here are items that you must not do, as they can cause unpredictable ABENDS, whether you are using COBOL/370, COBOL II, or VS/COBOL:

* Don't use any facility that requires a FILE SECTION (e.g., REPORT WRITER, OPEN, CLOSE, READ, WRITE).

* Don't specify any compile option that requires system services performed outside of CICS. This includes COUNT, DYNAM, ENDJOB, FLOW, STATE, SYMDMP, and TEST. (A review of proper compile options is in Chapter 10.)

* Don't use statements that implicitly require system-provided I/O, such as DISPLAY, EXHIBIT, ACCEPT from input device, or MERGE.

If you are using VS/COBOL, here are additional no-no's:

* Don't use STRING, UNSTRING, INSPECT, or TRANSFORM verbs.

* Don't execute GOBACK, EXIT PROGRAM, or STOP RUN statements.

* Don't use any form of the ACCEPT verb.

Looking back through these restrictions, there are some subtle issues that you may not have seen. For example, COBOL II and COBOL/370 may use the ACCEPT statement format for DATE and TIME, while it is not recommended for VS/COBOL. (Despite IBM's documentation, however, I have seen that ACCEPT format used in VS/COBOL applications successfully. My interpretation is that, while some restricted statements may function for an application, they cause memory fragmentation within the CICS environment.)

Also, COBOL II and COBOL/370 may use the SORT verb. Since that requires special consideration at your shop, not to mention severe performance degradation. I make no further reference to SORT within the book.

Finally, while COBOL II and COBOL/370 may use GOBACK, EXIT PROGRAM, and STOP RUN, I encourage you to use the proper CICS command if a program was invoked via a CICS command (e.g., from CICS directly, via XCTL, LINK, or START).

5.2.2. COBOL II and COBOL/370 Program Design Differences

When writing COBOL II or COBOL/370 applications, you will find that several differences appear. For one, you don't need to manipulate BLL cells as you did with VS/COBOL. Also, you don't need to provide the length of data elements that are already defined within your program. Detailed information on converting to COBOL II is in the *Power Programming* series, but many of the issues are apparent in this book just by comparing examples.

More important than the technical details themselves is the knowledge that these compilers work hand in hand with CICS, eliminating the need for some coding techniques and participating in the execution and debugging of applications. If you peruse an IBM reference for these compilers, you will find information there on the various environments in which CICS runs. That wasn't true for VS/COBOL where the environment (such as CICS) was foreign to COBOL.

One of the more visible differences is that there is more flexibility in program-to-program communications, such as in the following examples:

- A run unit must not have a mix of VS/COBOL , COBOL/370, and COBOL II. (That means that you cannot mix old and new programs together in the same phase (VSE) or loadmodule (MVS).)

- Dynamic CALLs are allowed with the CALL *identifier* format of the CALL statement.

- CALLed subprograms may contain EXEC CICS commands if running under CICS/MVS, CICS/VSE, or CICS/ESA. (Remember to pass the DFHEIBLK and DFHCOMMAREA as the first two parameters.)

- You may use GOBACK, in place of RETURN, to return to an invoking application. STOP RUN returns control to CICS.

These are general considerations, although you will also find information on differences in Chapter 6.

5.3. CONVERTING FROM VS/COBOL TO COBOL II OR COBOL/370

Probably the hardest thing you will find in converting to COBOL II or COBOL/370 is not coping with any of the newer coding techniques. More likely, your difficulty will be in recoding many antiquated statements that just don't compile correctly anymore. For example, CICS programs written in VS/COBOL always seem rife with EXAMINE statements, a throwback to the ANSI 68 standard. So, if your shop is about to convert some CICS transactions to COBOL II, don't worry about the newer COBOL II statements; just get the dinosaurs to compile correctly by converting out-of-date statements.

True conversion issues that separate the compilers fall in the area of memory management, usually where a program is allocating memory at run time in the LINKAGE SECTION. (Examples in the prior chapters did not do this, and many companies don't allow that technique.) More on that in Chapter 6.

SUMMARY

Although this chapter contained no CICS commands, the information is critical. If you disregard the issues presented here, you may find that, while your programs compile successfully, they will not run. If your shop uses COBOL II, don't miss the opportunity it provides to let you develop better, more structured applications.

6

CICS Programming Techniques

Up to this chapter, you have been struggling with learning how to develop programs that work as pseudoconversational within the world of CICS. I kept the programs simple to let you focus on MAPs and dialogue. Knowing how to structure the dialogue is key to your mastery of CICS. This chapter will present some commands and considerations to assist you as you build applications. As an example, you need to understand some I/O commands, some ways to save data between dialogues with the terminal, and some miscellaneous commands could be useful, too. Also, since DL/I programs need some extra help in a CICS environment, I included some information on that, too.

6.1. DOING VSAM I/O

Although CICS can work with all of IBM's database products, VSAM is still preferred at many shops. This book doesn't explain how to define and manipulate VSAM datasets (there are other books for that), but it must assume that you do understand the concept of keyed (or indexed) files. By that, I mean that an I/O command to a keyed file will retrieve, add, or update only that specific record. CICS can access purely sequential files, but that isn't usually the charter of online applications. Instead, they are used to access specific records for a terminal user.

There are two basic approaches to handling VSAM files. One is to access specific records using READ and WRITE commands. This set of commands (described in 6.1.1) is the commands most often used for random inquiry and file management. The other approach is to browse through the records in a sequential fashion (covered in 6.1.2). This technique is most often used when the user (or program) needs to scan through a range of records for the desired information. The READ command could, of course, do that, but the browse commands are more efficient.

Notice: In most cases throughout this book, where there is a difference among the several versions of CICS, I point it out for each occurrence. This will be an exception. FILE I/O commands in CICS/VS used the keyword DATASET to identify the file being accessed. The keyword used by CICS/MVS, CICS/ESA, and CICS/VSE is FILE. DATASET is still accepted but, since FILE is the preferred keyword, FILE is used in this book. If you review other programs at your shop, you will probably see DATASET used. Both keywords accomplish the same thing, but I encourage you to use FILE.

6.1.1.   Reading and Writing VSAM Files

Accessing VSAM records in CICS is actually easier than doing it in a batch program. After all, you don't need to OPEN or CLOSE the file. CICS does that for you. (*Note*: You can also do that with the CEMT transaction, described in Chapter 7.)

Before getting into the specifics of the commands, let me review the implications of doing I/O within the confines of a CICS task. You should recall that a task ends when a RETURN command is issued. When that happens, all data is lost unless you did something with it to keep it. For example, you can't READ a record during one task and expect the data to be waiting for you when the next task is initiated. Everything that must be done must be done during a task.

That means that, if you plan to read and update a record, do it within a task. If that is not possible, you will need to consider the implications of reading a record in one task for information, then rereading it in a following task. For one thing, some other transaction could have read and updated or even deleted that record. In CICS, no one "owns" a record beyond one task. We'll pick up on this again, but I wanted to sensitize you first.

The basic commands that manage VSAM I/O are the following:

- READ, which reads a specified record, depending on key selection.
- WRITE, which adds a new record to the file.

- REWRITE, which rewrites a record that had previously been READ with UPDATE specified.

- DELETE, which removes a record from the file.

- UNLOCK, which releases a record from a hold status, allowing other transactions to access it.

You will find the READ, WRITE, and DELETE commands similar to their COBOL equivalent statements. The update process is similar to batch but needs to be reviewed. Here are the steps to update a record:

1. First, read the record with UPDATE specified. This prevents other transactions from accessing the record until either the end of task occurs, the record is updated with a REWRITE command, or an UNLOCK command is issued to release the record from update status.

2. If the record is to be updated, issue a REWRITE command within the same task. The command will be invalid (INVREC) if no READ with UPDATE was issued in the task.

The READ with UPDATE may also be used in combination with the DELETE command, but we'll see that later. Let's look at the commands themselves.

READ command. The READ command is straightforward, shown in Figure 6.1. The command is normally used to retrieve a specific record,

---

```
FUNCTION: Read a record from a VSAM file
EXEC CICS  READ
           FILE(datavalue)
           SET(pointer) | INTO(dataname)
        [ LENGTH(dataname) ]
           RIDFLD(dataname)
        [ KEYLENGTH(datavalue) [ GENERIC ] ]
        [ RBA | RRN ]
        [ GTEQ | EQUAL ]
        [ UPDATE ]
        [ HANDLE | NOHANDLE [ RESP() ] ]
END-EXEC
Most probable error conditions: DUPKEY, NOTFND, LENGERR
```

Figure 6.1. READ command.

although it can also be used to access records sequentially, starting with a specified location.

FILE() identifies the eight-byte name of the file as defined in the FCT.

SET() I INTO() specifies where the record is to be stored. INTO names a data area that has been allocated, such as in WORK-ING-STORAGE. The use of SET is covered in topic 6.2.

LENGTH() identifies the length of the record, using a PIC S9(4) COMP field. After the READ is complete, this field contains the actual length of the record, which may be different than specified.

RIDFLD() specifies the data area that contains the key for the READ. Since CICS accesses VSAM directly (where the key location and length are defined from the IDCAMS utility), you do not need to specify the location of this field. Except for RBA and RRN (below), this must always be as long as the key field for the file (even for GENERIC).

KEYLENGTH() [GENERIC] specifies the length of the key field. If a dataname, it should be PIC S9(4) COMP. KEYLENGTH must be used when GENERIC is specified and MUST specify a length that is less than the actual key. Do not use with RBA or RRN. GENERIC specifies that only part of the key is used. If GENERIC is not specified and KEYLENGTH is omitted also, CICS uses the key length specified in the VSAM cluster for the dataset. Not valid if RBA or RRN is specified.

RBA I RRN If either of these is specified, RIDFLD must point to a PIC S9(8) COMP field. RBA indicates that the RIDFLD is a relative byte address (RBA). RRN specifies that RIDFLD is the relative record number (RRN), beginning with 1 for the first record in the file.

GTEQ I EQUAL Of the two, EQUAL is the default. EQUAL means that the key of the retrieved record must be an exact match to RIDFLD. GTEQ specifies that the first record that is greater than or equal will be retrieved.

UPDATE specifies to CICS to hold the record retrieved for the remainder of the task or until the record is deleted or rewritten (DELETE and REWRITE commands) or an UNLOCK command is issued. This allows a program to read a record for update and immediately (within the task) make the decision on how to proceed. Technically, it is not just this record that is locked. VSAM locks the entire control interval, which may contain other records. All records in the control interval are locked out from access during this process. *Notice*: Only one record can be in UPDATE status at one time within a transaction.

Here is an example of reading a record. In this example, I am assuming that the record search key was entered on the screen into a field called EMPNOI. Following the READ command, the primary condition that should be checked is NOTFND, as that is the condition that will be raised if the specified record is not found. Otherwise, I normally expect the condition to be NORMAL (i.e., no condition was raised).

```
WORKING-STORAGE SECTION.

01   RECORD-WORK-AREAS.
     05   FILE-ID        PIC  X(8)     VALUE  'EMPAYFL'.
     05   FILE-REC-LEN   PIC  S9(4)  COMP   VALUE  +300.
     05   FILE-KEY-LEN   PIC  S9(4)  COMP   VALUE  +10.
     05   FILE-KEY       PIC  X(10).

01   FILE-DATA-AREA    PIC  X(300).

     MOVE  EMPNOI  TO  FILE-KEY
     EXEC  CICS  READ
           FILE        (FILE-ID)
           INTO        (FILE-DATA-AREA)
           LENGTH      (FILE-REC-LEN)
           RIDFLD      (FILE-KEY)
           KEYLENGTH (FILE-KEY-LEN)
           EQUAL
           NOHANDLE
           RESP        (CICS-RESP-CODE)
     END-EXEC

     IF  CICS-NOTFND
         MOVE  'Record  not  found'  TO  MSGO
     ELSE
         IF  NOT  CICS-NORMAL
             EXEC CICS ABEND ABCODE ('1234') END-EXEC
         END-IF
     END-IF
```

The use of END-IF is, of course, COBOL II. It allows logic to continue without an intervening period. In the prior example, the LENGERR condition could be raised if the record length was greater than what was specified — in this case, 300. This is rarely a problem if your program specifies the maximum record length for a given file. Since CICS reinitializes programs at the beginning of each task, I know that the value 300 will always be in FILE-REC-LEN at the beginning of the READ command. (Remember, CICS updates this field after the READ. If, for example, the record actually read was only 250 bytes, FILE-REC-LEN would contain 250 after the READ.)

The normal situation where LENGERR occurs is where, within one task, a program does more than one READ command. Where that happens, you can prevent LENGERR from occurring by always moving the maximum value to the dataname specified in LENGTH prior to each READ. Otherwise, here is what could happen:

1.   Using our example above, FILE-REC-LEN contains 300 prior to the first READ.

2.   The first READ returns a record that is 250 bytes. Since this is less than 300, that is okay. FILE-REC-LEN now contains 250.

3.   The READ command is executed a second time without resetting FILE-REC-LEN to 300. This time, the record read is 275 bytes. Since this is larger than 250, CICS assumes an error has occurred and raises the LENGERR condition. What is frustrating about this problem is that your application may be executed hundreds of times before this combination occurs. It happened to me and that's why I always use a MOVE instruction to set the value. In our example above, I would insert this command prior to the READ command:

```
MOVE 300 TO FILE-REC-LEN
```

Cheap insurance? You bet!

If the processing logic might cause the record to be updated, I would have included UPDATE in the command. This will prevent any other transaction from accessing the record until my program makes a decision. If the program does nothing with the record during the task, the update hold status is released and other transactions can then access the record. (Incidentally, if another transaction attempted to READ the record while my program has the record in UPDATE status, no error occurs. The other transaction is delayed until my task terminates or my program updates, deletes, or unlocks the record.)

You may have noticed that I tend to group related work fields together, such as my 01-level named RECORD-WORK-AREAS. CICS doesn't *require* this way of organizing data fields. I do it as a matter of personal style. I find that it simplifies debugging and improves application documentation. Also, while the RIDFLD may specify the key field within the data record, I always keep the key field separate. Why? Sometimes I do READ with the SET option (covered in 6.2) and, in that situation, the RIDFLD must be separate. My approach is always to try to find one way that works all the time and stick with it.

WRITE command. The WRITE command (Figure 6.2) is simpler than the READ command because it isn't subject to as many considerations.

```
FUNCTION: Write a record to a VSAM file
EXEC CICS WRITE
          FILE(datavalue)
          FROM(dataname)
        [ LENGTH(datavalue) ]
          RIDFLD(dataname)
        [ KEYLENGTH(datavalue) ]
        [ RBA | RRN ]
        [ MASSINSERT ]
        [ HANDLE | NOHANDLE [ RESP() ] ]
END-EXEC
Most probable error conditions: DUPREC, NOSPACE
```

Figure 6.2. WRITE command.

Since most of the keywords are the same as for a READ command, I won't repeat them here. The new keyword is MASSINSERT, so I'll just review it.

   MASSINSERT specifies that there will be several sequential WRITE operations within this task. This causes VSAM to do more efficient control interval splits, since this notifies it of upcoming WRITE operations. All WRITE commands involved in the mass insertion must use the MASSINSERT, not just the first WRITE. MASSINSERT status stays in effect until either the end of the task occurs or an UNLOCK command is issued.

Using the same file description used in the READ command, here is an example of a WRITE operation. The main condition you will want to check for is DUPREC. This is because this condition occurs when your program attempts to insert a new record and the record already exists. Since NOHANDLE causes CICS to ignore the situation, you need to ensure this isn't happening.

```
WORKING-STORAGE SECTION.

01  RECORD-WORK-AREAS.
    05  FILE-ID          PIC X(8)    VALUE 'EMPAYFL'.
    05  FILE-REC-LEN     PIC S9(4)   COMP  VALUE +300.
    05  FILE-KEY-LEN     PIC S9(4)   COMP  VALUE +10.
    05  FILE-KEY         PIC X(10).

01  FILE-DATA-AREA       PIC X(300).

    EXEC CICS WRITE
              FILE        (FILE-ID)
              FROM        (FILE-DATA-AREA)
              LENGTH      (FILE-REC-LEN)
              RIDFLD      (FILE-KEY)
              KEYLENGTH   (FILE-KEY-LEN)
              NOHANDLE
              RESP        (CICS-RESP-CODE)
    END-EXEC
    IF CICS-DUPREC
        MOVE 'Record already exists' TO MSGO
    ELSE
        IF NOT CICS-NORMAL
            EXEC CICS ABEND ABCODE ('1234') END-EXEC.
```

REWRITE command. The REWRITE command (Figure 6.3) is a simple command (Figure 6.3), used after a READ with UPDATE command was executed. Since the record already exists, we should expect few problems in executing this command.

This command introduces nothing new. After executing the REWRITE command, the record can, once again, be accessed by other transactions. The INVREC condition is raised if the record had not been previously read with UPDATE or if the FCT does not allow updating this file.

```
FUNCTION: Update  a  record  in  a  VSAM  file

EXEC  CICS   REWRITE
               FILE(datavalue)
               FROM(dataname)
           [ LENGTH(dataname)  ]
           [ HANDLE  |  NOHANDLE  [ RESP()  ]  ]
END-EXEC

Most  probable  error  condition:    INVREQ
```

Figure 6.3. REWRITE command.

DELETE command. The DELETE command (Figure 6.4) serves an obvious purpose. It deletes one or more records from a file. Despite that, there are several ways to use the command.

```
FUNCTION: Delete  a  record  from  a  VSAM  file

EXEC  CICS   DELETE
               FILE(datavalue)
           [ RIDFLD() [ KEYLENGTH() [ GENERIC [ NUMREC() ] ] ] ]
           [ RBA  |  RRN  ]
           [ HANDLE  |  NOHANDLE  [ RESP()  ]  ]
END-EXEC

Most  probable  error  conditions:  INVREQ,  NOTFND
```

Figure 6.4. DELETE command.

The definition of most of these fields were documented for the READ command and are not repeated here. Where there are differences, I will note them.

RIDFLD() Although documented in the READ command, this option is not always needed. If the record to be deleted was read with UPDATE, then this field isn't needed. If the DELETE command is to locate and delete the record, then it is required.

NUMREC() This specifies the name of a PIC S9(4) COMP field where CICS will store the number of records deleted. Use this field when doing GENERIC deletes if your program wants to know this value.

If a record had been read with UPDATE, using the earlier examples, here is the DELETE command that would be valid. Since the record was successfully read by the READ command, no conditions should be raised (unless the READ did not include UPDATE, in which case the INVREQ would be raised).

```
EXEC CICS DELETE
    FILE (FILE-ID)
END-EXEC
```

If the record had not been read, the DELETE command would be coded this way.

```
EXEC CICS  DELETE
    FILE (FILE-ID)
    RIDFLD      (FILE-KEY)
END-EXEC
```

Notice that the KEYLENGTH keyword was not used. I used KEYLENGTH in earlier examples, but, if you check the syntax, it isn't required except with the GENERIC option. I usually use it for better documentation, but KEYLENGTH is rarely required with DELETE. Check with your shop's standards, however, to see how optional keywords should be treated.

UNLOCK command. The UNLOCK command (Figure 6.5) has been discussed already. The command is needed only if (1) your program issued a READ with UPDATE command, you do not want to DELETE or REWRITE the record, and you want to issue another READ with

---

FUNCTION: Unlocks a control interval

```
EXEC CICS UNLOCK
        FILE(datavalue)
        [ HANDLE | NOHANDLE [ RESP() ] ]
END-EXEC
```

Most probable error conditions:

Figure 6.5. UNLOCK command.

UPDATE command, or (2) your program issued a WRITE with MASSINSERT command and you want to revert to writing without mass insert logic. Since ending the task with any form of RETURN command also accomplishes this function, you may rarely find that you need it.

6.1.2. Browsing VSAM Files

Browsing files is a technique that isn't often needed. Usually, you will see it when a program presents a list of information, such as customers, employees, parts, or whatever on screen. Menu-driven applications often use this approach to let a terminal user browse through a file onscreen and then, by a select field or by cursor positioning (described in Chapter 4), specify which record to process.

Browsing requires that commands be issued in a predetermined sequence, much as we saw for updating records or doing mass insertion in prior topic. The commands we will review are the following:

* STARTBR, which signals to CICS that a browse operation is to begin. This command also specifies the record location in the file at which the browse will start. No record is read.

* READNEXT, which causes the next sequential record to be read.

* READPREV, which causes the previous record to be read, in other words, read backwards through the file.

* RESETBR, which resets the location in the file for following READNEXT or READPREV commands. Not needed unless the browse operation initiated by a STARTBR needs to jump to a different file position.

* ENDBR, which signals to CICS that the browse operation is now over. Up to now, we have seen that most situations, such as a READ with UPDATE, are cancelled by just ending the task. Not true for browse operations. Always issue the ENDBR command prior to terminating the task.

The browse operation ties up more resources than do most other CICS commands, so you should consider efficiency when doing a browse operation. For example, I don't recommend that your program browse through hundreds of records within one task. Your shop may have rules or guidelines on this. Also, the entire browse operation must be done within one task.

STARTBR command. Many of the keywords used in the VSAM READ
are repeated here and have the same meaning. See Figure 6.6.

```
FUNCTION: Start a Browse operation
EXEC CICS STARTBR
          FILE(datavalue)
          RIDFLD(dataname)
        [ KEYLENGTH(datavalue) [ GENERIC ] ]
        [ REQID(dataname) ]
        [ RBA | RRN ]
        [ GTEQ | EQUAL ]
        [ HANDLE | NOHANDLE [ RESP() ] ]
END-EXEC
Most probable error conditions: NOTFND, INVREC
```

Figure 6.6. STARTBR command.

Since most of these keywords are defined elsewhere in the READ
command, I will document what is new or different.

RIDFLD() specifies the key field that *must* be used by all
commands in the browse operation. This is mandatory, as
CICS maintains the data field with the appropriate key value.

REQID() specifies a PIC S9(4) COMP field that contains the
number of this browse operation. This should only be used
if your program is concurrently browsing two different files,
or the same file but in two different locations. Since browse
operations tie up CICS resources, I don't encourage that you
do this. Besides, the program complexity could be over-
whelming.

As a reminder, a GENERIC browse requires that the KEYLENGTH
specify a length that matches the portion of the key that is to be used.
Also, all following READNEXT and READPREV commands must not
specify a different KEYLENGTH as that will cause incorrect results. My
recommendation is to omit KEYLENGTH from those commands.

As with other commands identified in this book, there are other
conditions that can be raised in addition to these two. These are the
most likely ones. NOTFND is what you should normally include

program logic to handle. I include the INVREC to remind you that, if the file is not authorized for browse operations (specified in the FCT), no browse operations may be done. Your systems programmers can change the entry, if needed.

Normally, if your program wants to start a browse operation at a specific point, you would move the appropriate value to the key field before issuing the STARTBR command. That would start the browse operation at a known record. Another example might be a generic browse. For our example, if your shop had a parts file where the key was formed by combining manufacturer code and part code, you might want to browse all parts from one manufacturer. That would be a generic browse. That might be coded this way to browse all entries for a manufacturer, assuming the manufacturer code was retrieved from the screen in a field called MANUCDI.

```
01   RECORD-WORK-AREAS.
     05   FILE-ID        PIC  X(8)    VALUE  'PARTFIL'.
     05   FILE-REC-LEN   PIC  S9(4)   COMP   VALUE  +300.
     05   FILE-KEY-LEN   PIC  S9(4)   COMP   VALUE  +10.
     05   FILE-KEY.
          10   MANUFAC-CODE   PIC  X(5).
          10   PART-CODE      PIC  X(5).

01   FILE-DATA-AREA    PIC  X(300).

     MOVE  MANUCDI  TO  MANUFAC-CODE
     EXEC  CICS  STARTBR  FILE  (FILE-ID)
                          RIDFLD  (FILE-KEY)
                          KEYLENGTH  (5)
                          GENERIC
                          EQUAL
     END-EXEC
```

The above technique, by specifying EQUAL, ensures that there is at least one record retrieved or a NOTFND condition is raised when the STARTBR is issued. This would be important if the program wanted to ensure that there was at least one record on file for the manufacturer. Notice that the KEYLENGTH specifies a length that matches the part of the key that my program is using. As with all GENERIC options in this chapter, the KEYLENGTH must specify a shorter length.

But, what if I had a different situation, one where I wasn't sure if a particular manufacturer code was on the file but wanted to start there anyway? This might occur if a company billed throughout the month, based on the first letter of the manufacturer. In that case, my application doesn't care whether there are any matches at all. One option would be to use the above approach but specify GTEQ instead of EQUAL. That would cause the first READNEXT to retrieve the first record in the file that began with that manufacturer code or a higher one. In that situation, you will sometimes see a different approach, a generic one that does not specify GENERIC. You need to be familiar with it, because many programmers never code GENERIC but fiddle with the key to accomplish a similar result. Look at this example.

```
01  RECORD-WORK-AREAS.
    05  FILE-ID          PIC  X(8)    VALUE  'PARTFIL'.
    05  FILE-REC-LEN     PIC  S9(4)   COMP   VALUE  +300.
    05  FILE-KEY-LEN     PIC  S9(4)   COMP   VALUE  +10.
    05  FILE-KEY.
        10  MANUFAC-CODE  PIC  X(5).
        10  PART-CODE     PIC  X(5).

01  FILE-DATA-AREA       PIC  X(300).

    MOVE  MANUCDI  TO  MANUFAC-CODE
    MOVE  LOW-VALUES  TO  PART-CODE
    EXEC  CICS  STARTBR  FILE  (FILE-ID)
                         RIDFLD  (FILE-KEY)
                         KEYLENGTH  (FILE-KEY-LEN)
                         GTEQ
    END-EXEC
```

This is almost the same as the prior example, except that it initializes the low-order bytes to LOW-VALUES, specifies the full length of the key, specifies GTEQ, and does not specify GENERIC. Still, this is a generic request because CICS will accept the first record that is greater or equal to the particular manufacturer code and low values. Since LOW-VALUES is the lowest value in the computer's collating sequence, there will be a record returned by the first READNEXT unless there are no more records in the file.

Okay, now let's do one more change, one that can be done by the STARTBR or prior to issuing a READNEXT or READPREV command. Let's replace the MOVE MANUCDI TO MANUFAC-CODE with MOVE

LOW-VALUES to MANUFAC-CODE (or replace both MOVE statements with MOVE LOW-VALUES TO FILE-KEY). You can probably guess what will happen. The first READNEXT will read the first record in the file. On a similar approach, moving HIGH-VALUES to FILE-KEY would be a good way to initialize a browse operation that will use the READPREV command to begin at the end of the file. You can mix and match this technique, also. That is, you can read forward for part of a browse and then read backwards.

READNEXT command. The READNEXT command (Figure 6.7) reads the next record sequentially. If this is the first READNEXT, it uses the key established by the STARTBR.

```
FUNCTION: Read next record in a browse operation
EXEC CICS READNEXT
          FILE(datavalue)
          SET(pointer) | INTO(dataname)
        [ LENGTH(dataname) ]
          RIDFLD(dataname)
        [ KEYLENGTH(datavalue) ]
        [ REQID(dataname) ]
        [ RBA | RRN ]
        [ HANDLE | NOHANDLE [ RESP() ] ]
END-EXEC

Most probable error condition: ENDFILE
```

Figure 6.7. READNEXT command.

There is nothing new here in the keywords, so I won't review them. As a reminder, the SET keyword is explained in topic 6.2. Also, don't forget that the KEYLENGTH, if specified, must match the full key length for the file.

Since CICS puts the key of the record that was read in the RIDFLD, this ensures that, if the same field is used for the next READNEXT, the file will be read sequentially. This gives you an opportunity to change the processing sequence. Often referred to as "skip-sequential processing," the technique is simple. If your application needs to change the file position where the browse operation is being executed, all you need to do is move the new key value to the RIDFLD and issue the next READNEXT command. It will read the record at that new location.

Since this is your traditional sequential read process, don't forget to check for the ENDFILE condition.

READPREV command. The READPREV command (Figure 6.8) is identical to the READNEXT except it works backwards. The ENDFILE condition is raised when the READPREV reaches the beginning of the file. The NOTFND occurs when the READPREV follows a STARTBR command and there is no such record. This occurs even if GTEQ was specified. My suggestion: Never issue a READPREV after a STARTBR unless you set the RIDFLD to HIGH-VALUES. ENDFILE will be the only normal condition to anticipate.

FUNCTION: Read the previous record in a browse operation

```
EXEC CICS READPREV
          FILE(datavalue)
          SET(pointer) | INTO(dataname)
        [ LENGTH(dataname) ]
          RIDFLD(dataname)
        [ KEYLENGTH(datavalue) ]
        [ REQID(dataname) ]
        [ RBA | RRN ]
        [ HANDLE | NOHANDLE [ RESP() ] ]
END-EXEC
```

Most probable error conditions: ENDFILE, NOTFND

Figure 6.8. READPREV command.

If you switch from READNEXT to READPREV, you need to remember the file positioning. For example, if after issuing a READNEXT, you issued a READPREV with the same RIDFLD, you would read the *same record* that you had just read. This is because the file pointer is now at the next sequential record. To read the record that was previous to the last record read with READNEXT, you must issue two READPREV commands.

RESETBR command. The RESETBR command (Figure 6.9) changes
the key value for the browse operation. A simpler way to accomplish
this is just to change the value prior to issuing a READNEXT or
READPREV command.

```
FUNCTION:  Reset  key  in  a  browse  operation

EXEC  CICS  RESETBR
           FILE(datavalue)
           RIDFLD(dataname)
        [  KEYLENGTH(datavalue)  [  GENERIC  ]  ]
        [  REQID(dataname)  ]
        [  RBA  |  RRN  ]
        [  GTEQ  |  EQUAL  ]
        [  HANDLE  |  NOHANDLE  [  RESP()  ]  ]
END-EXEC

Most  probable  error  conditions:  INVREC,  NOTFND
```

Figure 6.9. RESETBR command.

The main value of this command is that it also lets you change
other aspects of the browse, such as changing from GTEQ to EQUAL,
or from specific to GENERIC. Unless your browse is especially complex, you will seldom need this command.

```
FUNCTION:  End  a  browse  operation

EXEC  CICS  ENDBR
           FILE(datavalue)
        [  REQID(dataname)  ]
        [  HANDLE  |  NOHANDLE  [  RESP()  ]  ]
END-EXEC

Most  probable  error  condition:  INVREQ
```

Figure 6.10. ENDBR command.

ENDBR command. This command (Figure 6.10) terminates a browse operation, thereby releasing the dedicated CICS resources. This command must be executed to terminate a browse operation. The INVREQ condition could be raised if no STARTBR had been issued.

BROWSE Example. Here is a basic example that ties several of the browse commands together. In this example, the program wants to browse up to 15 records or until ENDFILE or NOTFND occurs. This is not uncommon where a program only wants to read enough records to display summary data for each on the screen. The repeated MOVE 300 TO FILE-REC-LEN would only be required if the records were variable-length.

```
01   RECORD-WORK-AREAS.
     05   FILE-ID        PIC  X(8)    VALUE  'PARTFIL'.
     05   FILE-REC-LEN   PIC  S9(4)   COMP   VALUE +300.
     05   FILE-KEY-LEN   PIC  S9(4)   COMP   VALUE +10.
     05   FILE-KEY.
          10   MANUFAC-CODE   PIC  X(5).
          10   PART-CODE      PIC  X(5).

01   FILE-DATA-AREA         PIC  X(300).

          .
          .

     MOVE  MANUCDI  TO  MANUFAC-CODE
     MOVE  LOW-VALUES  TO  PART-CODE
     EXEC  CICS  STARTBR  FILE (FILE-ID)
                          RIDFLD (FILE-KEY)
                          KEYLENGTH (5)
                          GENERIC
                          EQUAL
     END-EXEC
     PERFORM 2000-READ-RECORDS VARYING REC-CNT FROM 1
          BY ONE UNTIL REC-CT > 15 OR CICS-NOTFND
     EXEC CICS ENDBR FILE (FILE-ID)
     END-EXEC
          .
          .
2000-READ-RECORDS.
     MOVE 300 TO FILE-REC-LEN
     EXEC CICS READNEXT
               FILE   (FILE-ID)
```

```
                RIDFLD (FILE-KEY)
                INTO   (FILE-REC-LEN)
                LENGTH (FILE-DATA-AREA)
                NOHANDLE
                RESP   (CICS-RESP-CODE)
        END-EXEC
        IF CICS-NORMAL
            PERFORM 2210-PROCESS-DATA
        ELSE
            IF CICS-ENDFILE OR CICS-NOTFND
                MOVE 16 TO REC-CT
            ELSE
                EXEC CICS ABEND ('1234') END-EXEC.
```

This example, because it uses GENERIC and EQUAL, ensures that no records are processed unless the first matches the first five bytes of the key. If the browse operation is to continue in the next task (for example, to access the next 15 records within the sequence), the application logic would need to store the full 10 byte key in the COMM area and restore it when the transaction is reexecuted.

6.2.   DYNAMICALLY MANAGING MEMORY

Many shops do not allow programmers to write code that dynamically allocates and deallocates memory. For one thing, it can be tricky for the novice programmer, and it exposes the application to a higher possibility of abending. Another reason not to use it is that it increases resource consumption for the task, having to request memory allocation by CICS. You may be wondering why the technique is required at all. Let me explain.

One of the major difficulties in the CICS world has been memory constraints caused by the unavoidable environment of managing many programs concurrently in memory. Eventually, you're just going to exhaust the memory allocated to the CICS environment. Certainly, CICS/ESA is the best avenue for a company to take to solve this concern, but many programs and shops just aren't there yet. Even when a shop is CICS/ESA, there may be situations where memory needs to be dynamically managed.

If you are using COBOL II or COBOL/370, there is much less concern for memory management, as COBOL II and COBOL/370 generate more efficient code than does VS/COBOL and have greater addressability. With VS/COBOL on MVS, for example, the WORK-ING STORAGE SECTION cannot exceed 64K. Once it does, the program abends when CICS attempts to load it. When that occurs, the VS/COBOL programmer must restructure the program before it will execute. (That's happened to me on several occasions, usually when the target date is near.)

Here is another possible situation where a program needs to manage memory. If a program is already quite large and has many different data areas and MAPs that are only occasionally used, the programmer might remove the areas from WORKING STORAGE and place them in the LINKAGE SECTION. This immediately reduces the size of the object code but leaves unanswered how to address those items in the LINKAGE SECTION. CICS provides facilities to do this, but the techniques are different for VS/COBOL and COBOL II. (Remember, what applies to COBOL II here also applies to COBOL/370.)

Before proceeding, you should remember that, up to now, all of the fields that you have addressed in the LINKAGE SECTION have been allocated either by CICS or by an invoking program using CALL, LINK, or XCTL. This is also true for non-CICS programs. Whenever a program attempts to use a data area in the LINKAGE SECTION that has not been allocated for use, the program immediately abends.

This technique, by the way, is generally referred to as *locate-mode I/O*. Using WORKING STORAGE for I/O is referred to as *move-mode I/O*. Each approach has its supporters. Some people prefer locate-mode because they believe it is more efficient. Supporters of move-mode believe it is safer.

6.2.1. Defining Dynamic Memory Areas in VS/COBOL

VS/COBOL is sensitive to whether a dynamically allocated area is greater or less than 4,096 bytes. The structure of 01-levels is the same for both, but the differences are enough to justify explaining them. In a later topic we will see how the addresses are computed/set. This topic is to present to you how the LINKAGE SECTION must be defined.

Memory areas not greater than 4096 bytes. VS/COBOL requires that you use a data element referred to as a BLL (Base Logical Locator). These are data fields that CICS (or your program) manipulates to construct an address for data areas. The requirements are rigorous and must be followed explicitly. Neither the CICS translator nor the VS/COBOL compiler can flag errors in the logic. Only the ABEND will confirm that you did it incorrectly. Here is the basic format that must appear in the LINKAGE SECTION. The WORKING-STORAGE entries may be in any order. The datanames are not critical; the structure and physical location in the LINKAGE SECTION are.

```
WORKING-STORAGE SECTION.

01  MY-WORK-AREAS.
    05  LEN-NXT-AREA  PIC  S9(4)  COMP  VALUE +2050.
    05  LEN-1ST-AREA  PIC  S9(4)  COMP  VALUE +3000.

LINKAGE  SECTION.

01  BLL-FIELDS.
    05  FILLER             PIC  S9(8)  COMP.
    05  ADDR-1ST-01-LVL    PIC  S9(8)  COMP.
    05  ADDR-NEXT-01-LVL   PIC  S9(8)  COMP.
    .
    .                                         address  of
    .                                         this  01-level
01  FIRST-01-LEVEL
    .                                         address  of
    .                                         next  01-level
01  NEXT-01-LEVEL
    .
    .
    .
```

When the CICS translator processes the program, the EIB (DFHEIBLK) and DFHCOMMAREA are inserted as the first two 01-levels, immediately following the LINKAGE SECTION statement. That will cause the 01 that I named BLL-FIELDS to be the third 01, the 01 named FIRST-01-LEVEL to be the fourth 01, and the last one shown to be the fifth. This order is critical. Notice that the second entry in BLL-FIELDS (the first is required but may be FILLER) will have the address of the following 01-level, and each succeeding entry in BLL-FIELDS will have the address of the next 01-level.

Now, the addresses are not inserted automatically. Before you can reference either of those 01-level areas called FIRST-01-LEVEL or NEXT-01-LEVEL, you must write code that causes the area to be allocated and the address stored in the corresponding BLL field. That is covered in topic 6.3.3.

Memory areas greater than 4096 bytes. All of the above information applies to data areas greater than 4096 bytes, but additional entries and steps are required. Let's compare an example where the 01-areas are larger than 4096 bytes.

```
01  MY-WORK-AREAS.
    05  LEN-LRG-AREA   PIC  S9(4)  COMP  VALUE +8692.
    05  LEN-BIG-AREA   PIC  S9(4)  COMP  VALUE +5700.

LINKAGE  SECTION.

01  BLL-FIELDS.
    05  FILLER              PIC  S9(8)  COMP.
    05  ADDR-LRG-01-LVLA    PIC  S9(8)  COMP.
    05  ADDR-LRG-01-LVLB    PIC  S9(8)  COMP.
    05  ADDR-LRG-01-LVLC    PIC  S9(8)  COMP.
    05  ADDR-NEXT-01-LVLA   PIC  S9(8)  COMP.
    05  ADDR-NEXT-01-LVLB   PIC  S9(8)  COMP.
    .
    .
    .                                        address of
                                             this 01-level
01  LARGE-01-LEVEL    PIC  X(8692)
    .                                        address of
    .                                        next 01-level
01  BIG-01-LEVEL      PIC  X(5700)
    .
    .
    .
```

If you do a little arithmetic, you will notice that I had to add additional BLL entries for each 4096 or fraction. Since the first 01-level is larger than two times 4096, I needed three BLL entries. The second 01-level requires two BLL entries. All of the BLL entries for any given 01-level must be set prior to accessing the data area. Now, read topic 6.3.3 to see how to allocate the areas.

6.2.2. Defining Dynamic Memory Areas in COBOL II

Compared to VS/COBOL, COBOL II and COBOL/370 make it easy. With COBOL II or COBOL/370, all that you have to do is define your 01-level entries, of any size and in any order, after the LINKAGE

SECTION statement. Not only do you not need BLL entries, they are not allowed. Easy? you bet!

Reminder: You still need to set the address prior to actually referencing the data areas. Remember, all that we are doing here is defining the area. Also, for both VS/ACOBOL and COBOL II, a precoded DFHCOMMAREA must precede dynamic areas.

6.2.3.   Allocating Memory in VS/COBOL, COBOL II and COBOL/370

In this topic, I assume you have read the prior topics that explained how to define the LINKAGE SECTION components. Now we will see how the areas are allocated for our use.

Using SET in I/O commands. Several commands that retrieve input data, such as the various READ and RECEIVE commands, provide an alternative to the INTO keyword. (Up to now, all such CICS commands that we have used included the INTO keyword, specifying the name of a data area in WORKING STORAGE to store the data.) A mutually exclusive keyword is the SET keyword. This keyword specifies that CICS is to allocate dynamically the required data area and store the address for future use. The examples shown use the READ statement, but the technique is identical for any similar CICS command (e.g., READQ, RECEIVE MAP).

An important item to remember is that memory allocated by SET is automatically freed at the end of the task. You don't need to take any action within the program to release this memory. As soon as your program issues a RETURN or RETURN TRANSID command, this memory will be released. Also, once you have executed these instructions to allocate a given data area within a task, they do not have to be repeated prior to the end of the task. That means that, if you needed to reuse the area again within the task (such as for a second READ to the same file), you could issue a READ command with the INTO option.

VS/COBOL use of SET. For VS/COBOL, the dataname specified in SET references the name of the BLL entry, *not* the name of the data area. As an example, if we wanted to READ data into the 01-level named NEXT-01-LEVEL, our READ command would look like this:

```
EXEC CICS READ FILE      ('fileid')
               SET       (ADDR-NEXT-01-LVL)
               LENGTH    (LEN-NXT-AREA)
               .
               .
END-EXEC
SERVICE RELOAD NEXT-01-LEVEL
```

The READ instruction made no reference to the true data area. Instead, CICS knew from the relative location of the BLL pointer, ADDR-NEXT-01-LVL, which 01-level area to use. This is why the physical layout is critical to VS/COBOL. If the BLL pointers are not in the proper order, CICS will use the wrong data area. The SERVICE RELOAD statement is required (only for VS/COBOL) after any instructions are executed that cause memory addresses to be set or modified. The SERVICE RELOAD statement is not required if the program was compiled with NOOPTIMIZE but, since almost all programs specify OPT (or OPTIMIZE) for efficiency, I assume that you do too.

What if the READ had been into LARGE-01-LEVEL? There would be some differences. Here goes:

```
EXEC CICS READ FILE      ('fileid')
               SET       (ADDR-LRG-01-LVLA)
               LENGTH    (LEN-LRG-AREA)
               .
               .
END-EXEC
COMPUTE ADDR-LRG-01-LVLB = ADDR-LRG-01-LVLA + 4096
COMPUTE ADDR-LRG-01-LVLC = ADDR-LRG-01-LVLB + 4096
SERVICE RELOAD LARGE-01-LEVEL
```

In this example, we must do some arithmetic. CICS provided the beginning address of the 01-level and stored it in ADDR-LRG-01-LVLA. Since each BLL points to 4,096 bytes, I added two COMPUTE statements to set the next two BLLs to the value contained in the previous BLL plus 4096. After we compute the addresses, we execute the SERVICE RELOAD statement so CICS can readjust its pointers.

COBOL II and COBOL/370 use of SET. After seeing what VS/ COBOL must do, you may be expecting a similar requirement for COBOL II and COBOL/370. Instead, just as with the simple defini- tion requirements that you encountered in topic 6.2.2, the allocation is also easy. There is no difference in whether the area is large or small, so let's see how we would handle the previous example with COBOL II or with COBOL/370.

```
01  MY-WORK-AREAS.
    05  LEN-LRG-AREA  PIC S9(4)  COMP  VALUE +8692.

LINKAGE SECTION.

01  LARGE-01-LEVEL  PIC X(8692).
    •
    •

EXEC CICS READ FILE    ('fileid')
               SET     (ADDRESS OF LARGE-01-LEVEL)
               LENGTH  (LEN-LRG-AREA)
               •
               •
END-EXEC
```

The LENGTH keyword is optional, except where a variable-length data area is involved. I recommend that the LENGTH keyword *always* be used for a CICS command that introduces data into the application. This allows CICS to store the actual length of the data received. Notice the new syntax in the SET keyword. COBOL II provides the ability to specify ADDRESS OF when referencing any data area. The address isn't stored for programmer access, but this isn't a value that you care about, anyway. Notice that, not only do we not need the BLLs, we don't need the SERVICE RELOAD statement, and we don't need those extra COMPUTE statements. Clearly, dynamic memory management with the SET keyword and COBOL II or COBOL/370 is simple, requiring no more code than if the data were in WORKING STORAGE.

Using GETMAIN/FREEMAIN. Sometimes you need to allocate memory without using a READ or RECEIVE command. For example, possibly you need to issue a WRITE command from the LINKAGE SECTION. The WRITE command does not have a SET keyword because it doesn't make sense. This is because you must first build an output record before issuing a WRITE command and the data area would need to be allocated before your program began assembling the output record. So, you need a different facility. To accomplish this, CICS provides two commands, GETMAIN to allocate memory and FREEMAIN to release previously allocated memory. As with the prior examples, memory allocated by GETMAIN is automatically released when the task terminates, unless released earlier by a FREEMAIN command.

FUNCTION: *Allocate memory in LINKAGE SECTION*

```
EXEC CICS  GETMAIN
           SET(pointer)
           LENGTH(datavalue) | FLENGTH(datavalue) [BELOW]
         [ INITIMG(dataname) ]
         [ SHARED ]              <== CICS/ESA & CICS/VSE only
         [ NOSUSPEND ]
         [ HANDLE | NOHANDLE [ RESP() ] ]
END-EXEC
```

Most probable error conditions: LENGERR, NOSTG

Figure 6.11. GETMAIN command.

The GETMAIN command (Figure 6.11) uses the same SET option that was provided earlier. The difference is that allocating memory is all that it does, but it provides more options. Here is a review of the options:

SET   Used the same as in prior examples.

LENGTH() | FLENGTH()   LENGTH is the more common choice, since FLENGTH was not always available. FLENGTH must either specify a literal or the name of a field defined as S9(8) COMP. LENGTH must be either a literal or the name of a field defined as S9(4) COMP. FLENGTH is preferred because it is upward compatible with CICS/ESA. Below are the possible values:

	CICS/VSE	CICS/VS	CICS/MVS	CICS/ESA
LENGTH	32,767	32,767	32,767	65,535
FLENGTH	65,504	65,504	65,504	no limit

MVS has special use of LENGTH and FLENGTH. Memory specified with LENGTH is allocated below the 16-megabyte line, while memory specified with FLENGTH is allocated above, if available (for COBOL II and COBOL/370). The option, BELOW, is applicable only for CICS/ESA, specifying that the memory should be allocated in 24-bit mode.

INITIMG()   specifies what value the memory area should be initialized to. This is normally blanks or LOW-VALUES. If the allocated memory is to be used for a symbolic MAP, specify LOW-VALUES here.

SHARED specifies that the memory is NOT to be deallocated at the end of the task. This might occur if the memory will be used by another task that was STARTed by this task. This is available only with CICS/ESA.

NOSUSPEND specifies that, if the requested memory is not available, do not suspend the task until it becomes available. In this situation, the error condition raised is NOSTG. This should be used only where your program has other alternatives. My recommendation is not to code this. More than likely, if your program needs memory allocated, you may as well wait a few seconds until it is available.

Using GETMAIN is straightforward, especially if you understand use of the SET keyword. Let's repeat our earlier examples, only in this case, we just want the memory allocated. Here is how the VS/COBOL and the COBOL II examples would be coded. For both examples, we need to specify the data area that contains the initialization value. That could be coded in WORKING-STORAGE with something like this:

```
05  INIT-VALUE     PIC   X     VALUE  LOW-VALUES.
```

Using GETMAIN with VS/COBOL:

```
EXEC CICS GETMAIN
          SET      (ADDR-LRG-01-LVLA)
          LENGTH   (LEN-LRG-AREA)
          INITIMG  (INIT-VALUE)
END-EXEC
COMPUTE ADDR-LRG-01-LVLB = ADDR-LRG-01-LVLA + 4096
COMPUTE ADDR-LRG-01-LVLC = ADDR-LRG-01-LVLB + 4096
SERVICE  RELOAD LARGE-01-LEVEL
```

Using GETMAIN with COBOL II or COBOL/370:

```
EXEC CICS GETMAIN
          SET      (ADDRESS OF LARGE-01-LEVEL)
          LENGTH   (LEN-LRG-AREA)
          INITIMG  (INIT-VALUE)
END-EXEC
```

In both cases, I did not use my traditional NOHANDLE approach. This is because if this amount of memory is not available, I may as well wait.

```
FUNCTION:   Release previously allocated memory

EXEC CICS FREEMAIN
          DATA(dataname)
END-EXEC

Most probable error conditions: none
```

Figure 6.12. FREEMAIN command.

FREEMAIN (Figure 6.12) is much easier and is coded the same
way for both VS/COBOL, COBOL/370, and COBOL II. The keyword,
DATA, contains the dataname of the area to be released. Since it
doesn't use BLLs, the command is the same for VS/COBOL COBOL/
370, and COBOL II. Freeing the area allocated by the previous
GETMAIN commands would require this:

```
EXEC CICS FREEMAIN DATA (LARGE-01-LEVEL)
END-EXEC
```

Earlier, I mentioned that I would use only the READ command
for the examples. Remember that all the techniques we discussed
here apply equally to any command that has the SET keyword. Also,
once the data has been allocated within the task, it should be treated
just as though it had been in WORKING-STORAGE. For example,
you might use GETMAIN to allocate an 01-level area in the LINK-
AGE SECTION and then use a WRITE or SEND MAP command
using the FROM keyword.

6.3.   COMMUNICATING WITH DL/I DATABASES

First, I assume you already know DL/I, as that is too big a topic for
this book. Next, this topic focuses on the use of the CALL 'CBLTDLI'
approach to DL/I databases. If you are using EXEC DLI commands,
that is beyond this book, as it is a skill set in itself. When you execute
DL/I applications in batch, you may never have noticed it, but your
EXEC JCL actually executed a DL/I module (from IBM). That module,
in turn, constructed a parameter list and issued a dynamic CALL to
invoke your application, passing all appropriate data to your program.
So, why should that concern us? Because those data areas were in the
LINKAGE SECTION and the memory was already allocated prior to

invoking your program. Unfortunately, we can't use the memory allocation techniques in the prior topics because we need help from the DL/I facilities to set the proper addresses into the field after the area is allocated (sort of a chicken and egg situation).

This is done in CICS applications by issuing what is known as a scheduling CALL. The scheduling CALL causes the proper processes to occur so our task can continue in a normal fashion, using DL/I commands as we would in batch. To do this, IBM provides a COPYbook called DLIUIB (listed in Appendix A). This COPYbook will be used to set the proper addresses of the PSB (Program Specification Block) and the related PCBs (Program Communication Block).

6.3.1. Using VS/COBOL

Before we review the code, let's review the necessary LINKAGE SECTION structure. In this example, I will assume a PSB with two logical views (PCBs), although there could be more or fewer.

```
        LINKAGE  SECTION.

    01  BLL-FIELDS.
            05   FILLER           PIC  S9(8)    COMP.
            05   DLIUIB-PTR       PIC  S9(8)    COMP.
            05   PSB-PTR          PIC  S9(8)    COMP.
            05   PCB1-PTR         PIC  S9(8)    COMP.
            05   PCB2-PTR         PIC  S9(8)    COMP.
                         .
                         .                   address  of
                         .                   DLIUIB
            COPY  DLIUIB.
                         .                   address  of
                         .                   PSB
    01  THIS-IS-PSB.
            05   ADDR-OF-PCBA     PIC  S9(8)  COMP.
            05   ADDR-OF-PCBB     PIC  S9(8)  COMP.

    01  FIRST-PCB.
                         .
    01  SECOND-PCB.
                         .
```

At first glance, this appears the same as the earlier example. Every 01-level is in the sequence that corresponds to the BLL entries. There is a difference, though. While CICS services will provide us with the address of DLIUIB, we will need to get the additional addresses from the DLIUIB. Here is the structure:

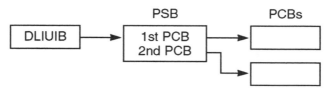

The DLIUIB itself contains the address of the PSB. Likewise, the PSB contains the addresses of the PCB(s). The field in the DLIUIB COPYbook that contains this address is named UIBPCBAL. After we allocate the DLIUIB COPYbook, we must then get addressability to the PSB and then to the PCBs. This process is true for both VS/COBOL, COBOL/370, and for COBOL II.

Using the above information, here is how we would do it for VS/COBOL:

```
CALL 'CBLTDLI' USING  PCB-SCHEDULE
                      psb-name
                      DLIUIB-PTR
SERVICE RELOAD DLIUIB
MOVE UIBPCBAL        TO PSB-PTR
SERVICE RELOAD THIS-IS-PSB
MOVE ADDR-OF-PCBA TO PCB1-PTR
MOVE ADDR-OF-PCBB TO PCB2-PTR
SERVICE RELOAD FIRST-PCB
SERVICE RELOAD SECOND-PCB
```

Remember, this is just to establish addressability to the DL/I control blocks. After doing this, our application can issue DL/I commands.

6.3.2.   Using COBOL II or COBOL/370

By now, you can guess that it will be simpler with COBOL/370 or COBOL II, but we will still need to set the addressability issues of the PSB and PCBs. To do this requires that we change some of the data elements from PIC entries to POINTER items.

```
LINKAGE SECTION.

    COPY DLIUIB.
 01 COBII-DLIUIB REDEFINES DLIUIB.
    05  COBII-UIBPCBAL        POINTER.
    05                        PIC XX.

 01 PCB-ADDRESSES.
    05  PCB-ADDR-1    POINTER.
    05  PCB-ADDR-2    POINTER.

 01 PCB-1.
    •
 01 PCB-2.
    •

CALL 'CBLTDLI' USING  PCB-SCHEDULE
                      psb-name
                      ADDRESS OF DLIUIB
    SET ADDRESS OF PCB-ADDRESSES TO COBII-UIBPCBAL
    SET ADDRESS OF PCB-1 TO PCB-ADDR-1
    SET ADDRESS OF PCB-2 TO PCB-ADDR-2
```

The POINTER facility is too involved for this book. The main fact you need here is just to know that POINTER indicates that the field contains an address of a data area. That signals to COBOL/370 or COBOL II to provide the same service that the earlier CICS commands provided for VS/COBOL.

6.4. COMMUNICATING BETWEEN TASKS AND PROGRAMS

We covered much of this when we developed a menu-driven application, but there are various techniques that should be reviewed. One of them is determining and using techniques to ensure data is available when the task next begins, and another is determining what commands or COBOL statements to use when transferring control between programs.

6.4.1. Data Storage Techniques

In our menu-driven application and our stand-alone application, we used the COMM area to save data from one execution of a transaction to the next. This is always my preference because it is simple to use and requires the fewest resources from CICS.

Using the DFHCOMMAREA. Unlike the dynamic memory techniques discussed earlier, the COMM area is maintained by CICS from one task to the next. By that, I mean that if a transaction issues a RETURN TRANSID or XCTL and specifies a COMMAREA, CICS will ensure that the next transaction receives it. The COMM area is not a fixed area throughout a dialogue. Instead, CICS allocates and deallocates it from task to task. This means that, if you specify a different area for COMMAREA in one program, the original COMM area is lost. As an example, assume that transaction A issues an XCTL to transaction B, pointing to a COMMAREA that is 3000 bytes long. Transaction B specifies a DFHCOMMAREA of only 2000 bytes because it doesn't need the other 1000 bytes. If transaction B then issues an XCTL back to transaction A, the COMM area is now 2000 bytes, not 3000.

That situation is not true for a CALL or LINK command. In that case, the original data area is passed to the subprogram and, even if the subprogram only defines and uses one byte, the original COMM area is still intact. So, you don't need to worry about protecting your COMM area when invoking a subprogram, but you do need to be concerned if a different task is going to access the COMM area.

Also, whether you use VS/COBOL, COBOL/370, or COBOL II, there is no need to fiddle with the memory management techniques in topic 6.2 to gain addressability to a COMM area. IBM recommends that COMM areas not exceed 24K, but most companies use much smaller areas. As companies migrate to CICS/ESA, they should consider reviewing this practice, as memory is much more plentiful.

Using temporary storage queues. When applications determine that the COMM area is insufficient to store the amount of data required to maintain a dialogue between tasks, or where transaction A issues an XCTL to transaction B, but does not wish to ask transaction B to preserve data that will be needed when control reverts back to transaction A (see COMM area discussion above), CICS provides a facility whereby your application can write some data to a temporary storage queue. Since the storage queue is temporary, it is not treated as a file by CICS and does not require an entry in the FCT.

Temporary storage queues, once written, remain in the CICS environment until either (1) a transaction DELETEs the queue by name, or (2) the technical support staff shuts down CICS for a restart. For that reason, you should always issue DELETE commands for temporary storage queues when they aren't needed. You can even issue DELETE commands for nonexistent queues, provided that you specify NOHANDLE. Temporary storage queues can have a name (determined by your program) of up to eight bytes. Since you usually want the queue to be known only to your program so that you can retrieve it later, you will often find that programmers use two four-byte fields in the EIB to name the queue. These two fields are EIBTRMID and EIBTRNID. EIBTRMID identifies the CICS code for the specific terminal that your program is accessing, and EIBTRNID is the transaction ID for your program. By using these two fields, you ensure that other programs don't accidentally READ or DELETE it, assuming that they follow the same approach to naming queues. Of course, you should check with your shop's standards first.

In handling queues, you may find it convenient to think of them as files. Each READ or WRITE processes one record. Now that I've said that, let me also tell you that most applications that use temporary storage queues write only one record to the queue. Why? Because, for most applications, one record (since you can specify its size) can contain all the information that a program wants to retrieve at a later time.

```
FUNCTION:  Read  a  temporary  storage  queue

EXEC  CICS  READQ  TS
            QUEUE(dataname)
            SET(pointer)  |  INTO(dataname)
        [   LENGTH(dataname)  ]
        [   ITEM(datavalue)  |  NEXT  ]
        [   HANDLE  |  NOHANDLE  [  RESP()  ]  ]
END-EXEC

Most probable error conditions: ITEMERR, LENGERR, QIDERR
```

Figure 6.13. READQ TS command.

The READQ TS command (Figure 6.13) reads a queue record. Since it has the SET keyword, you may use it in the LINKAGE SECTION, if desired. (Using the LINKAGE SECTION was covered in topic 6.2.)

The ITEMERR condition is raised if the specified record does not exist in the queue. QIDERR is raised if the queue itself is not there, and LENGERR is raised if the queue record is longer that the specified LENGTH value. None of these necessarily means a logic error and you may find situations where these are acceptable. For example, a program might issue a READQ TS command just to determine if a particular queue is present.

QUEUE()   specifies the data area that contains the queue name, up to eight bytes.

SET()|INTO()   specifies whether the memory needed to store the record must be dynamically allocated (SET) or preexists (INTO).

LENGTH()   Specifies the data area that contains the length of the record, defined as PIC S9(4) COMP.

ITEM()|NEXT   specifies whether the READQ should read a specific record (ITEM) or the next sequential record (NEXT). ITEM is normally used and must be defined as PIC S9(4) COMP or be a numeric literal.

Here is an example, where the queue name is terminal ID, followed by transaction ID. *Note*: This is just an example. Your shop may have specific standards for naming queues, or your application may need special codes. I encourage you always to include EIBTRMID to ensure that the queue can be quickly identified.

```
WORKING-STORAGE SECTION.
01   QUEUE-WORK-AREAS.
     05   QUEUE-NAME.
          10   1ST-FLD   PIC  X(4).
          10   2ND-FLD   PIC  X(4).
     05   QUEUE-LENGTH   PIC  S9(4)  COMP  VALUE  +300.
     05   QUEUE-ITEM     PIC  S9(4)  COMP  VALUE  +0.

01   QUEUE-RECORD        PIC  X(300).
     MOVE  EIBTRMID  TO  1ST-FLD
     MOVE  EIBTRNID  TO  2ND-FLD
     MOVE  1  TO  QUEUE-ITEM

     EXEC  CICS  READQ    TS
                 QUEUE  (QUEUE-NAME)
                 INTO   (QUEUE-RECORD)
```

```
                    LENGTH  (QUEUE-LENGTH)
                    ITEM    (QUEUE-ITEM)
                    NOHANDLE
                    RESP    (CICS-RESP-CODE)
          END-EXEC
```

FUNCTION: Write, or rewrite, a temporary storage queue

```
EXEC CICS WRITEQ TS
          QUEUE(dataname)
          FROM(dataname)
        [ LENGTH(datavalue) ]
        [ ITEM(datavalue) [ REWRITE ] ]
        [ MAIN | AUXILIARY ]
        [ NOSUSPEND ]
        [ HANDLE | NOHANDLE [ RESP() ] ]
END-EXEC
```

Most probable error conditions: ITEMERR, QIDERR, INVREQ

Figure 6.14. WRITEQ TS command.

The WRITEQ TS command (Figure 6.14) complements the READQ TS command. Where the WRITEQ TS command is unique is that this command may be used to write new records into a queue (this automatically creates a queue if the queue does not exist) or this command can REWRITE a modified record back into the queue.

QUEUE() specifies the data area containing the eight-byte name of the queue.

FROM() specifies the name of the data area where the queue record exists or a literal. Since the READQ command requires a data area, not a literal, I recommend that you use a data area for both commands.

LENGTH() specifies the PIC S9(4) COMP field that contains the length of the record.

ITEM() is normally used in conjunction with REWRITE. If REWRITE is specified, this indicates a data area containing the record number to rewrite. If REWRITE is not specified, the contents of the field are ignored, and CICS returns the number of the record written. This is PIC S9(4) COMP.

REWRITE specifies that the record identified in ITEM is to be rewritten. This process should follow a READQ TS command.

MAIN|AUXILIARY is used to identify to CICS whether the queue should be written to memory (default) or to auxiliary storage (DASD). Normally, I leave the default, but, if your application will want the queue stored for an extended time (whatever that is), then specify AUXILIARY. Check with your shop's standards or guidelines.

NOSUSPEND specifies that the application does not want to be suspended if there is insufficient space to store the record in the queue. Instead, CICS will immediately return control to the application with a NOSPACE condition raised.

The following example would rewrite the first (or only) record to the queue, assuming the prior READQ TS had been executed within the same task. If this were the first command to create a record in the queue, then REWRITE should be removed from the command.

```
EXEC CICS WRITEQ   TS
          QUEUE   (QUEUE-NAME)
          LENGTH  (QUEUE-LENGTH)
          ITEM    (QUEUE-ITEM)
          FROM    (QUEUE-RECORD)
          REWRITE
          NOHANDLE
          RESP    (CICS-RESP-CODE)
END-EXEC
```

Whenever you are writing the first record for a queue, you should always issue a DELETEQ TS command first. This ensures that, if the queue remained from a previous transaction, any data is destroyed. This could happen if your program does not delete queues, or if the program abended prior to deleting the queue. As you might suspect, I recommend that your programs always clean up the environment before the final RETURN to CICS by deleting any queues that were established.

FUNCTION: *Delete* *a* *temporary* *storage* *queue*

```
EXEC CICS DELETEQ TS
          QUEUE(dataname)
        [ HANDLE | NOHANDLE [ RESP() ] ]
END-EXEC
```

Most probable error conditions: QIDERR

Figure 6.15. DELETEQ TS command.

The DELETEQ TS command (Figure 6.15) deletes an entire queue, not just one record. You will frequently see it in programs just preceding the first WRITEQ TS command, something like this:

```
MOVE EIBTRMID TO 1ST-FLD
MOVE EIBTRNID TO 2ND-FLD
EXEC CICS DELETEQ TS QUEUE (QUEUE-NAME)
          NOHANDLE RESP     (CICS-RESP-CODE)
END-EXEC
EXEC CICS WRITEQ TS   QUEUE (QUEUE-NAME)
    .
    .
```

The example does not test for QIDERR, although it was surely raised. The reason is that, in this common example, the application does not care. Just because you anticipate that a condition will be raised does not mean that you must interrogate it.

To review the logic where you might use queues, here is a brief summary of the logic path within a dialogue:

1. After initial RETURN TRANSID command, user enters data on first screen and presses Enter key.

2. On first time through subsequent logic path (EIBCALEN > 0), the program uses the data from the screen to read data from a file. Part of this data is formatted to the screen, but the rest of it will be needed later. This data is stored in a temporary queue by issuing first a DELETEQ TS command, followed by a WRITEQ

TS command. To set a reminder that the queue now exists, the program might set a flag byte in the COMM area. The program then issues a SEND MAP and a RETURN TRANSID command.

3. On the next iteration with the user, the program checks the COMM area and finds the flag byte set, indicating that the queue already exists. The program now issues a READQ TS command to retrieve the data record. If the record is modified and the dialogue is still incomplete, the program will issue a WRITEQ TS command with the REWRITE option. The program ends with a SEND MAP and a RETURN TRANSID command.

4. On the next iteration, the program determines that this is the end of the dialogue. The program issues a DELETEQ TS command, followed by a RETURN command.

6.4.2. Interprogram Techniques

You are already familiar with the XCTL and LINK commands. Let's review the tradeoffs there and also contrast with the COBOL CALL statement, as well as the COBOL GOBACK and STOP RUN statements (which can be used if you are using COBOL II).

The XCTL command. The XCTL command is primarily useful where the application is decomposed into several transactions, possibly so the same program can be used by several other applications. This is especially useful where a separate program provides a useful function and is sufficiently well documented so it can return to the invoker. If you recall our menu application, I stored the program name in the COMM area to simplify identification. If a second field were placed in the COMM area, the applications could keep track of the program that should receive control on the next RETURN TRANSID command and which program should receive control on an XCTL command. This is normally handled by specifying FROM and TO fields in the COMM area. Most important, your shop needs explicit COMM area usage standards before extensive use of XCTL can be effective.

The CALL statement (with COBOL II and COBOL/370). The LINK command used to be the only way to pass control to a subprogram that will execute CICS commands. (You could always use the CALL statement for static CALLs to subprograms that did a calculation or other non-CICS functions — and did no I/O.) Now, with COBOL II and COBOL/370, you will often find improved performance by replacing

LINK commands with CALL statements. The difference is that you must include DFHEIBLK and DFHCOMMAREA as the first two parameters being passed to the subprogram, thereby allowing the subprogram to use CICS commands. The CALLed subprogram, since it was invoked by a CALL statement, should return control with a GOBACK statement, not a CICS RETURN statement that would return control back to CICS instead of back to the calling program. The subprogram could also use STOP RUN if it wanted to terminate the transaction. I don't recommend this because CICS has no way of recording why the transaction ended.

The subprogram still needs to be processed by the CICS translator, because it contains CICS commands. If additional information needs to be passed to the subprogram, identify only those fields on the PROCEDURE DIVISION USING statement. (Remember, the translator will automatically insert DFHEIBLK and DFHCOMMAREA as the first two.) The resulting structure would appear something like this, assuming we had two areas called FIELDA and FIELDB that should be passed:

Main program:

```
CALL 'subproga' USING DFHEIBLK DFHCOMMAREA FIELDA FIELDB
    .
    .
```

CALLed program:

```
LINKAGE SECTION.
01  LS-FIELDA    PIC X(200).

01  LS-FIELDB    PIC X(300).

PROCEDURE DIVISION USING LS-FIELDA LS-FIELDB.
    .
    application logic, including CICS commands
    .
    .
    GOBACK.
```

The example shown is a static CALL. If the main program used the CALL dataname format, where dataname contained the name of the subprogram, then this could be a dynamic CALL. Static CALLs have higher performance.

The LINK command. The LINK command is still useful, even with less performance, because it maintains a link with CICS and the invoking program. If an error occurs, CICS facilities can assist. Since COBOL II and VS/COBOL programs cannot be in the same run unit, this is a way to mix VS/COBOL and COBOL II in the same transaction. In such situations, the COMM area should be allocated below the 16-megabyte line by the COBOL II or COBOL/370 program (done by DATA option at compile time or by LENGTH option if COMM area is allocated via GETMAIN).

6.5.   MISCELLANEOUS FUNCTIONS

There are many CICS commands that you may never see. What I have done here is include some of the common ones that you may routinely see or need. Because they don't affect program structure, I don't list them in any particular order. Also, a complete list of commands is in Appendix A, should you need to see the basic syntax of commands other than those used in this book.

```
FUNCTION: Establish absolute time

EXEC CICS ASKTIME
       [ ABSTIME(dataname) ]
END-EXEC

Most probable error conditions: none
```

Figure 6.16. ASKTIME command.

The ASKTIME command (Figure 6.16) can be used whenever your program needs to compute the exact time. ASKTIME is often used in conjunction with FORMATTIME.

> **ABSTIME()** contains the name of a PIC S9(15) COMP-3 field where an absolute time can be stored for subsequent use by the FORMATTIME command. This value is the number of milliseconds that have elapsed since January 1, 1900.

The ASSIGN command (Figure 6.17) is useful when your application needs information from CICS, either about the network, the terminal user, or many other fields (see Appendix A for the full command).

FUNCTION: Provide system information to the program

```
EXEC  CICS  ASSIGN
        [  NETNAME(dataname)  ]
        [  USERID(dataname)  ]
END-EXEC
```

Most probable error conditions: none

Figure 6.17. ASSIGN command.

NETNAME() This is the name of an eight-byte field where the SNA address of the terminal will be stored. This is often useful to display on screens in case the terminal user needs to call a help desk for assistance.

USERID() contains the name of an eight-byte field where the user's logon ID will be returned. This is also a field that some companies like to display on screen so it is immediately obvious if a person is using someone else's logon ID.

FUNCTION: Deedit a numeric field

```
EXEC  CICS  BIF  DEEDIT
            FIELD(dataname)
        [  LENGTH(datavalue)  ]
END-EXEC
```

Most probable error conditions: none

Figure 6.18. BIF DEEDIT command.

BIF DEEDIT (Figure 6.18) is a little-used command (for good reason, I think). This command strips all nonnumeric entries from a DISPLAY field and right justifies whatever is left. For example, a nine-byte field containing A1B2C6.A7 would be converted to 000001267.

FIELD() specifies the name of a data field that contains alpha-numeric data that is to be converted to numeric-only format.

LENGTH() specifies the length of the data element identified in FIELD.

FUNCTION: Format time and/or date fields

```
EXEC CICS FORMATTIME
          ABSTIME(dataname)
     [ YYDDD(dataname) ]
     [ YYMMDD(dataname) ]
     [ YYDDMM(dataname) ]
     [ DDMMYY(dataname) ]
     [ MMDDYY(dataname) ]
     [ DATE(dataname) [ DATEFORM(dataname) ] ]
     [ DATESEP(datavalue) ]
     [ DAYCOUNT(dataname) ]
     [ DAYOFWEEK(dataname) ]
     [ DAYOFMONTH(dataname) ]
     [ MONTHOFYEAR(dataname) ]
     [ YEAR(dataname) ]
     [ TIME(dataname) [ TIMESEP(datavalue) ] ]
END-EXEC
```

Most probable error conditions: none

Figure 6.19. FORMATTIME command.

FORMATTIME (Figure 6.19) is, despite the many keywords, a simple command. You may use as many of the keywords as desired. This command must be preceded by the ASKTIME command, as it uses the ABSTIME value from ASKTIME to compute the various date and time formats.

ABSTIME() specifies the name of the field used by a previous ASKTIME command.

YYDDD() specifies the name of a six-byte field where CICS places the date, separated by a space, as yy ddd (see DATESEP).

YYMMDD() YYDDMM() DDMMYY() MMDDYY() These fields are each 8-bytes and will receive the date according to the specified name. The year, month, and date, are separated by a space (see DATESEP).

DATE() specifies an eight-byte field to receive the date in the installation standard format.

DATEFORM() specifies a six-byte field to receive the date in the installation standard format

DATESEP() specifies either a literal or the name of a one-byte field that contains the value to be used to separate date fields. If DATESEP is coded with no variable, a "/" is used.

DAYCOUNT() names a PIC S9(8) COMP field to receive the number of days since January 1, 1900.

DAYOFWEEK() DAYOFMONTH() MONTHOFYEAR() YEAR() Each field is PIC S9(8) COMP where CICS places the appropriate value. DAYOFWEEK receives a value of 0 through 6 corresponding to Sunday through Saturday; DAYOFMONTH and MONTHOFYEAR are self-explanatory; YEAR receives the four-digit year value.

TIME() is an eight-byte field where the time will be placed as hh mm dd, separated by spaces (see TIMESEP).

TIMESEP() specifies either a literal or name of a one-byte value to use as a separator for time values. If TIMESEP is coded with no variable, a ":" is assumed.

Here is an example of how ASKTIME and FORMATTIME could be combined.

```
EXEC CICS ASKTIME
          ABSTIME (WS-ABSTIME)
END-EXEC

EXEC CICS FORMATTIME
          ABSTIME (WS-ABSTIME)
          MMDDYY  (WS-MMDDYY)
          TIME    (WS-TIME)
          TIMESEP ('.')
          DATESEP ('/')
END-EXEC
```

SUMMARY

This chapter covered many new CICS commands, as well as CICS techniques. You should have a grasp of VSAM I/O commands, considerations for coding VS/COBOL or COBOL II applications, considerations and techniques to use to save data when communicating with other tasks or programs, and feel comfortable with some basic CICS commands. For more CICS commands, or to practice them, see Chapter 7, which introduces many transactions that can be entered directly from the terminal, including some that let you experiment directly with CICS commands.

7

Using the IBM-Supplied CICS Transactions

Using the IBM-supplied CICS transactions can eliminate any remaining "black magic" that you thought existed. Wondering what CICS condition code you will get for a particular command? Curious about a CICS command's syntax but don't have a manual nearby? Want to step through a transaction to see how it works with CICS? All these questions and more (much, much more) can be answered by developing a basic awareness of the IBM CICS transactions. Since they all share the same syntax, it will be mostly a matter of trial and error on your part as you master these CICS facilities.

One of the areas of CICS where many programmers never venture is in the area of IBM's own CICS transactions. They are provided with each release of CICS and are there to improve your own productivity. This chapter will focus on these transactions as they would normally be used by application developers. (As I've mentioned earlier, learning about each CICS feature would require a book much larger and would not be a productive use of your time. Most CICS applications use only a small percentage of possible commands and options.)

Additionally, since the format in this chapter will assume some hands-on contact, you will need to experiment some to become sufficiently familiar with these CICS transactions. This section won't address every facility, since some features are of little use or are seldom needed. Only by actively "playing" with these transactions will you learn them. Many programmers never learn or use these helpful tools until they have a problem. By practicing with these transactions, you will start to feel more confident of your CICS skills. I find new uses for them each week.

By the time you arrive at this chapter, you probably have already developed or worked with CICS transactions and programs. If, perchance, you haven't, see your supervisor, instructor, coach, or teammate to get names of some transactions and programs that you could execute without causing harm. The transactions discussed here are best learned by sitting at a terminal as you read the material, allowing you to participate by experimenting with the commands yourself.

The transactions all begin with the letters "CE," and all share the same format on-screen. Some interact with each other, but each has its special strengths. As you build a mastery of these transactions, you will never (well, almost never) be at a loss in CICS. The basic transactions that we will review are the following:

CEDA (and CEDB and CEDC): This transaction is normally used by systems programmers who administer the CICS software environment. There are several versions of this transaction, as each version has different levels of authority. For our work, we will use the lowest level, CEDC, as it provides adequate inquiry access to several CICS tables.

CEMT: This operator-oriented transaction has significant power, but we will limit our use to its features that are normally used by application programmers. After all, we have little need to control the online environment.

CEDF: This is a debugging facility from IBM that many programmers never learn. It doesn't have the power of some of the major proprietary debugging packages, but it is always available and is one of your *best* sources of CICS feedback.

CECI and CECS: These two transactions may appear to be "overkill." One allows you to check syntax of any CICS command, while the other allows you to execute any CICS command. As you will see, they look almost identical on-screen, and maybe, just maybe, IBM could have achieved the goal of online assistance with only one of them. Still, I like having them both. Sometimes I just want to test syntax without worrying about the CICS command actually executing.

CEBR: This is the simplest of the IBM transactions we will review. Also, it is the least powerful for that reason. However, when you need to see data in a CICS queue, CEBR makes quick work of it. Naturally, you need to understand queues before this command is useful. If your application doesn't use queues, this will be of little value.

CESN, CSSN, and CSSF: Are these transactions in the normal sense? I think not. Still, you may need to use them every day for the housekeeping issues of working within CICS. For that reason, I include them in this book. In fact, you may find that your shop has developed menus that are activated during the logon process that preempt the need for these commands.

Unlike most other sections in this book, this is one section where you may want to be sitting at a CICS terminal while reading the material. Having the ability for direct feedback can be immensely rewarding while learning these transactions. As I mentioned earlier, many programmers never grasp any of these commands — but the commands are always there for your use.

7.1. TRANSACTION SYNTAX AND STRUCTURE

The syntax for each transaction is almost identical. Each transaction and all its possible operands may be typed onto a single line (when you know what you're doing) or may be entered only after prompts (when you're not sure). While I show you all the options for each CICS command in this book, I avoid the first approach for the CICS transactions. That is because their options are so extensive and because they are readily available on-screen. Following the screen-by-screen technique will serve you well. Usually, I use the "not-sure" method that I mentioned earlier just to see all the various options (I enter a transaction name and then respond to listed options). All transactions provide access to some common functions via PF keys. Some of the common PF keys are in Figure 7.1.

Don't worry about learning the PF keys; CICS always displays on screen the options available at that time. If you're familiar with some other online software packages, you may notice some differences. For example, PF7 and PF8 are slightly different, scrolling only half a screen. While PF1 is of limited use, only by experimenting will you learn all that a transaction can do.

```
PF1:   Display help screen(s)
PF2:       varies with transaction
PF3:   Terminate transaction
PF4:       varies with transaction
PF5:       varies with transaction
PF6:       varies with transaction
PF7:   Scroll back one half screen
PF8:   Scroll forward one half screen
PF9:   Display error messages (if any)
PF10:  Scroll back one screen
PF11:  Scroll forward one screen
PF12:      varies with transaction
```

Figure 7.1. Basic PF keys for IBM-supplied CICS transactions.

As you learn the transactions, you will frequently encounter error messages and other warnings. This occurs because some of the transactions are constantly evaluating what you've entered. Don't be alarmed. Just keep typing and checking until you get the results you want. (For example, you might see a SEVERE error message after entering only the rudiments of a command. That is because CICS always assumes you may have meant it to be a complete command. Since I use the "not-sure" technique, I ignore the error messages until I have responded to all the prompts. As we progress, it will be more obvious — and if you are sitting at a terminal, it will be immediately apparent.)

Figure 7.2 displays a typical screen format. PF keys are at the bottom of the screen, the command options entered so far are displayed near the top of the screen, and additional options that are available are shown below. Sometimes the options are not followed by ==>, indicating that, if you need them, you must type them on the top command line where the cursor is positioned.

Also, wherever you do need to enter information, you may use wild card characters. These are the "*" for "any characters" and the "+" for "any single character." For example, the letters *test** in Figure 7.2 would mean that, for this command, use only those groups at the company that begin with the word *test*. I use wild cards frequently, and you will see several in the examples that follow.

```
D                        <== option entered
OVERTYPE TO MODIFY
  CEDC   Display         <== combination of options entered
    Group       ==> test* <== choices to make
    List        ==>




S   GROUP OR LIST MUST BE SPECIFIED.   <== warning message(s)

PF 1 HELP 3 END    6 CRSR 7 SBH 8 SFH 9 MSG 10 SB 11 SF 12 CNCL
```

Figure 7.2. Example of CICS transaction screen format.

Although it might not have been apparent in Figure 7.2, the top line shows the single character, D, and the third line shows a combination of options entered, *CEDC Display*. As you will discover in the commands, you may abbreviate the spelling of all shown options, usually to a single character. In many commands, you will see the minimum number of characters displayed in upper case to assist you in reducing the required number of keystrokes.

One last item on the general syntax: As the comment in Figure 7.2 indicates, you may overtype most fields to change the command, rather than exiting from the screen and starting over. This will take a little trial and error on your part. If you are using a color monitor, it will be more obvious, as any green or red field may be modified (assuming a standard four-color monitor).

As we review various transactions, you will find additional PF keys and options. While it may seem complex, you will find that the screen layout and the immediate accessibility of information will allow you to feel like an expert quickly. The important thing is to experiment, experiment, experiment. A woman with whom I work is exceptional in her ability to use these transactions, primarily because she realizes that a few error messages or other complaints from the transactions are harmless.

One last reminder: When executing CICS transactions, *always* press the CLEAR key first as this resets the terminal to its base status. While the transaction ID you enter may perform properly anyway, a clear screen ensures that you won't be subjected to any spurious data. In fact, I offer this suggestion for any CICS command you may enter.

7.2.   CEDA

As I mentioned earlier, this command has several flavors: CEDA (butterscotch-almond), CEDB (chocolate), and CEDC (vanilla). I presume that IBM designed it this way to simplify the allocation of authority throughout an organization. CEDA has the most capability and is usually assigned only for use by systems programmers because CEDA allows a user to assign, modify, and install resources to a CICS system. (Remember our discussion of the various application tables, such as the PCT and PPT?) CEDB is almost as capable as CEDA, and CEDC (the one we will review) is the passive version of the command. With CEDC, you can "look but not touch." That is normally all the authority an application programmer needs (and all the authority that many shops will allow).

7.2.1.   Overview of CEDC

Application programmers can find CEDC a useful tool to answer questions such as "What is the name of the program that is executed when transaction ID A250 is entered?" "Is program PAYR0250 a COBOL or Assembler program?" "Is there a MAP in the CICS system by the name of PAY250?" "Is program PAYR0250 enabled (authorized to execute) or disabled (shutdown due to problems or operator action)?" and "What are all the transactions that begin with PAY?"

Such questions are usually posed by maintenance programmers or those programmers who are attempting to reconstruct documentation for a current system. Either way, this is a sure way to be sure of the appropriate transaction ID or program name when asked to fix a problem. (Okay, okay, I confess. Once I was asked to make a change to a specific program because a particular transaction had abended. I wasted several hours on the problem before I decided to use CEDC, whereby I confirmed that I was working on the *wrong program*.)

An additional use for CEDC is when you are developing a new transaction and need to request that a new transaction ID be established. You may feel that, because your new program is named PAYR2500, you can use PY25 for a transaction ID, only to learn later that PY25 is already established for program PAY00250. When in doubt, check.

CEDC has three capabilities:

- The ability to DISPLAY groups and lists within the CICS system
- The ability to EXPAND a group or list (i.e., display the contents of the group or list)
- The ability to VIEW the contents of a member of a group or list

First, let's review groups and lists. A group is a name assigned by a systems programmer to a set of programs, transactions, MAPs, and other CICS components. This allows the systems programmers to tune the CICS system and specify what groups are allowed in different CICS regions. The only reason you and I need to know about groups is that the application components we develop (programs, transactions, and MAPs) are stored according to their group name. Normally, you won't be told the name of the group where your team's components are stored, so you can use CEDC to tell you this. Once you know the group name, just remember it so you can type it in where its name is requested.

I mention *lists* in this book only because you will see it appear as an option on the screen. Lists are a special packaging technique for systems programmers to organize groups, so don't worry about them. Once you know your group name, everything you may need to know about your programs, your transactions, and your maps can be quickly located.

7.2.2. Using CEDC

Okay, let's do it. To use CEDC, enter the letters CEDC at the top left of your screen, just as you would for any other transaction. Later, if you've memorized one or more of the desired options, they can also be entered. For now, don't worry about it. The screen you will see is in Figure 7.3. (*Note*: Entering CEDC, followed by the first letter of any of the choices, D, E, or V, would cause you to bypass this opening screen.)

There are two new PF key options here. One is PF6, which will move the cursor to the first available position to enter data. I generally ignore PF6 because the cursor is already positionedthere. The second is PF12, which will cancel the most recently entered information and return to the previous screen. This can be useful when you want to back up one screen. (*Note*: You may want to experiment with PF12 and PF3. While they seem quite different, PF3 ends the transaction but preserves all variables entered, so pressing the Enter key accomplishes a similar result to that achieved by PF12.)

```
 ┌─                                                              ─┐
  ENTER  ONE  OF  THE  FOLLOWING
  Display
  Expand
  View




  PF  1  HELP    3  END    6  CRSR     9  MSG      12  CNCL
 └─                                                              ─┘
```

Figure 7.3. Opening screen for CEDC.

Of the three options, you will normally find that VIEW is what
you want, although the other options can — eventually, after enough
keystrokes — provide the same information. (Incidentally, CEDC has
an excellent help facility. Try PF1 and you'll agree. Most of its information is addressed to the person using CEDA or CEDB, but it is a
good refresher on what is covered here.)

The VIEW Option. Assuming you may or may not have followed my
suggestion to experiment with the help facility, let's begin our study
of CEDC by choosing the VIEW option. Enter either V or VIEW (upper or lower case is fine) and press Enter. As mentioned previously,
each command immediately lists more options (if any) depending on
what choice you selected. For the VIEW options, see Figure 7.4.

As Figure 7.4 shows, after entering V, there are several options
that may be viewed. Abbreviations are shown in upper case. We won't
review all these options, as most don't apply. Application programmers are usually concerned about MAPs, programs, and transactions,
so that will be our focus. Should you later need to inquire about the
other facilities, the process would be similar. Let's check out the MAP
option. Press M (or enter MAP). The screen in Figure 7.5 will appear.
Here is where you must enter variable information.

Most of the information is familiar to you by now. Options entered so far (V and M) are listed on the top line, with options below.
Here, the options are followed by ==>, indicating that you must press
the Tab key and then enter data before the transaction can continue.
Notice the useless (to me) error message. The message means there
are two severe errors with the command. (If you want to see them,

press PF9. This applies to all the transactions.) I say it is useless at this point in time only because I know that I still must enter more data. If the error message is still there after responding to the ==> prompts, I will attend to it. Otherwise, I ignore the error messages.

```
  V
   ENTER  ONE  OF  THE  FOLLOWING
  Connection
  Mapset
  PArtitionset
  PROFile
  PROGram
  Sessions
  TErminal
  TRansaction
  TYpeterm




  PF  1  HELP    3  END    6  CRSR    9  MSG    12  CNCL
```

Figure 7.4. Opening screen for CEDC VIEW.

```
  V  M
  OBJECT  CHARACTERISTICS
   CEDC   View
     Mapset  ==>
     Group   ==>



   MESSAGES:  2  SEVERE
  PF  1  HELP    3  END    6  CRSR    9  MSG    12  CNCL
```

Figure 7.5. CEDC with VIEW MAPSET.

Remember my review of groups earlier? It is here that you need to know something of your own to help CICS provide you with useful information. (Yes, you could use the wild card characters and enter an * beside both prompts, but that would be requesting CICS to list all MAPs in all groups. That might be hundreds or thousands — and all virtually useless to you. For our study, let's assume you know the group name and the first three letters of the MAPs you need to identify. Now we can proceed. For our example, assume that you knew the group name was TESTPAY and that the first few characters you wanted to search on was PY7. To the prompts, you could have entered the following:

```
Mapset    ==>  PY7*
Group     ==>  TESTPAY
```

The screen you might have seen, assuming the group name was valid and the MAPs existed, would be in Figure 7.6.

```
ENTER COMMANDS
   NAME        TYPE        GROUP         DATE      TIME
   PY70000     MAPSET      TESTPAY       92.211    13.46.14
   PY70500     MAPSET      TESTPAY       92.211    13.46.15
   PY70600     MAPSET      TESTPAY       91.105    12.15.15
   PY70700     MAPSET      TESTPAY       92.351    08.23.19



   RESULTS:  1 TO 4 OF 4     TIME:  15.31.09     DATE:  92.361
   PF 1 HELP 3 END 6 CRSR 7 SBH 8 SFH 9 MSG 10 SB 11 SF 12 CNCL
```

Figure 7.6. Listing of MAPSETs with CEDC VIEW.

Did you notice that more PF keys appeared? The information in Figure 7.6 is common among many other screens. The bottom of the screen shows that there were four entries in total and that 1 through 4 are shown on screen. (Yes, I've sometimes used the wild cards too enthusiastically and seen messages such as: *RESULTS: 1 to 15 of 2048.* This is an abuse of the transaction and wastes valuable system resources. Please don't follow my example.)

What is interesting on this screen is the statement at the top of the screen, ENTER COMMANDS. Admittedly, most of the time, this may have been all the information you needed. You now have the names of all the MAPs that interest you and the last date and time they were changed.

If that is all you needed, just press PF3 or PF12. However, if you wanted more information (there isn't much more to provide for MAPs), you need to know one of the tricks of using the CICS commands. Whenever you anticipate that more commands are allowed, yet no options are listed (as in this case), just press the Tab key. If it moves you to a blank portion of the screen (as will occur on this screen), then additional commands are available.

Since you won't always have this book with you (you could buy several copies, you know), you either need to memorize the available commands on any given screen, or you must know a trick whereby CICS will explain them to you. IBM suggests using the "?" whenever more information is desired. That usually works okay, but I prefer to enter trash. Somehow, the explanatory message always seems clearer. (Maybe it's just me...)

Anyhow, pressing the Tab key takes you to a space just to the right of the first listed item. Pressing it again takes you to the next listed item and so on. At the line where you want more information and don't remember the command, just enter something obviously invalid, such as "xx." CICS will respond with an error message that tells you the xx is incorrect and also (most important) tells you what would have been acceptable. Normally, it is VIEW or EXPAND. If we enter the acceptable option, VIEW, shown below, we will see the final (for this search) screen in Figure 7.7.

```
PY70000   MAPSET   TESTPAY   view 92.211 13.46.14
```

```
OBJECT CHARACTERISTICS
   CEDC    View
   Mapset         :  PY70000
   Group          :  TESTPAY
   Rsl            :  00              0-24 | Public
   Status         :  Enabled         Enabled | Disabled



PF 1 HELP  3 END  6 CRSR  7 SBH  8 SFH  9 MSG  10 SB  11 SF  12 CNCL
```

Figure 7.7. Expansion of MAPSET with CEDC VIEW.

With MAPs, our main concern is determining when they were changed (Figure 7.6) and whether they are enabled or disabled (Figure 7.7). If we were to press PF3 here, we would see the screen as shown below. Notice that it preserved the basic information on the screen, setting the stage to allow us just to press the Enter key (if desired) and immediately be in the same mode (VIEW MAPSET).

```
CEDC  V  M
        STATUS:    SESSION ENDED
```

A full exit obviously requires pressing the CLEAR key. If we want to reenter CEDC but execute different options, we need only to overtype the information on the first line. Overtyping data is common among all the transactions.

Up to this point, we have been looking at MAP information. Let's assume we want information about a specific transaction. Instead of selecting M in Figure 7.4, let's assume we entered TR (for transaction). In that case, we would have been presented with Figure 7.8.

```
V  TR
OBJECT  CHARACTERISTICS
  CEDC    View
    TRansaction    ==>  P7*
    Group          ==>  TESTPAY


  S    AN  OBJECT  MUST  BE  SPECIFIED.

PF  1 HELP  3 END  6 CRSR  7 SBH  8 SFH  9 MSG  10 SB  11 SF  12 CNCL
```

Figure 7.8. Opening screen of CEDC VIEW for transactions.

In Figure 7.8, I entered P7* as I wanted to see all transactions with this prefix (I could have entered a single, specific transaction) and the group name (I could have entered a partial name and wild card character or just a wild card character). Because my request was not specific, CICS responds with a list of all transactions that meet the request. See Figure 7.9.

```
ENTER COMMANDS
    NAME   TYPE            GROUP            DATE      TIME
    P700   TRANSACTION     TESTPAY          92.211    13.46.31
    P705   TRANSACTION     TESTPAY          91.211    13.46.31
    P706   TRANSACTION     TESTPAY          92.211    13.46.31
    P707   TRANSACTION     TESTPAY          92.351    08.23.19



    RESULTS:  1  TO  4  OF  4   TIME:  15.35.50      DATE:  92.361
  PF  1  HELP  3  END  6  CRSR  7  SBH  8  SFH  9  MSG  10  SB  11  SF  12  CNCL
```

Figure 7.9. Listing of CEDC VIEW for transactions.

Yes, Figure 7.9 is almost identical in layout to Figure 7.6. In fact, I hope you can figure out by now that you can do the same thing you did back there: tab to the line of interest and enter VIEW. Doing that will present Figure 7.10. (*Note:* If you had entered a single transaction ID originally, you would have bypassed the screen shown in Figure 7.9.)

If you're thinking, "Uh-oh, looks like more information that I don't need," you're right. Usually, you will be interested in the name of the program and the enable/disable status. Using the same techniques shown here, you could return to the initial CEDC screen (PF12) or exit (PF3) and repeat the process for the program name. (*Note:* From Figure 7.4, the option to pursue program information is PROG.)

The DISPLAY and EXPAND options. What we've just done with the VIEW option can also be accomplished with the DISPLAY option. The difference is that both DISPLAY and EXPAND require more system resources, more keystrokes, and more time. For example, if you select DISPLAY instead of VIEW, the first screen is a prompt for group name. If you enter the specific group (or a combination of characters and wild card characters), you will be rewarded (?) with a listing of the group names that fits the specification. Then, if you press the Tab key and enter EXPAND, you will see *everything* defined to the group. That could be hundreds of entries. Then, after scrolling through all the entries to the one you wanted, you could press the Tab key and type VIEW and see the same information. Usually, this is overkill for application needs.

```
╭─────────────────────────────────────────────────────────────╮
│ OBJECT CHARACTERISTICS                                        │
│   CEDC   View                                                 │
│    TRansaction      :  P700                                   │
│    Group            :  TESTPAY                                │
│    PROGram          :  PAYR7000                               │
│    TWasize          :  00000           0-32767                │
│    PROFile          :  DFHCICST                               │
│    PArtitionset     :                                         │
│    STatus           :  Enabled         Enabled | Disabled     │
│    PRIMedsize       :  00000           0-65520                │
│   REMOTE ATTRIBUTES                                           │
│    REMOTESystem     :                                         │
│    REMOTEName       :                                         │
│    TRProf           :                                         │
│    Localq           :                  No | Yes               │
│   SCHEDULING                                                  │
│    PRIOrity         :  001             0-255                  │
│    TClass           :  No              No | 1-10              │
│  + ALIASES                                                    │
│                                                               │
│ PF 1 HELP 3 END 6 CRSR 7 SBH 8 SFH 9 MSG 10 SB 11 SF 12 CNCL  │
╰─────────────────────────────────────────────────────────────╯
```

Figure 7.10. Transaction information for CEDC VIEW.

Since you will usually know a transaction ID or program/MAP name, the VIEW option uses fewer resources and can provide you with the same information. Just enter * for group name the first time and, from then on, you can save time by entering the full name.

7.3.   CEMT

The CEMT transaction is normally used by application programmers for maintenance of their work environment. This includes verifying that files are allocated, opening or closing files, setting programs to usable (enable) or nonusable (disable) status, and similar functions.

CEMT reacts somewhat differently than other transactions in this section do. This is because CEMT was developed for use by computer operators who were responsible for administering the CICS environment. It still serves that primary role. As such, you will find that some options are not available to you, a programmer, or that some options execute for the entire shop, without prompting for your specific concern (e.g., doing a file inquiry with CEMT without entering the name of the desired file causes CEMT to list information for every file in the region).

7.3.1.   Overview of CEMT

As stated previously, CEMT was originally intended for operator-only usage. Over time, it became common knowledge that programmers also needed access to some of its functions. When developing and testing new applications, for example, a programmer may need to make some modifications to the CICS environment without needing to involve a computer operator. For example, you may have a CICS transaction that reads a file called EMPMASTR. The CEMT transaction can tell you the actual dataset name for the file and whether it is accessible or not. Although CEMT is not a debugging tool, it helps you keep informed of your CICS world. Let's walk through a few examples.

7.3.2.   Using CEMT

To execute the CEMT transaction, just enter CEMT as you would any other transaction. The screen you will then see is Figure 7.11. (*Note*: As with CEDC and the other transactions here, once you are familiar with CEMT, you can type in all necessary variables on the command line.)

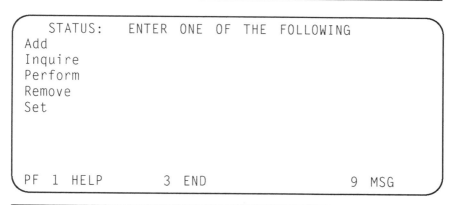

```
   STATUS:    ENTER  ONE  OF  THE  FOLLOWING
Add
Inquire
Perform
Remove
Set




 PF  1  HELP         3  END               9  MSG
```

Figure 7.11. Opening screen for CEMT.

For our purposes with CEMT, we will limit our use of CEMT to the Inquire and Set options. (Besides, you may find that the CEMT transaction is not authorized for your use at your shop. If so, many companies provide a neutered version for the Inquiry function.) For the application programmer, the Inquire and Set functions provide most of the routine needs that you will face. The Inquire function lets you determine the current status of a resource (e.g., whether a file is open). The Set function allows you to change the status of a resource (e.g., set a program to enabled status). If you press "I" (or type Inquire), you will see the screen in Figure 7.12.

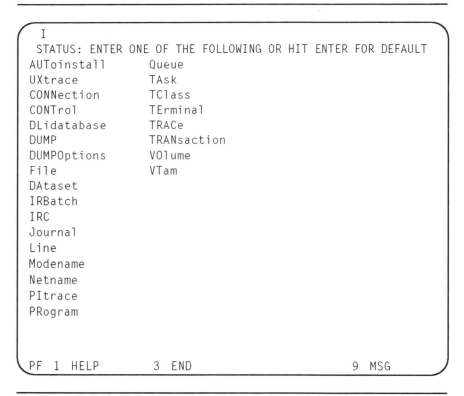

```
  I
  STATUS: ENTER ONE OF THE FOLLOWING OR HIT ENTER FOR DEFAULT
  AUToinstall        Queue
  UXtrace            TAsk
  CONNection         TClass
  CONTrol            TErminal
  DLidatabase        TRACe
  DUMP               TRANsaction
  DUMPOptions        VOlume
  File               VTam
  DAtaset
  IRBatch
  IRC
  Journal
  Line
  Modename
  Netname
  PItrace
  PRogram




 PF  1  HELP          3  END                      9  MSG
```

Figure 7.12. Opening screen for CEMT Inquiry.

A benefit of using the Inquiry mode is that, in addition to seeing all the status items of the selected resource, you can also change them by overtyping. Often, this is preferable to using the Set option, as the

Set option requires that you enter more information. With Inquiry, CICS shows you all the status variables, allowing you to overtype only those of interest.

Note: If you were to press the Enter key after viewing the screen in Figure 7.12 and had entered no information, you would be presented with a screen that showed processing limits for various CICS elements. Since those elements are normally outside the concerns of applications programmers, I omitted the screen from this book, but go ahead and press the Enter key so you will see the options. Perhaps at your installation these variables may be changed. If so, check with your supervisor for more information on how they are used for your team.

Processing FILES. As you might imagine, the CEMT transaction assumes you know about the category of your inquiry, so we will keep it to topics that are familiar to us. Where CEMT's Inquiry function is somewhat different from other transactions is that it attempts to satisfy your query immediately instead of waiting for more specifics. For example, if you were to enter "F" (to do a file inquiry) in response to Figure 7.12, CEMT would immediately show you the status of *all* files in the region, not necessarily what you wanted.

My suggestion when presented with Figure 7.12 is to enter *only* the information necessary for your inquiry. If we wanted to determine the datasets allocated in the CICS region that had FCT names beginning with PY, we might enter

```
F(PY*)
```

That would present Figure 7.13. In this screen, we see the status of all files that are part of our interest, without wasting system resources to list the many others. Notice that some are open and others are closed. This might be an indication that some files, while allocated within the CICS region, aren't used with regular frequency. If there were more files than would list on a single screen, CEMT places a plus sign (+) at the first/last line on the screen to indicate that more information is available by scrolling either forward or backward.

When viewing a screen from CEMT, you should know that you can determine all fields that can be modified by simply pressing the Tab key. That moves you to each field of opportunity. Remember that I mentioned you can overtype information? Let's assume you entered information for a specific file (e.g., PYHRRATE). The screen would predictably show what we see in Figure 7.14. Instead of a list of many files, we see a single file.

```
I  F(PY*)
STATUS:    RESULTS - OVERTYPE TO MODIFY
  Fil(PYEMPLOY) Vsa Clo Une Rea Upd Add Bro Del          Sha
     Dsn( PAYROLL.EMPLOYEE.MAST                              )
  Fil(PYJOURNL) Vsa Clo Une Rea Upd Add Bro Del          Sha
     Dsn( PAYROLL.JOURNAL                                    )
  Fil(PYCHKRGR) Vsa Clo Une Rea Upd Add Bro Del          Sha
     Dsn( PAYROLL.CHECK.REGISTER                             )
  Fil(PYHRRATE) Vsa Ope Ena Rea Upd Add Bro Del          Sha
     Dsn( PAYOLL.HOUR.RATES                                  )
  Fil(PYSUMMAR) Vsa Ope Ena Rea Upd Add Bro Del          Sha
     Dsn( PAYROLL.SUMMARY                                    )



  RESPONSE: NORMAL      TIME: 7.52.04    DATE: 92.260
 PF 1  HELP    3  END      7  SBH  8  SFH  9  MSG  10  SB  11  SF
```

Figure 7.13. Status screen for CEMT Inquiry.

Additionally, whenever CEMT has more information to show you than will fit on a single screen, it places a + at the lower left of the screen if there are entries to be viewed by scrolling forward. For additional entries to be viewed by scrolling backward, it places a + sign at the upper left of the screen.

```
I  F(PYHRRATE)
STATUS:    RESULTS - OVERTYPE TO MODIFY
  Fil(PYHRRATE) Vsa Ope Ena Rea Upd Add Bro Del          Sha
     Dsn( PAYROLL.HOUR.RATES                                 )




  RESPONSE: NORMAL      TIME: 8.52.04    DATE: 92.260
 PF 1  HELP    3  END      7  SBH  8  SFH  9  MSG  10  SB  11  SF
```

Figure 7.14. Status screen for CEMT Inquiry with one file.

As we see in Figure 7.14, the file is open. To close it, we could (a) press PF3 and start over with the S (for Set) option, move the cursor back over the I and overtype it with S and then move the cursor to the right of the file name and enter CLO, or (b) just overtype *Ope* with *Clo*.

This ability to modify resources from the Inquiry mode is a major strength of CEMT. While the Set option prompts you for all major variables, the Inquiry option shows you what is set and lets you modify it. My personal preference is to use the Inquiry mode and then overtype what I want. That's much simpler that using the Set option and attempting to guess what options are required. The top line, using the Set option, would look like this:

```
S  F(PYHRRATE)  CLO
```

On pressing the Enter key, we would see the status of the file change from open (ope) to closed (clo). I use this command frequently when a test file is to be updated by a batch program (batch programs can't update allocated online files) and then use the next command to reopen it:

```
CEMT  S  F(PAYHRRATE)  OPE
```

Yes, it takes some practice, but you can see that it isn't hard to figure out the command line entries after doing it a few times. When you are not sure, I always encourage that you back up with PF3 and allow the transaction being used to help you. For example, instead of using the overtype mode to change the file status, we could have used the CEMT Set function. If we had overtyped the command line in Figure 7.14 to just " S F," we would have seen the supportive information in Figure 7.15. This screen presents a menu of all the possible settings for a file that can be set.

Completing the prompt in Figure 7.15 requires only that we enter the file name in parentheses and the appropriate setting. In truth, we will probably enter the same information overtyped earlier, but this menu ensures that we see all the options.

Note: When using the OPEN or CLOSE options of CEMT, you should also be aware of the ENABLE and DISABLE options. ENABLE and DISABLE are options that signal to CICS if a file is even available, while OPEN and CLOSE specify its accessibility. For example, if a file is ENABLEd and CLOSEd, there is no problem, as the first request for access to the file will cause CICS to open the file. Likewise, if a file is DISABLEd, an open of the file will fail.

```
S F
STATUS:   COMMAND SYNTAX CHECK
 CEMT   Set File()
   < ALl >
   < OPen | Closed | Forceclose >
   < ENabled | DIsabled >
   < REAd | NORead >
   < UPdate | NOUpdate >
   < ADd | NOAdd >
   < BRowse | NOBrowse >
   < DElete | NODElete >
   < EXclusive | NOEXclusive >
   < EMptyreq | NOEMptyreq >
   < OLd | Share >
   < DSname() >



 PF  1 HELP   3 END    7 SBH 8 SFH 9 MSG 10 SB 11 SF
```

Figure 7.15. Status screen for CEMT set function.

Using the NEWCOPY facility. Finally, CEMT serves a function that is often provided in various utilities that your shop may or may not have. That is the function of updating the CICS in-memory directories of programs and MAPs. *Reminder*: When CICS is started by your shop's technical staff, CICS opens the various libraries that contain executable code. Should you recompile and linkedit a module after startup, CICS won't have access to it. This isn't a fault of CICS but a trait of partitioned data sets. Since CICS loads the directory into memory for fast access, any changes you make to the actual partitioned dataset will *not* be known to CICS. What is required is the ability to update the in-memory directory entry. This is known as a NEWCOPY.

To use the NEWCOPY facility, you use the CEMT Set function. This is done by entering "S PR" (or just "S" and then adding "PR" at the next screen prompt). The screen you will see is in Figure 7.16.

You don't need me to fill in here, do you? All you need to do is fill in the program name within parentheses and add "N" or "NEWCOPY" to the command line. Doing so will present results as shown in Figure 7.17. Here we have loaded a new copy of program

PY002500. (*Reminder*: This is only needed if a program or MAP is recompiled after the CICS region is started.)

```
S  PR
  STATUS:   COMMAND  SYNTAX  CHECK
   CEMT    Set  PRogram( )
   <  CLass( )   |  AL1  >
   <  Enabled   |  Disabled  >
   <  Newcopy  >



 PF  1  HELP    3  END     7  SBH  8  SFH  9  MSG  10  SB  11  SF
```

Figure 7.16. Prompt screen for CEMT set function for NEWCOPY.

Note: As a writer, I sometimes color the facts to communicate a concept. With the NEWCOPY function, you should know that this does not actually create a new copy of the program/MAP in memory. It actually does just the opposite. Yes, it removes the in-memory directory entry for the prior version of the program/MAP. Then, when CICS attempts to locate the MAP or program, CICS finds the address missing and creates a new copy of the entry at the first request for it. This is a minor issue, but I didn't want to mislead you.

```
S  PR(PY002500)  N
 STATUS:   RESULTS  -  OVERTYPE  TO  MODIFY
   Pro(py002500)  Len(0065968)  Res(000)  Use(000000)  Cob  Ena  NEW  COPY




   RESPONSE:  NORMAL       TIME:  7.57.35    DATE:  92.160
 PF  1  HELP    3  END     7  SBH  8  SFH  9  MSG  10  SB  11  SF
```

Figure 7.17. Status screen for CEMT set function for NEWCOPY.

As a CICS programmer, you will frequently need the NEWCOPY function, but it is often provided by other utility programs. I include it here so you will always have some access to it.

In wrapping up the CEMT transaction, you may be thinking that I didn't cover all its power. You're right, I didn't, but the issues addressed in this topic are the ones most likely to be needed by you.

7.4.   CEDF

The CEDF transaction is probably my favorite. CEDF (often referred to as just EDF) is unique in its ability to help new CICS programmers grasp how CICS works. CEDF was designed to help programmers step through their work in a debugging mode. While I also use proprietary debugging software, I always revert to CEDF when I want to know how CICS views a transaction. If you master nothing else, I encourage you to master CEDF. All it takes is a basic knowledge of CICS commands and knowing the name of a working CICS transaction at your shop. As I have said before, practice, practice, practice. It is only by getting your hands dirty that you will learn the capabilities of CEDF.

7.4.1.   Overview of CEDF

CEDF is a transaction that establishes a working environment; it must be executed *before* you execute the transaction that you want to debug or walk-through. CEDF does not trap each COBOL instruction, but focuses instead on every CICS command, showing the status both before and after executing the instruction. Not only can this help you debug an application, it can also educate you in the ways of CICS.

Since CEDF only stops to display information at each designated CICS instruction, you will typically be more successful when you use a pencil and paper as you progress. In other words, don't look for CEDF to analyze and document why things go wrong. Instead, look to CEDF to help you gather information as a transaction progresses.

A color monitor is especially valuable when using CEDF, even more so than with other transactions. Why? Because you will be immediately aware of the myriad of data fields that may be overtyped. Assuming you are using a standard four-color monitor, any green or red field may be modified by you. Just seeing these colors can help you realize the power available to you. (For example, the command to be executed appears in red, identifying that even this can be changed.)

Stepping through a transaction with CEDF can be time-consuming, as you will see every ASKTIME, every FORMATTIME, every WRITEQ, and so on. If you want to proceed at a faster pace, CEDF offers you options that let you specify only the command(s) that interests you. Also, if you have a program that is so squeaky clean that you don't want it to clutter up the screen while in a debug session, you need to specify the NOEDF option when running the CICS translator for the specific program.

The importance of being able to control the screens should not go lightly with you. Recently, I wanted to check the status of a READ command in program x. Unfortunately, to reach program x, there was a main menu program that XCTLed to a subordinate menu program that XCTLed to a processing program that then LINKed to program x. Stepping through all the CICS commands of three programs before reaching the program in question can try your patience.

Unlike the other CICS transactions, CEDF offers you the option to specify whether CEDF is still needed. Depending on your response to its prompt (or how you set options with PF9), CEDF will continue to intercede or will allow itself to terminate, leaving your transaction still operable.

Using the CEDF screens. As you are presented with each screen, many of the variables may be modified by simply placing the cursor over a field and typing what you want to happen. For example, I was testing a transaction that experienced the MAPFAIL error condition. Since I wanted to see how the logic flowed without such an error, I overtyped NORMAL over MAPFAIL and pressed the Enter key. The transaction still had the issue of the MAPFAIL condition, but it now followed the logic of the NORMAL condition. Obviously, you can paint yourself into a corner if you tell CICS to overlook serious conditions. Still, it is useful to be able to override errors that don't apply to the part of the program in which you are interested.

As you use CEDF, you will also periodically see the application data screen while CICS is performing its functions. Don't attempt to instantly interact with the screens. Normally, CICS hasn't relinquished control but is just exercising its components. As with other CICS transactions, part of their mastery is learning their idiosyncrasies.

Finally, as each transaction prepares to RETURN to CICS, you will be given the option of continuing in CEDF mode or resorting to normal transaction flow. As we will see, the default is NO, so don't idly just keep pressing the Enter key for long dialogues.

Understanding the PF keys. While other transactions have the basic keys (see Figure 7.1), CEDF offers a richness not approached by the other transactions. Some of the keys you may never need, but others will be used consistently. Pressing the Enter key afterwards will keep the transaction moving forward. Let's review their basic functions (although some will vary in different displays). Each key that requires some additional practice or understanding will be covered in more detail in later topics:

PF2: SWITCH HEX/CHAR This useful key does just what it implies: It changes alphanumeric displays to hex displays and hex displays to alphanumeric displays. This can be useful when you want to locate addresses of data areas as the transaction executes.

PF3: END EDF SESSION Don't let this confuse you into thinking that pressing PF3 ends the transaction. It only terminates EDF's monitoring of the transaction. Once I am comfortable that I understand a transaction issue, I press PF3 to restore full control to the application program.

PF4: SUPPRESS DISPLAYS A clumsy title for a function key, but this is a major productivity key to use. Pressing this key tells CEDF *not* to display information in which you have no interest. This speeds up a debugging session considerably. (You specify what interests you with PF9. Together, these keys reduce your time spent watching irrelevant displays.)

PF5: WORKING STORAGE If the name of this key hints that it displays COBOL WORKING STORAGE, you're right. That means also that when you are still at the first screen and the COBOL program hasn't yet been loaded, you will receive a message that WORKING STORAGE is not yet available. When you press PF5, you will also see a different set of PF keys. I use these for special functions that aren't always accessible. (For example, one of the PF keys displayed on the WORKING STORAGE screen displays the EIB area. Since I often want to see that, I press PF5 and then press the PF key for the EIB area.)

PF6: USER DISPLAY This little-used key is still valuable. Pressing it causes the current user screen to display. While not often useful, there are times when you are so involved in debugging that you forget what the screen is showing.

PF7 and PF8 These two PF keys are just as stated — used for scrolling forward and backward where appropriate. For example, these are quite useful after pressing PF5 to see WORKING STORAGE.

PF9: STOP CONDITIONS One of my favorite keys now, it wasn't always, as I didn't understand it. PF9 is there so you can specify what conditions (if any) you want to monitor. This can be especially important if you simply want to monitor a RECEIVE MAP command at a particular point in your application and want to bypass all other CICS commands. If you sometimes feel that CEDF is just too darn slow, then you are probably not using PF9 effectively.

PF10: PREVIOUS DISPLAY This lets you back up through prior screens (up to ten) to see transaction progress. The screens you see are now history, so overtyping accomplishes nothing.

Other PF keys develop meaning at various points, but the screen will always show their availability. As I mentioned previously, many of the keys will never be useful to you, but a few will always be important.

7.4.2. Using CEDF

Much of what we have covered in previous transactions is true of CEDF. All of the screen mannerisms are there. For example, to start CEDF, just type CEDF on a blank screen. If CEDF has not been previously activated, you will receive a response message stating that EDF mode is on. Following that message, type the transaction identifier of the transaction that you want to evaluate. It's that simple. To build familiarity, just type in the trans ID of any working transaction at your shop. What we're after here is basic awareness.

Assuming we did just that, the first screen that we would see would be similar to that shown in Figure 7.18. This displays the CICS environment BEFORE the program itself is loaded. What you see here is the EIB, as it exists just before loading the application program.

Notice in Figure 7.18 how the CICS elements come alive. While we have discussed various EIB components prior to this, CEDF shows them to be alive and responsive. If the labels on the PF keys indicate a richness of function, you're correct. CEDF is the most powerful of the supplied CICS transactions from IBM. Let's play a bit with the PF keys to get some familiarity. Pressing PF2 at the first screen would transform it into what is shown in Figure 7.19. This does not change major information but presents it in hex format. Pressing PF2 again would restore what was shown in Figure 7.18.

```
TRANSACTION: P250  PROGRAM: PY002500  TASK  NUMBER: 0002633  DISPLAY: 00
STATUS:    PROGRAM INITIATION

    EIBTIME     = 153940
    EIBDATE     = 92361
    EIBTRNID    = 'P250'
    EIBTASKN    = 2633
    EIBTRMID    = 'E000'

    EIBCPOSN    = 27
    EIBCALEN    = 0
    EIBAID      = X'7D'                         AT  X'0009E182'
    EIBFN       = X'0000'                       AT  X'0009E183'
    EIBRCODE    = X'000000000000'               AT  X'0009E185'
    EIBDS       = '........'
    EIBREQID    = '........'


ENTER: CONTINUE
PF1  : UNDEFINED          PF2 : SWITCH HEX/CHAR PF3 : END  EDF  SESSION
PF4  : SUPPRESS DISPLAYS  PF5 : WORKING STORAGE PF6 : USER DISPLAY
PF7  : SCROLL BACK        PF8 : SCROLL FORWARD  PF9 : STOP CONDITIONS
PF10: PREVIOUS DISPLAY    PF11: UNDEFINED       PF12: UNDEFINED
```

Figure 7.18. Opening screen for CEDF.

The hex format is useful when you need to determine memory addresses for variables and I/O areas or just to determine the hex configurations of various variables. While not an earth-shaking PF key, PF2 is a good day-to-day warrior.

Setting STOP conditions. Earlier, I mentioned that you will often want to bypass screens that aren't relevant to what you are interested in. To bypass screens, press PF4. (*Note*: To see every CICS command, press Enter.) Pressing PF4 causes CEDF to bypass the display of all CICS commands that do not fit the specific STOP conditions. To see the specific STOP conditions (and modify them, if desired) press PF9. This key helps us reduce the data we will see while browsing through our transaction in action. (Unless you use PF9 to set options, you may see every CICS command, something you may not want.)

```
TRANSACTION: P250 PROGRAM: PY002500 TASK NUMBER: 0002633 DISPLAY: 00
STATUS:    PROGRAM INITIATION

    EIBTIME    = X'0153940C'                        AT  X'0009E168'
    EIBDATE    = X'0092361F'                        AT  X'0009E16C'
    EIBTRNID   = X'D7F2F5F0'                        AT  X'0009E170'
    EIBTASKN   = X'0002633C'                        AT  X'0009E174'
    EIBTRMID   = X'C5F0F0F0'                        AT  X'0009E178'

    EIBCPOSN   = X'001B' AT  X'0009E17E'
    EIBCALEN   = X'0000' AT  X'0009E180'
    EIBAID     = X'7D'   AT  X'0009E182'
    EIBFN      = X'0000' AT  X'0009E183'
    EIBRCODE   = X'000000000000'                    AT  X'0009E185'
    EIBDS      = X'0000000000000000'                AT  X'0009E18B'
    EIBREQID   = X'0000000000000000'                AT  X'0009E193'


ENTER: CONTINUE
PF1 : UNDEFINED          PF2 : SWITCH HEX/CHAR PF3 : END EDF SESSION
PF4 : SUPPRESS DISPLAYS PF5 : WORKING STORAGE PF6 : USER DISPLAY
PF7 : SCROLL BACK        PF8 : SCROLL FORWARD  PF9 : STOP CONDITIONS
PF10: PREVIOUS DISPLAY   PF11: UNDEFINED       PF12: UNDEFINED
```

Figure 7.19. Opening screen for CEDF in hex.

```
TRANSACTION: P250 PROGRAM: PY002500 TASK NUMBER: 0002633 DISPLAY: 00
DISPLAY ON CONDITION:-

    COMMAND:                        EXEC CICS
    OFFSET:                         X'......'
    LINE NUMBER:                    ........
    CICS EXCEPTIONAL CONDITION:
    ANY CICS ERROR CONDITION        YES
    TRANSACTION ABEND               YES
    NORMAL TASK TERMINATION         YES
    ABNORMAL TASK TERMINATION       YES



ENTER: CURRENT DISPLAY
PF1 : UNDEFINED          PF2 : UNDEFINED       PF3 : UNDEFINED
PF4 : SUPPRESS DISPLAYS PF5 : WORKING STORAGE PF6 : USER DISPLAY
PF7 : UNDEFINED          PF8 : UNDEFINED       PF9 : UNDEFINED
PF10: UNDEFINED          PF11: UNDEFINED       PF12: REMEMBER DISPLAY
```

Figure 7.20. CEDF STOP condition screen.

Refer to Figure 7.20. One item of interest is that there is a new PF key shown, PF12. This key, PF12, can be helpful in a debugging session because it can capture a data screen (remember, the backward review only supports ten screens). Using PF12, you can store certain screen images for later recall when you use PF10. In this screen, you may also set many options. Here is how you can use them:

COMMAND: EXEC CICS

This is where you can type in the name of a CICS command where you want to cause CEDF to pause.

This is useful if, for example, you want to analyze what is occurring in a transaction for a specific CICS command, for example, SEND.

OFFSET:
X'......'

This option is useful if you want to stop at a hexadecimal offset. Remember, it must come from the CICS listing, not from the compile. If the offset is not a CICS command, it will be ignored.

LINE NUMBER: ....

I find this useful when stepping through a program when I also have a printed listing of the program available. This is the line number of the CICS command from the CICS translator listing (*not* from the COBOL listing). Combining the line number option with the command option would let you pinpoint the specific command you want information from, for example, a SEND command on line 135. This significantly reduces your debug time because you don't need to see all the other CICS commands appear on your screen. The line number facility requires that you code the DEBUG option when running the CICS translator.

CICS EXCEPTIONAL CONDITION:

ANY CICS ERROR CONDITION   YES

I suggest always setting this to NO, depending on how your applications are written. If set to YES, any command that returns a condition code other than NORMAL will cause CEDF to stop and display the screen. Often, programmers code CICS commands, such as READQ, just to check the environment and treat the resulting QIDERR as insignificant.

TRANSACTION ABEND   YES

Always leave this set to YES. After all, if the transaction ABENDs, you certainly want the option of looking around, don't you?

NORMAL TASK TERMINATION   YES

Since CEDF prompts you when a transaction is about to terminate, I always leave this set to YES, just so I can decide whether CEDF should remain active.

ABNORMAL TASK TERMINATION   YES

Again, here is an option that I always leave set to YES. The whole concept of monitoring a transaction is to intercept unusual situations.

```
TRANSACTION: P250  PROGRAM: PY002500  TASK  NUMBER: 0002633  DISPLAY: 00
DISPLAY ON CONDITION:-

     COMMAND:              EXEC CICS SEND    <=== stop at this command
     OFFSET:                  X'......'
     LINE NUMBER:             00127...       <=== if on this line
     CICS EXCEPTIONAL CONDITION:
     ANY CICS ERROR CONDITION      no        <=== ignore error conditions
     TRANSACTION ABEND             YES
     NORMAL TASK TERMINATION       YES
     ABNORMAL TASK TERMINATION     YES


ENTER: CURRENT DISPLAY
PF1 : UNDEFINED           PF2 : UNDEFINED        PF3 : UNDEFINED
PF4 : SUPPRESS DISPLAYS   PF5 : WORKING STORAGE  PF6 : USER DISPLAY
PF7 : UNDEFINED           PF8 : UNDEFINED        PF9 : UNDEFINED
PF10: UNDEFINED           PF11: UNDEFINED        PF12: REMEMBER DISPLAY
```

Figure 7.21. CEDF STOP condition screen example.

By setting the options in Figure 7.21, I can now press PF4 to accelerate CEDF through the CICS screens, or I may just press Enter to see each screen. Even if you do not use the PF9 options, pressing PF4 will always improve your speed in moving through transactions.

In this topic, you saw how a combination of PF9 (to set STOP conditions) and PF4 (to bypass them) can improve your use of CEDF. The next topic will help you cope with issues as they arise.

Overriding Conditions. As you step through CEDF, it will show
you each command of interest, both before and after execution. That
can be useful, allowing you to modify information to see what will
happen. My suggestion is, when in doubt, attempt to override whatever
appears in error. Often, CEDF will allow it. Besides, it sure can't hurt
you. Let's see an example of doing a RECEIVE where a return code
occurs that was not expected. The programmer wants to proceed with
the program despite the unexpected return code. (*Remember*: Unexpected return codes are errors to your program *only* if they cause the
program to proceed incorrectly.)

In our example (Figure 7.22), a RECEIVE is about to be done.
From the information on the screen, it is from line 65 from the application program. If we wished, we could overtype any field that seemed
important. Let's just press Enter and see what happens. This RECEIVE
command is expecting a data field with a length of nine bytes.

```
TRANSACTION: P250  PROGRAM: PY002500  TASK  NUMBER: 0002633  DISPLAY: 00

STATUS:    ABOUT  TO  EXECUTE  COMMAND
EXEC  CICS  RECEIVE
  INTO  ('.........')
  LENGTH  (9)
  NOHANDLE



OFFSET:X'000B0A'        LINE:00065            EIBFN=X'0402'

ENTER:  CONTINUE
PF1  :  UNDEFINED          PF2  :  UNDEFINED        PF3  :  UNDEFINED
PF4  :  SUPPRESS DISPLAYS  PF5  :  WORKING STORAGE  PF6  :  USER DISPLAY
PF7  :  UNDEFINED          PF8  :  UNDEFINED        PF9  :  UNDEFINED
PF10:  UNDEFINED           PF11:  UNDEFINED         PF12: REMEMBER DISPLAY
```

Figure 7.22. CEDF about to execute a command.

As often happens in testing, the anticipated condition codes are
not what were expected. In our example, the received data had a
length other than 9. That causes an error condition to be raised. The
resulting screen is in Figure 7.23. This is the result of the command.

CEDF always presents the results of a command immediately after executing the command. The resulting condition code can help us modify our program to anticipate it for productional use. In this example, the condition code is not what was expected, so the programmer needs to override it to see if the program's processing logic would have continued in an appropriate fashion, anyway.

Refer to Figure 7.23 to see the status after the RECEIVE operation. Clearly, an error has occurred. The issue now is for the programmer either to let the transaction terminate because the condition code was not expected, or to intercept the condition code to see what would have happened had the program anticipated the condition code. Let's override the result. After all, we're here to achieve results — right?

```
TRANSACTION: P250  PROGRAM: PY002500  TASK  NUMBER: 0002633  DISPLAY: 00

STATUS:   COMMAND EXECUTION COMPLETE
EXEC CICS RECEIVE
   INTO ('P250,DAVE.................')
   LENGTH (27)
   NOHANDLE




OFFSET:X'000B0A'     LINE:00065      EIBFN=X'0402'
RESPONSE: LENGERR                    EIBRESP=22

ENTER: CONTINUE
PF1 : UNDEFINED         PF2 : UNDEFINED         PF3 : UNDEFINED
PF4 : SUPPRESS DISPLAYS PF5 : WORKING STORAGE   PF6 : USER DISPLAY
PF7 : UNDEFINED         PF8 : UNDEFINED         PF9 : UNDEFINED
PF10: UNDEFINED         PF11: UNDEFINED         PF12: REMEMBER DISPLAY
```

Figure 7.23. CEDF after executing a command.

As a debugging programmer seeing the information in Figure 7.23, I have two options. The first is to accept the error and attempt to solve it with pencil and paper. The alternative is to intercept the error to see what would happen if the condition code had been NORMAL. Since that is usually preferable, let's just overtype the word LENGERR with NORMAL. Piece of cake.

Yes, it's that simple. Move the cursor to LENGERR and type NORMAL and then press Enter. This simple act resets the CICS condition code to zero, allowing your transaction to proceed as though the condition code had been zero. Nice touch, eh? (*Reminder*: The problem still exists and could become more serious as processing continues. Overriding condition codes assumes you know what condition codes are being tested for in the program and how the program proceeds based on the condition code. For example, if the condition code was NOTFND or LENGERR after a READ command, overtyping with NORMAL could be disastrous.)

Ignoring CICS Commands. Sometimes, you may want to bypass or ignore CICS commands. For example, maybe your transaction is attempting to read a file that doesn't exist or is unavailable. One option is to bypass the command entirely. How do you do that? No problem. On the screen that shows the message ABOUT TO EXECUTE COMMAND, just tab to the command line and press the EraseEOF key, or type NOOP and press Enter. Either choice will cause CICS to display NOOP in place of the original command. The CICS command is still there, but, for this one execution, it won't occur. As stated above, how the program tests for condition codes is still important.

Checking WORKING STORAGE. As a final touch with CEDF, let's review its strength with WORKING STORAGE. Accessing WORKING STORAGE is done via the PF5 key. This allows you to check and modify the contents of data elements in the application. As you can see in Figure 7.24, the options vary somewhat from other CEDF screens. This is because the browse of WORKING STORAGE is dependent on the availability of the COBOL storage areas.

This option is (obviously) most valuable for transactions that need to analyze or modify contents of data areas. It is also useful for transactions that need to see decisions made from contact with other transactions. I usually use it after using PF2 to determine the hex addresses of a CICS command. Then, by pressing PF5 and overtyping the address field, I can review the data area before or after the command was executed.

Viewing WORKING STORAGE is usually done after determining the hex addresses with PF2. This isn't necessary, of course. It is useful, however, to see memory areas during execution to make appropriate decisions. *Note*: The ADDRESS area on the second line may be overtyped by simply entering the address of the desired data area and then pressing the Enter key. Also, *any value* in the WORKING STORAGE display may be changed by overtyping. You may do this by either overtyping the hex portion with hex values or the character portion with character values.

```
TRANSACTION: P250 PROGRAM: PYO02500 TASK NUMBER: 0002633 DISPLAY: 00
ADDRESS:  0009504C                    WORKING  STORAGE
00095040 000000                                 000A001B
00095050 000004   00290283  7330350C  F1F261F2  F761F9F1  ...c....12/27/92
00095060 000014   F1F54BF4  F24BF1F0  4040E3D9  C1D5E2C1   15.42.10 TRANSA
00095070 000024   C3E3C9D6  D540E3C5  D9D4C9D5  C1E3C5C4  CTION TERMINATED
00095080 000034   4B40E4E2  C540D7C6  F16B40D7  C6F26B40  . USE  PF1,  PF2,
00095090 000044   D7C6F36B  40D6D940  D7C6F440  D6D5D3E8  PF3, OR PF4 ONLY
000950A0 000054   C5F4F2F0  6BC4C1E5  C5000000  00000000        P250,DAVE
000950B0 000064   00000000  00000000  00000000  007D6D6A  ............'_.
000950C0 000074   7EE6E788  7F6C6E6B  F1F2F3F4  F5F6F7F8  =WXh"%>,12345678
000950D0 000084   F97A7B7C  C1C2C3C4  C5C6C7C8  C94A4B4C  9:#@ABCDEFGHIð.<
000950E0 000094   00000000  00000000  00000000  00000000  ...............
000950F0 0000A4   00000000  00000000  00000000  00000000  ...............
00095100 0000B4   00000000  00000000  00000000  00000000  ...............
00095110 0000C4   00000000  00000000  00000000  00000000  ...............
00095120 0000D4   00000000  00000000  00000000  00000000  ...............
00095130 0000E4   00000000  00000000  00000000  00000000  ...............

ENTER: CURRENT  DISPLAY
PF1 : UNDEFINED        PF2 : BROWSE TEMP STORAGE PF3 : UNDEFINED
PF4 : EIB DISPLAY      PF5 : WORKING STORAGE      PF6 : USER DISPLAY
PF7 : SCROLL BACK HALF PF8 : SCROLL FORWARD HALF PF9 : UNDEFINED
PF10: SCROLL BACK FULL PF11: SCROLL FORWARD FULL PF12: REMEMBER DISPLAY
```

Figure 7.24. CEDF with view of WORKING STORAGE.

You should notice in Figure 7.24 that there are two hex offsets: one for the relative location of the data areas within the program and one for the relative offset within WORKING STORAGE.

PF key options. Notice also that the WORKING STORAGE PF key commands provide some important entries to CICS information. One is PF2, allowing direct access to temporary storage queues (as provided by the CEBR transaction). The other is PF4, allowing access to all entries in the EIB. This can be especially useful when attempting to debug a transaction where the programmer has little or no experience.

This opportunity to view the EIB should be used frequently for new transactions. For example, the length of the COMMAREA may be incorrect (more common than you may imagine).

You will most often use PF5 to browse WORKING STORAGE after having completed a command that alters WORKING STORAGE (such as RECEIVE MAP or READ). By using PF2 to determine the hex address, PF5 gives you the opportunity directly to see (and modify, if desired) the data area. Use this technique as part of your debugging arsenal of tools. I do — frequently.

Since you will frequently want to use CEDF for program debugging, I suggest you practice with CEDF until

- you can locate the EIB with two keystrokes.

- you can locate WORKING STORAGE with one keystroke.

- you can bypass any CICS command.

- you can change the status after executing any CICS command.

- you can set conditions to stop CEDF.

Knowing how to do these tasks won't make you a guru, but you will certainly be on your way.

7.5. CECI

The CECI command and the CECS command are sisters (cousins?). One executes a CICS command immediately; the other only ensures that you coded it correctly. If you ever plan to master CICS, you will want these two commands in your corner. Why? Because these commands let you play with the CICS commands and get direct feedback from CICS itself on whether the command will work. A side blessing is that CICS provides richer feedback with these two commands. For example, even when I do not code a command completely, these commands still provide useful feedback. In summary, they always give you constructive information.

7.5.1. Overview of CECI

CECI is the CICS transaction that executes CICS commands. While this may seem of little value, CECI is one of my favorites. For one, it seldom requires that all variables be entered. When unsure, just press the Enter key. More often than not, you will receive enough feedback for your efforts. CECI also allows a great deal of shorthand to minimize your keystrokes.

A special advantage of knowing CECI is that you have the power to execute any CICS command directly from a terminal without the need to imbed the command in a COBOL program. As you progress in learning CICS, you will find this is a plus.

7.5.2. Using CECI

As with other commands, just press the Clear key and then type CECI. Also, as with other commands, once you know the allowable keywords, you may type them immediately. This technique is especially valuable when you know a specific command to execute.

CECI is often useful when (a) you have a temporary storage queue to browse or delete, (b) you want information on your terminal environment, (c) you want to experiment with status codes from various transactions, or (d) you want to see what the various keyword elements contain after executing certain CICS commands. The possibilities go on and on.

After entering CECI and pressing the Enter key, the first screen we will see will be that shown in Figure 7.25.

```
STATUS:    ENTER  ONE  OF  THE  FOLLOWING

ABend        ENDbr         POSt          SPOOLClose
ADdress      ENQ           PURge         SPOOLOpen
ALlocate     ENTer         PUSh          SPOOLRead
ASKtime      EXtract       READ          SPOOLWrite
ASSign       FOrmattime    READNext      START
BIf          FREE          READPrev      STARTBr
BUild        FREEMain      READQ         SUspend
CAncel       Getmain       RECeive       SYncpoint
CONNect      Handle        RELease       Trace
CONVerse     IGnore        RESEtbr       Unlock
DELAy        INquire       RESYnc        WAit
DELETE       ISsue         RETRieve      WRITE
DELETEQ      Journal       RETUrn        WRITEQ
DEQ          LInk          REWrite       Xctl
DIsable      LOad          ROute
DUmp         POInt         SENd
ENAble       POP           SET

PF  1  HELP  2  HEX  3  END  4  EIB  5  VAR  6  USER      9  MSG
```

Figure 7.25. CECI opening options.

From Figure 7.25, as with other CICS transactions from IBM, you need only to code the necessary characters from a keyword that are in upper case. For example, you only need to code REC to activate the RECEIVE command. To experiment with CECI, I suggest that you only use commands with which you are already familiar. All will function properly, but you may not understand the outcome.

One of the first things you should always do for a transaction that offers help is to press the proper PF key, PF1 in this case. That will help you understand the shorthand for all possible PF keys and other command options. Pressing PF1 brings up Figure 7.26. In that figure, you will see mostly familiar PF keys. Some that are especially beneficial are PF4 (shows the EIB area) and PF5 (shows a user defined area — we'll cover that in a moment).

```
Enter command on the first line and press ENTER
   (after returning from HELP).
Options can be abbreviated to the minimum to make
   them unique.
? before command gives COMMAND SYNTAX CHECK and
   prevents execution.
To expand a value or variable to full screen,
   position cursor using TAB key and press ENTER

PF KEY HELP INFORMATION

   PF01    HELP     HELP INFORMATION
   PF02    HEX      SWITCH HEX/CHAR
   PF03    END      END SESSION
   PF04    EIB      EXEC INTERFACE BLOCK
   PF05    VAR      VARIABLES
   PF06    USER     USER DISPLAY
   PF07    SBH      SCROLL BACK HALF
   PF08    SFH      SCROLL FORWARD HALF
   PF09    MSG      MESSAGES
   PF10    SB       SCROLL BACK
   PF11    SF       SCROLL FORWARD
   PF12             UNDEFINED
USE ENTER TO RETURN
```

Figure 7.26. CECI help screen.

As shown in Figure 7.26, any command can be neutered by placing a ? to the left of the command. For now, we won't worry about that, but it is always nice to know that you can prevent accidental execution by such a simple process. As discussed, most of the functions are familiar to you by now, especially if you have used CEDF.

Using a TS queue. For a simple example, let's practice writing and reading a temporary storage queue. No, this serves no productive purpose from a corporate standpoint, but we need some simple exercises in which we can express ourselves. Since we've discussed the concept of temporary storage queues previously, let's create one here and then read it. No sweat.

First, we select WRITEQ from the options in Figure 7.25. This presents us with Figure 7.27. One of CECI's strengths is that it always prompts you when there are choices. Here is your first one.

```
 WRITEQ

  ENTER ONE OF THE FOLLOWING OR HIT ENTER FOR DEFAULT

 TD
 TS




  MESSAGES:  2  SEVERE

PF  1 HELP  2 HEX  3 END  4 EIB  5 VAR  6 USER      9 MSG
```

Figure 7.27. CECI WRITEQ prompt screen.

In Figure 7.27, did you notice that you received a "severe" error message? That occurs because CECI is always prepared to move ahead, treating even your first tentative entries as complete commands. Unless I am attempting to execute the command with what I believe are all necessary operands, I just ignore the errors. For example, in our example we know that WRITEQ is insufficient information for a complete command. (If we were to press PF9 for the error messages, we would see a message to that effect. So, who cares?) Your real goal is to select from one of the two options, TD or TS. (Yes, if you had entered WRITEQ TS originally, you would have bypassed this screen. That is *always* true for the IBM CICS transactions.)

Assuming you entered TS (for Temporary Storage queue), you will see Figure 7.28. Here are all the options for this command. I know, you're still seeing that doggone error message. Well, press PF9 to see what it's warning you about. Nothing new or special, but this is an easy way to confirm your required keywords for a command. Pressing PF9 will present you with Figure 7.29. As seen, the information isn't all that useful, but it is a good reminder, at least.

From Figure 7.29, you know that QUEUE and FROM are required. Well, it's not difficult to think up a queue name that is less than nine characters long (you may recall that, from earlier chapters, using the terminal ID and a unique identifier are usually sufficient). But what about establishing the FROM area? After all, this isn't a COBOL program where you have WORKING STORAGE or LINK-AGE sections to define an area to write to a queue. So, you need to be able to define a temporary work area for some commands. CECI provides the facility with PF5. Watch how we do it.

```
WRITEQ TS
STATUS:   COMMAND SYNTAX CHECK                    NAME=
   EXEC CICS   WRITEQ TS
   Queue()
   < Sysid() >
   From()
   < Length() >
   < Item() < Rewrite > >
   < Main | Auxiliary >
   < Nosuspend >




   MESSAGES:  2 SEVERE
 PF1 HELP 2 HEX 3 END 4 EIB 5 VAR 6 USER 7 SBH 8 SFH 9 MSG 10 SB 11
```

Figure 7.28. CECI WRITEQ option screen.

```
WRITEQ  TS
SYNTAX  MESSAGES
  S  QUEUE  MUST  BE  SPECIFIED.
  S  FROM  MUST  BE  SPECIFIED.



Line  showing  PF  keys  omitted  for  clarity
```

Figure 7.29. CECI WRITEQ error messages from PF9.

Establishing temporary areas. Following our current example of a WRITEQ command (although any would do), let's set up a temporary data area. Normally, this would be done with a COBOL program, but we don't have one here, do we?

We invoke this facility by pressing PF5 (appears on most of these CICS transactions as VAR (for VARiable data). What we get is shown in Figure 7.30. Whereas other screens are somewhat self-explanatory, this screen isn't.

```
  WRITEQ  TS
  VARIABLES
&DFHC   +00016   THIS  IS  A  SAMPLE
&DFHW   +00046   EXEC  CICS  WRITEQ  QUEUE('""CIE000')  FROM(&DFHC)
&DFHR   +00045   EXEC  CICS  READQ  QUEUE('""CIE000')  INTO(&DFHC)



PF  1  HELP  2  HEX  3  END  4  EIB  5  VAR  6  USER        9  MSG
```

Figure 7.30. PF5 screen from CECI.

Notice that each temporary variable has a four-character name preceded by an ampersand, has a specified length, and a value. First, remember that the values are meaningless, only serving to demonstrate that a variety of characters may be used. Second, know that the shown variables may be used for our own purposes if their lengths are sufficient (that is my normal choice).

For example, if we wanted to write a temporary queue of 15 bytes, we could complete the command line by entering any of the variables, as all of them are at least 15 bytes long. That would give us any of these possibilities:

```
WRITE  TS  QUEUE(&DFHC)
WRITE  TS  QUEUE(&DFHW)
WRITE  TS  QUEUE(&DFHR)
```

Obviously, each would write a queue record of a different length, but if we only want to experiment, that is of no consequence.

For our tests, let's assume that we want a specific value and length to be manipulated in our test transaction. (Learning this trick is just one of many ways to set your skills apart from the masses.) First, we must revisit Figure 7.30. To establish a new variable, we must tab to a new line and enter a name for our temporary area and then tab and enter a value. See Figure 7.31 (abbreviated).

```
WRITEQ  TS
VARIABLES
&DFHC    +00016    THIS  IS  A  SAMPLE
&DFHW    +00046    EXEC  CICS  WRITEQ  QUEUE('""CIE000')  FROM(&DFHC)
&DFHR    +00045    EXEC  CICS  READQ   QUEUE('""CIE000')  INTO(&DFHC)
&test    25
```

Figure 7.31. Setting up a temporary area, phase 1.

In Figure 7.31, we have tabbed to the next available line, entered a name for a temporary area (&TEST), then tabbed and entered the desired length. Doing this yourself will reinforce this exercise.

After we enter these two pieces of information, we can press the Enter key. That will cause the data to become legitimate (&test becomes &TEST and 25 becomes +00025). Finally, we complete the exercise by tabbing to the data field to the right of the +00025 and entering our data. This required pressing the Enter key twice, not once, but we now have our personal data element, as shown in Figure 7.32.

```
WRITEQ  TS
VARIABLES
&DFHC   +00016   THIS  IS  A  SAMPLE
&DFHW   +00046   EXEC  CICS  WRITEQ  QUEUE('""CIE000')  FROM(&DFHC)
&DFHR   +00045   EXEC  CICS  READQ  QUEUE('""CIE000')  INTO(&DFHC)
&TEST   +00025   THIS  IS  A  SAMPLE  OF  TEST
```

Figure 7.32. Setting up a temporary area, phase 2.

We can finish our command now by inserting a queue name. (For my textbook example I used DAVEK, but you should *never* be so flippant. As mentioned previously, use meaningful names such as terminal ID and trans ID, as they virtually guarantee uniqueness.) When CECI displays the statement, ABOUT TO EXECUTE COMMAND, you know that it has enough information to proceed, even though that might be somewhat different from what you need in a COBOL program. Our final screen for this example, just prior to execution, is in Figure 7.33.

```
WRITEQ  TS  QUEUE(DAVEK)  FROM(&TEST)
STATUS:    ABOUT  TO  EXECUTE  COMMAND                NAME=
 EXEC  CICS    WRITEQ  TS
   Queue(  'DAVEK      '  )
   <  Sysid()  >
   From(  'THIS  IS  A  SAMPLE  OF  TEST  '  )
   <  Length(  +00025  )  >
   <  Item()  <  Rewrite  >  >
   <  Main  |  Auxiliary  >
   <  Nosuspend  >



PF1 HELP 2 HEX 3 END 4 EIB 5 VAR 6 USER 7 SBH 8 SFH 9 MSG 10 SB 11
```

Figure 7.33. CECI prior to executing a command.

If you stayed with me through the exercise of writing a temporary storage queue record, you should now use CECI to construct and execute a READQ command to confirm your efforts. (Don't forget also to execute a DELETEQ command to remove the queue.)

Getting system information. From the previous information on the CECI transaction, you might infer that it is only to test new CICS commands for an application. Not true. As you become confident with CICS, you may find yourself using it daily for basic housekeeping information. For example, here are some situations where I regularly use CECI.

Finding basic system information. There are times when you need to know your terminal ID, your terminal's attributes, or other basic system information. Since the CICS command, ASSIGN, obtains this information, why not use it with CECI? Great idea! If, after entering CECI, we type ASSIGN, look at what we get in Figure 7.34.

```
  ASSIGN
  STATUS:    COMMAND EXECUTION COMPLETE                      NAME=
    EXEC CICS   ASSign
      < ABcode( '        ' ) >
      < APplid( 'CICSTEST' ) >
      < Btrans( '.' ) >
      < COlor( '.' ) >
      < CWaleng( +00640 ) >
      < DELimiter( '5' ) >
      < DESTCount( +00000 ) >
      < DESTID( '            ' ) >
      < DESTIDLeng( +00000 ) >
      < Extds( '.' ) >
      < FAcility( 'E002' ) >
      < FCi( '.' ) >
      < GCHars( +00000 ) >
      < GCOdes( +00000 ) >
      < Hilight( '.' ) >
      < Inpartn( '    ' ) >
  +   < Katakana( '.' ) >

      RESPONSE: INVREQ                          EIBRESP=+0000000016
    PF1 HELP 2HEX 3END 4EIB 5VAR 6USER 7SBH 8SFH 9MSG 10SB 11SF
```

Figure 7.34. ASSIGN command with CECI.

Getting EIB information. Okay, so normally you don't need this information, but when you do, you do. Knowing such mundane items as the terminal ID can be important if you're up to your neck in alligators and trying to drain the swamp. To get this information, just execute CECI and immediately press PF4 (yes, you can get the same information from the CEDF transaction, but it requires that you execute a 'real' program and obtain EIB information from within that program. CECI makes it easier. All the basic system information about your environment is presented to you with minimal keystrokes. What you will see is in Figure 7.35.

```
EXEC  INTERFACE  BLOCK
   EIBTIME       =  +0133924
   EIBDATE       =  +0092017
   EIBTRNID      =  'CECI'
   EIBTASKN      =  +0001210
   EIBTRMID      =  'E002'
   EIBCPOSN      =  +00041
   EIBCALEN      =  +00000
   EIBAID        =  X'7D'
   EIBFN         =  X'0000'
   EIBRCODE      =  X'000000000000'
   EIBDS         =  '........'
   EIBREQID      =  '........'
   EIBRSRCE      =  '
   EIBSYNC       =  X'00'
   EIBFREE       =  X'00'
   EIBRECV       =  X'00'
   EIBATT        =  X'00'
   EIBEOC        =  X'00'
 + EIBFMH        =  X'00'

 PF1 HELP  2HEX  3END  4EIB  5VAR  6USER  7SBH  8SFH  9MSG  10SB  11SF
```

Figure 7.35. EIB area from CECI.

Is CECI a command that you will routinely need? Who knows. I only know that I find it immensely useful. CECI's sister/cousin, CECS, is next. All that CECI does is done by CECS, but only to check syntax.

7.6. CECS

CECS is the poor cousin of the CECI transaction. Where CECI actually executes a CICS command, CECS only checks the syntax. I like CECS for those occasions where I want to know what parameters are needed for a command but don't have this book handy. While a strength of CECI is that it executes CICS commands with minimal information supplied, CECS helps you understand the various keywords that are required for proper execution in a productional environment.

A trick I often use is to make CECI perform like CECS. How to do it? Simple. Just place a ? before the CECI command and it reverts to just a syntax-checking role. For more information on the keywords for CECS, see the previous topic on CECI.

I've been encouraging you to experiment a bit. Well, with CECS, you can't possibly do any harm, so do try it out. I've admitted that, in this book, I have not even attempted to show you all the CICS commands that are available nor all the keyword options available. Here's your chance to find out all about the areas of CICS that I omitted.

As you experiment, you should find that CECS and CECI present similar menus and offerings.

7.7. CEBR

The CEBR transaction is, as I mentioned earlier, one of CICS's "lesser" transactions. Don't get me wrong, it's very useful. It's just that its strengths are so narrowly focused that many programmers never learn about it. CEBR is designed to let you browse existing storage queues and first searches for one named after your termID (e.g., if your terminal ID was A006, it would search for one named CEBRA006). Normally, such a queue would not exist. In such cases, the screen you would see is that shown in Figure 7.36.

Since the opening screen for CEBR is normally useless, IBM made a wise decision when developing the debugging facilities for COBOL II. Instead of sending abend information to a newly named queue, IBM decided to use the CEBR default. This means that, if you abend a COBOL II application (compiled with the appropriate options, such as TEST or FDUMP), the abend information can be quickly perused via the CEBR transaction. This was a good move by IBM and simplifies the debugging of COBOL II applications. (*Note*: This does *not* apply to COBOL/370, which uses different debug techniques.)

```
 ╭───────────────────────────────────────────────────────────────────────
 │  CEBR    TS QUEUE    CEBRA006 RECORD    1  OF  0    COL  1  OF  0
 │  ENTER  COMMAND  ===>
 │  *********************** TOP  OF  QUEUE  ***********************
 │  ******************* BOTTOM  OF  QUEUE   *******************
 │
 │
 │
 │
 │
 │
 │
 │
 │  TEMPORARY  STORAGE  QUEUE  CEBRA006      IS  EMPTY
 │  PF1 : HELP          PF2 : SWITCH HEX/CHAR    PF3 : TERMINATE BROWSE
 │  PF4 : VIEW TOP      PF5 : VIEW BOTTOM        PF6 : REPEAT LAST FIND
 │  PF7 : SCROLL BACK HALF  PF8 : SCROLL FORWARD HALF PF9 : UNDEFINED
 │  PF10: SCROLL BACK FULL  PF11: SCROLL FORWARD FULL PF12: UNDEFINED
 ╰───────────────────────────────────────────────────────────────────────
```

Figure 7.36. CEBR opening screen.

An additional strength of CEBR is that it allows you to browse any named queue. Finally, all of the instructions are in a good help screen, accessed via PF1. The Help screen for CEBR is one of CICS's better help screens. Not only does it explain functions available, it also shows the syntax of various commands. See Figure 7.37.

7.8.   CESN, CSSN, AND CSSF

These were briefly covered earlier in the book. I include them here only for completeness, as the section title indicates that CICS transactions are located here. Usually, you will not need any specific knowledge of them. Here are the basics for them:

CESN — the preferred transaction to log onto CICS. I say *preferred* because IBM says so. This transaction is designed to interface with various security and other system functions that don't directly require our involvement.

CSSN — the logon transaction that is replaced by CESN. Whether your shop uses CESN or CSSN is an issue to refer to your supervisor, coach, or instructor.

CSSF — the transaction to log you off of CICS. There are some options for CSSF, including LOGOFF and GOODNIGHT. How they are used at your shop should be reviewed with your supervisor, coach, or instructor.

With CICS/ESA there are two new CICS commands, SIGNON and SIGNOFF. I haven't had the opportunity to use them, but your shop may be using them in applications if you are using CICS/ESA.

```
CEBR    TS QUEUE   CEBRA006  RECORD   1 OF 0   COL 1 OF 0
ENTER COMMAND ===>
These commands are available to you (abbreviations in UPPER CASE):
Find /string/              - Keyword optional. Final delimiter
                             optional if string has no blanks.
                             Any other delimiter is OK.
Line line-number
Column column-number
Top
Bottom
TERMinal terminal-id       - Browse temp. storage queue for
                             anotherterminal
Queue temp-stg-queue       - Browse a named temp. storage queue
                             (name may be in hex - e.g.,
                             X'C134')
Put transient-data-queue   - Copy current queue into a transient
                             data queue.
Get transient-data-queue   - Fetch a transient data queue for
                             browsing.
PURGE                      - Destroy the current queue.

*********************** TOP OF QUEUE ***********************
******************** BOTTOM OF QUEUE  ********************
TEMPORARY STORAGE QUEUE CEBRA006     IS EMPTY
PF1 : HELP          PF2 : SWITCH HEX/CHAR    PF3 : TERMINATE BROWSE
PF4 : VIEW TOP      PF5 : VIEW BOTTOM        PF6 : REPEAT LAST FIND
PF7 : SCROLL BACK HALF  PF8 : SCROLL FORWARD HALF PF9 : UNDEFINED
PF10: SCROLL BACK FULL   PF11: SCROLL FORWARD FULL PF12: UNDEFINED
```

Figure 7.37. CEBR Help Screen.

SUMMARY

This was an important chapter. While it didn't improve your program coding skills, I hope it opened up a powerful assortment of CICS aids for your use. As I mentioned previously, most programmers never master these transactions and suffer for it. Make your own learning schedule for these, and, when you have a few minutes here and there, experiment until you feel comfortable with their features.

VOCABULARY REVIEW

Since this chapter focused on hands-on facilities instead of building your vocabulary, use this as an opportunity to review your understanding of the transactions. Here are some questions to help, but write a few of your own.

List two ways to locate the EIB information.

Which two transactions are most useful for debugging applications?

What transaction is useful to see command syntax when this book isn't handy?

What do the terms DISABLE and ENABLE mean?

What transaction would you use to close a file?

8

CICS Debugging
Facilities and
Techniques

In previous sections, I emphasized that I would provide no in-depth information on application debugging. For that, QED has other reference textbooks that cover the issue in far greater detail. Even so, I feel an obligation to ensure that you have some basic information. Over the years, I have always found that well-defined programs, using structured techniques, rarely required that the programmer use a dump to solve a problem. I haven't needed a dump in many years (knock on wood) and I hope that you share similar success.

What is presented here are some common facilities that are often overlooked and that may be of assistance to you. The first item is an overview of CICS abend codes. The next topic explains some COBOL II techniques and, if you are using COBOL II, then you should experiment with these facilities (yes, if that means forcing an 0C7 abend, then do it). The topic on COBOL/370 is informational, but I have not had an opportunity to test a COBOL/370 program.

The final topics are a brief review of some CICS commands that are covered in greater detail elsewhere in this book. So, will this information solve your abends? No. The only easy solution to problems is to code it right the first time. Good luck.

8.1. CICS ABEND CODES

When talking with CICS programmers, you don't hear the term abend often. Instead, you will usually hear the term *ASRA*. So, did the world change? No, ASRA is the abend code that CICS provides anytime the

283

application ABENDs with what is known as a program check. Program check abends are those abends that are preceded with the characters "0C," such as 0C4, 0C7. Receiving an ASRA abend, then, means that your program committed one of 16 common errors. That code is a single byte that appears in the dump. This generally prints on the same line as the PSW. I encourage you to review a dump with your supervisor, coach, or team member to locate where this code appears.

ASRA Abend Description	ASRA code	Batch abend equivalent
Operation exception	1	0C1
Privileged operation	2	0C2
Execute exception	3	0C3
Protection exception	4	0C4
Addressing exception	5	0C5
Specification exception	6	0C6
Data exception	7	0C7
Fixed-point overflow	8	0C8
Fixed-point divide overflow	9	0C9
Decimal overflow	A	0CA
Decimal divide overflow	B	0CB
Exponent overflow	C	0CC
Exponent underflow	D	0CD
Significance exception	E	0CE
Floating-point divide exception	F	0CF

Figure 8.1. List of ASRA abend codes.

If your abend code is not ASRA (Figure 8.1), then it is probably a code that relates to the execution of a CICS command. A list of most of those possible codes is in Appendix A.

8.2.   COBOL II FACILITIES

COBOL II provides some debugging facilities that are rarely taught or explained — certainly not to CICS programmers. Here is a brief overview of each option:

FDUMP Specifying this option at compile-time ensures that, should your transaction abend, you will receive useful information on the affected statement and affected data items without needing to do hex arithmetic. The dump is produced to a CICS queue that can be reviewed with the CEBR command. In fact, it is written to the CEBR default queue name.

TEST This invokes the interactive debug facility and, while you can't interact directly with it as a TSO programmer might, you can still prepare a batch script that CICS will apply to your transaction. Learning the interactive debug facility is beyond this book, so I suggest you see the *COBOL II Power Programmer's* text.

SSRANGE This compile option traps any subscripts that exceed the stated range. It increases run time, but it can be useful if you are introducing new OCCURS clauses to an application.

As with most new techniques in your professional career, you will learn them best if you take a simple program and force an error in it. These compile options can help you.

8.3.   COBOL/370 FACILITIES

While COBOL/370 is a superset of COBOL II, supporting the same COBOL source statements, COBOL/370 users different debug techniques. For this reason, much of what was reviewed in topic 8.2 does not apply. Like COBOL II, COBOL/370 debug facilities can be established with compile-time options. Here is an overview of those options:

TEST=(optiona, optionb) Unlike COBOL II, which can be tested in CICS via a batch script with the IBM COBTEST product, COBOL/370 provides no support for COBTEST. Instead, the TEST option for COBOL/370 specifies a choice of features available for use with the Debug Tool (part of CODE/370). Since CODE/370 is the software that runs from the programmer workstation, a full discussion of those features is not part of this book. The options that apply from a mainframe perspective are

TEST=(NONE,SYM)   for the equivalent of the COBOL II FDUMP option. Output is sent to a transient data queue (not a temporary storage queue) named CESE. Check with your supervisor, coach or a peer in your team for information on how this is handled for your shop.

FDUMP This is not supported for COBOL/370. See prior information on TEST.

SSRANGE This is identical to the SSRANGE option for COBOL II. See topic 8.2 for information.

Although this topic may imply that COBOL/370 has fewer debug facilities than COBOL II, the opposite is true. COBOL/370 uses CODE/370 for a rich variety of debug facilities, including the ability to debug CICS programs interactively. Since CODE/370 is a separate topic in itself, it is not part of this book.

8.4.   USING CEDF AND CEBR

We've already covered these two CICS transactions, so you might think this is nothing new. You're right. My concern, however, is that many CICS programmers do not know how to use either of them. As I just explained, CEBR can directly access the debug information from FDUMP. From earlier discussions, you now know that CEDF can help you trap many problems in a CICS program, especially if you omitted the code to check for various CICS condition codes.

8.5.   USING CEMT AND TRACE

One of the CEMT options that can assist you in debugging is the trace facility. The trace facility uses a predefined (for your shop) trace table that is appended to your dump. If you are having difficulty following the logic of a transaction and other tools aren't helping, you might want to try this. It can create more output than you want to see, but it just may be the only way to isolate a complex situation within your transaction. Here is how you do it:

- Before running your transaction, enter CEMT SET TRACE ON.

- Now execute your transaction. When it abends, the trace will be there for you to follow. The trace is limited to CICS commands, of course, and does not list the COBOL statements executed.

- Since the CEMT command set the TRACE option for your terminal, don't forget to enter CEMT SET TRACE OFF when you are through.

Personally, I don't like this approach because I can get confused with too much information in any trace format. I prefer to use CEDF and walk through the transaction, step by step. But, that's my preference. You may find the TRACE feature is right for your application. I omitted this feature from Chapter 7 because I felt it was specifically for debugging.

SUMMARY

You got no instruction here on debugging, did you? That's because I don't believe in teaching such skills, especially to those new to an environment. Why teach a person how to fix a flat tire when it's easier to explain the importance of tire maintenance? If mastery of the debugging process is your goal, I recommend that you read Eugene Hudders's book, *CICS/VS: A Guide to Application Debugging,* from QED. My approach is to equip you with some tools to help you analyze and plan your approach to resolving the problem. CICS is a complex product and, over time, you will probably face some complicated situations. I avoid such pursuits in this book because I am attempting to assist you, a newcomer, to the world of CICS.

Additional MAP and Screen Techniques

I decided to include this chapter because I know you have only so many dollars to spend for CICS books, you're hoping that this book will last awhile and, maybe more important, there are some changes beginning to happen in the CICS world and I wanted a chance to sensitize you to them. The area of change is in screen and transaction design. I'm still studying the techniques, so I can't present all the choices here. Still, this is an area that could have a major impact on future CICS applications. IBM has produced several publications in recent years on what they call a Common User Access (CUA) that document this direction and I've included the title of one in the publications chapter of this book. A full discussion of CUA would require a book much larger than this one, so I will present only the basic concept to you.

Did you ever use one of the earlier PC word processors? If you did, you may recall that each menu kept reducing your options. At the time, I thought it was great because I only had to select from the menu offerings. One of the first word processors that I used was IBM's DisplayWrite 3. For the time (mid-1980s), this was one of the more powerful word processors available, and I had a happy relationship with it. Now, several years later, I would be frustrated if I had to use it. Why? Let me describe the basic process to you.

The opening menu was simple, letting me decide whether I wanted to create a document, edit an existing document, print a document, or pick from several other options that I've forgotten. I think some of the other options let me copy files and do some other maintenance. What would frustrate me today is that, if I selected a document to edit, I would need to return to the opening menu to use any functions available there. That meant that I could not, for example, print a document while I was in the midst of editing it. Instead, I had to exit from the edit menu back to the opening menu and then select the print menu.

So, why I am talking about an older word processor? This book is about CICS, right? Think about that menu structure and compare it to many current CICS menu-driven applications. Do you see the similarity? Most CICS menu-driven applications use the menu to continually reduce the options available to the user, just as that early word processor did. Now, word processors have come a long way since then. For example, IBM replaced DisplayWrite 3 with DisplayWrite 4 years ago, followed it with a major upgrade, to be followed again by DisplayWrite 5. During those years, however, CICS applications (unfortunately) remained the same.

There are alternatives to this type of transaction design, but we've just never pursued them. Part of that is, admittedly, because the development costs may be higher, but I've always found that, when a development technique was restricted due to costs, technology eventually brought the cost down. As PCs become more prevalent as CICS terminal workstations, this change will accelerate. IBM already has a high-function version of CICS (CICS/OS2) that runs on a desktop workstation, so the future is closer than many people realize.

9.1.   ALTERNATE SCREEN DESIGN APPROACH

So, what is the alternative design technique? To explain the concept, I must return again to PC word processors for the example. The high-end word processors of today have no menus at all. Instead, they present an open screen to the user. The user can immediately start typing a document without responding to any menu choices. Then, when additional services are desired, such as spell checking, reformatting, printing, or merging with other documents, the user presses a key that activates a choice of pull-down menus (menus that appear in small areas from the top of the screen).

This technique reverses the earlier design, allowing the user to directly access the desired data, using pull-down menus to perform certain functions. As an example, our sample menu in Chapter 4 required that a user select an option of ADD, UPDATE, or DELETE from a menu. With an alternate transaction design approach, the user would be presented immediately with the screen to identify a record to create. Then, after entering any desired information (if any), the user could press a key that presented the choices available (such as ADD, UPDATE, DELETE).

Transactions designed this way will require more sophisticated MAPs and a more sophisticated program-to-program interface. As an example, each program would only contribute a portion of what is displayed on the screen instead of being in sole charge of screen contents. Accomplishing this will require that we develop MAPs that can overlay each other — not a trivial task. It will also require more attention to the concepts presented in Chapter 2.

9.2. CREATING PULL-DOWN MENUS

Yes, it can be done. You can develop MAPs that overlay other MAPs. An important consideration is to ensure some areas, such as the error message fields, are in the same place so the terminal user sees some consistency. I am not suggesting that you overturn all of your old applications. Instead, I want you to start thinking about how you might use your design skills to design applications with newer, CUA-type techniques. IBM's book is a good place to start.

To get you thinking, I prepared some sample help menus that might apply to our earlier MAP application for an employee data base. Instead of a single help MAP, here are three separate pull-down screens, each specializing in acceptable data formats allowed for each of the data fields.

There are better menus than what I did in Figure 9.1. My goal is to get you thinking. Executing programs with pull-down menus will require higher data traffic over the communication lines, but the productivity aspects may overcome the higher traffic costs. The three MAPs in Figure 9.1 can all be displayed at the same time, assuming that no SEND MAP with the ERASE option is used. The three menus appear as pull-down menus, overlaying the existing data.

To test the approach, your program should issue a traditional SEND MAP to the terminal. Then, with each pull-down menu selected by a different AID key, the test program should issue a SEND MAP for each MAP, but not using the ERASE option. Also, the program could con-

tinue to issue error messages because the message area of all four
screens is the same screen area. After sending the fourth MAP, the
screen will contain data from each of them. Naturally, application logic
to control them is critical and issuing a SEND MAP with ERASE will
be needed more frequently than with the traditional approach.

```
          TITLE  'MAPSET for pull down screens'
          PRINT  NOGEN
PULLDWN   DFHMSD TYPE=&SYSPARM,                                    X
                 MODE=INOUT,                                       X
                 LANG=COBOL,                                       X
                 TIOAPFX=YES,                                      X
                 CTRL=(FREEKB)
PULLDN1   DFHMDI SIZE=(24,80)
          DFHMDF POS=(01,05),LENGTH=15,                           X
                 INITIAL='| Departments:    |'
          DFHMDF POS=(02,05),LENGTH=15,                           X
                 INITIAL='|=============    |'
          DFHMDF POS=(03,05),LENGTH=15,                           X
                 INITIAL='| Acntg = 05      |'
          DFHMDF POS=(04,05),LENGTH=15,                           X
                 INITIAL='| MIS    = 06     |'
          DFHMDF POS=(05,05),LENGTH=15,                           X
                 INITIAL='| HR     = 07     |'
          DFHMDF POS=(06,05),LENGTH=15,                           X
                 INITIAL='| Sales = 10      |'
          DFHMDF POS=(07,05),LENGTH=15,                           X
                 INITIAL='| Manuf = 12      |'
          DFHMDF POS=(08,05),LENGTH=15,                           X
                 INITIAL='|_____    |'
MSGH1     DFHMDF POS=(20,01),LENGTH=79,ATTRB=(PROT,BRT)
PULLDN2   DFHMDI SIZE=(24,80)
          DFHMDF POS=(01,25),LENGTH=15,                           X
                 INITIAL='| Job Code:       |'
          DFHMDF POS=(02,25),LENGTH=15,                           X
                 INITIAL='|=============    |'
          DFHMDF POS=(03,25),LENGTH=15,                           X
                 INITIAL='| Salaried = S    |'
```

Figure 9.1. Example of pull-down menus.

```
          DFHMDF  POS=(04,25),LENGTH=15,                          X
                  INITIAL='| Temp       = T |'
          DFHMDF  POS=(05,25),LENGTH=15,                          X
                  INITIAL='| Comm       = C |'
          DFHMDF  POS=(06,25),LENGTH=15,                          X
                  INITIAL='| Contr      = P |'
          DFHMDF  POS=(07,25),LENGTH=15,                          X
                  INITIAL='| Hourly    = H |'
          DFHMDF  POS=(08,25),LENGTH=15,                          X
                  INITIAL='|_____|'
MSGH2     DFHMDF  POS=(20,01),LENGTH=79,ATTRB=(PROT,BRT)
PULLDN3   DFHMDI  SIZE=(24,80)
          DFHMDF  POS=(01,45),LENGTH=15,                          X
                  INITIAL='| Education:     |'
          DFHMDF  POS=(02,45),LENGTH=15,                          X
                  INITIAL='|=============   |'
          DFHMDF  POS=(03,45),LENGTH=15,                          X
                  INITIAL='| High  Sch= HS  |'
          DFHMDF  POS=(04,45),LENGTH=15,                          X
                  INITIAL='| 2-Yr Col= AS   |'
          DFHMDF  POS=(05,45),LENGTH=15,                          X
                  INITIAL='| Col  = BS/BA   |'
          DFHMDF  POS=(06,45),LENGTH=15,                          X
                  INITIAL='| Adv Deg:       |'
          DFHMDF  POS=(07,45),LENGTH=15,                          X
                  INITIAL='|      MA/MS/PH   |'
          DFHMDF  POS=(08,45),LENGTH=15,                          X
                  INITIAL='|_____|'
MSGH3     DFHMDF  POS=(20,01),LENGTH=79,ATTRB=(PROT,BRT)
          DFHMSD  TYPE=FINAL
          END
```

Figure 9.1. (cont'd). Example of pull-down menus.

From an application perspective, your program will need to rewrite the screen after returning from displaying a help MAP and will need to determine how the menus are selected. One option is to have an intermediate MAP, consisting of one line at the top of the screen identifying what PF keys are needed to invoke the pull-down menus. For example, a user may be working at a screen that has only information about the application. By pressing PF10, a single horizontal bar could be sent to the terminal listing options available. Then the user could select from the available AID keys and pick a pull-down option. This is very close to how many major PC software packages work today.

SUMMARY

As I stated, this chapter is conceptual, intended only to make you aware of an alternative approach to designing CICS applications. There isn't a lot of knowledge out there, as few people have experimented with overlaying MAPs.

Part 3

CICS Reference

Compiling a CICS Program

Unfortunately, most CICS programmers assume that the compile/link process is a "black box," not to be modified. Nothing could be so untrue. IBM consciously developed an extensive array of options, yet many programmers never learn or use any of these features. While it's true that you don't need to modify the options frequently, I believe that any person who receives monetary compensation for developing CICS programs should understand the options. Also, while I wrote the sample JCL in this chapter for MVS, the options and considerations apply to both VSE and MVS.

Normally, your technical staff will have prepared a set of options that fits most circumstances, but there are often various additional options that can be useful to you. (Also, many systems programmers are so overloaded in their own assignments that they just don't understand what options you need. Surprisingly, this is not uncommon.)

10.1. A LOOK AT THE JCL

In an earlier chapter, you saw that developing CICS programs was a three-step process. First, the CICS translator must evaluate the CICS commands and translate them as appropriate. Second, the COBOL compiler must generate the proper application code. Third, the Linkage Editor must create an executable module. Simple? Usually, but such issues as performance and debugging options are often overlooked. Let's review an example of a JCL PROC for CICS programs (see Figure 10.1).

```
   //DFHEITCL PROC OUT='*',MEMBER=
   //*
   //*       THIS PROCEDURE CONTAINS 3 STEPS
   //*       1.   EXEC THE COBOL TRANSLATOR
   //*       2.   EXEC THE COBOL II COMPILER
   //*       3.   LKED O/P FROM COBOL COMPILER
   //*            TO CICS.LOADLIB
   //*
1. //TRN     EXEC    PGM=DFHECP,PARM='COBOL2'
   //STEPLIB  DD      DSN=your.shops.cicslib,DISP=SHR
   //SYSPRINT DD      SYSOUT=&OUT
   //SYSPUNCH DD      DSN=&&SOURCE,DISP=(,PASS),UNIT=SYSDA,
   //          DCB=BLKSIZE=12000,SPACE=(TRK,(70,25))
2. //COB     EXEC PGM=IGYCRCTL,COND=(0,LT)
3. //SYSLIB  DD      DSN=your.shops.cobol.library,DISP=SHR
   //        DD      DSN=your.shops.IBMCICS.library,DISP=SHR
   //SYSPRINT DD      SYSOUT=&OUT
   //SYSIN    DD      DSN=&&SOURCE,DISP=(OLD,DELETE)
   //SYSLIN   DD      DSN=&&LOADSET,DISP=(MOD,PASS),
   //          UNIT=SYSDA,SPACE=(TRK,(20,10)),
   //          DCB=(RECFM=FB,BLKSIZE=3200)
   //SYSUT1   DD      UNIT=SYSDA,SPACE=(CYL,(1,1))
   //SYSUT2   DD      UNIT=SYSDA,SPACE=(CYL,(1,1))
   //SYSUT3   DD      UNIT=SYSDA,SPACE=(CYL,(1,1))
   //SYSUT4   DD      UNIT=SYSDA,SPACE=(CYL,(1,1))
   //SYSUT5   DD      UNIT=SYSDA,SPACE=(CYL,(1,1))
   //SYSUT6   DD      UNIT=SYSDA,SPACE=(CYL,(1,1))
   //SYSUT7   DD      UNIT=SYSDA,SPACE=(CYL,(1,1))
4. //LKED    EXEC PGM=IEWL,COND=(4,LT,COB),
   //          PARM='SIZE=(2000K,900K),XREF,LIST,RENT'
   //SYSLIB   DD      DSN=your.application.library,DISP=SHR
   //         DD      DSN=your.cobol.subroutine.library,DISP=SHR
   //SYSLMOD  DD      DSN=your.cics.loadlibrary(&MEMBER),DISP=SHR
   //SYSUT1   DD      UNIT=SYSDA,SPACE=(CYL,(3,2))
   //SYSPRINT DD      SYSOUT=&OUT
5. //SYSLIN  DD      DSN=your.shops.cics.library(DFHEILIC),
   //          DCB=BLKSIZE=3200,DISP=SHR
   //         DD      DSN=&&LOADSET,DISP=(OLD,DELETE)
   //         DD      DDNAME=SYSIN
```

Figure 10.1. Sample CICS compile PROC for MVS.

The JCL in Figure 10.1 may be different from that used in your shop, but this JCL is probably (based on many comparisons) much more efficient than that used in your shop. This isn't because I'm a genius. It's because the JCL supplied by IBM is a compromise, intended to accomplish the function with minimal resources. Since most shops have more resources than assumed in the IBM defaults, those shops can reduce the time and cost of CICS compiles. *Note*: While Figure 10.1 shows an example of JCL for COBOL II, the JCL for OS/VS COBOL or COBOL/370 would be equivalent, specifying the appropriate compiler in the second step and some different options specified.

The specifics are reviewed in detail in the *MVS Power Programming* book and in the *VSE Power Programming* book that I mentioned earlier (each book contains complete JCL examples also), but here is a brief review of what is important for CICS development:

Statement 1: The first step is the CICS translator. It's important that you are consistent in specifying the COBOL version used (we'll cover the options later). For example, specifying to the translator that you are using COBOL II, while the next step executes the VS/COBOL compiler, would cause major errors.

Statement 2: The second step executes the COBOL compiler (COBOL II in this example). It is in this step that you specify any application-oriented options that are important (again, we will review options available in the next section).

Statement 3: This should point to your normal COPY PDS library, but it must also include the IBM-supplied library so the IBM COPYbooks that are mentioned in this book can be used.

Statement 4: The Linkage Editor is often ignored or misunderstood. The options presented ensure optimum performance. I included the RENT option, but you should check with your technical staff to determine whether it will benefit your application. Often, it accomplishes nothing. (*Note*: For VS/COBOL programs, RENT is meaningless. Use REUS if memory management is an issue. Again, your technical staff should have more information.) Incidentally, the equivalent for the VSE Linkage Editor is to specify SVA on the PHASE statement.

Statement 5: This structure for the SYSLIN ddname is normal, intended to ensure that the IBM CICS interface module appears first within the loadmodule. (You can accomplish the same with the ORDER statement, but this is simpler.)

The PROC in Figure 10.1 would be executed as follows, assuming the source program was in a PDS named DAVES.TEST.COBOL with a member name of SAMPLE.

```
//COMPILE   EXEC DFHEITCL,MEMBER=SAMPLE
//SYSIN     DD   DSN=DAVES.TEST.COBOL(SAMPLE),DISP=SHR
```

As I reviewed in an earlier chapter, this JCL will produce three listings. The first will be a listing of the program as written with any CICS errors flagged. The second will be the normal COBOL listing, and the third will be the Linkage Editor listing. Each offers specific documentation for an application.

Be sure to review the following sections on CICS options and COBOL options to determine if your shop's default options are appropriate for you (the options always appear on listings from each step, so you don't need to ask anyone). I find it common for some of the installed default options to be either inefficient, inappropriate, or both. You can fix this, at least for your programs.

10.2. CICS OPTIONS

Few programmers realize that the translator options can affect their program's performance and their ability to debug it. For a long time, I blindly used my employer's defaults before I realized the benefits of modifying them to my own needs. In this section, I list the primary options that you can specify (yes, you may see additional options on your listing, but they shouldn't be modified). You will find that some of the listed options require further understanding of COBOL II, topics that are covered in my *COBOL II Power Programming* texts.

> **ANSI85** (available only with CICS/VSE, CICS/MVS, and CICS/ESA) Specify this option if you are using the following ANSI 85 features of COBOL/370 or COBOL II
>
> - Use of lower-case text for the source program
> - Batched compilations
> - Nested programs
> - GLOBAL variables
> - Reference modification
>
> These are some of the most powerful features of COBOL/370 and COBOL II, yet I rarely find a company that understands them or uses them. Setting ANSI85 also forces the

COBOL2 option. Do *not* use this option just because you are using COBOL/370 or COBOL II, as it affects the generated object code.

CICS This is a confusing option, implying that one option of the translator is to *not* process EXEC CICS commands. Well, that's what it is for, but you may be wondering what purpose it serves. This option will normally be the default, but it should *not* be used for batch DL/I programs that use EXEC DLI commands. Otherwise, leave this alone.

COBOL2 (Not available prior to CICS/VS 1.7) This specifies that the program being translated is for the COBOL/370 or COBOL II compiler. It signals to the translator to omit some imbedded statements (such as SERVICE RELOAD statements) and to generate different COBOL statements for some of the EXEC CICS commands (such as MOVE LENGTH OF dataname to ...). Specifying COBOL2 forces LANGLVL(2).

DBCS (not available with CICS/VS) This specifies that the double-byte character set is used. You probably will never need this unless you work with character sets that require two bytes per character.

[NO]DEBUG This tells the translator that source line numbers of EXEC CICS statements are to be accessible by the CICS debug transaction, CEDF. This was reviewed in a prior chapter. Since there is no degradation of performance, I always specify DEBUG. (Remember, the line number used is that from the translator listing, not that from the COBOL compiler listing. Also, it only works for the EXEC CICS commands, not your other statements.)

DLI This specifies that EXEC DLI commands are to be processed.

[NO]EDF Earlier in the book, when we reviewed how to use the CEDF transaction, you probably got the impression that CEDF tracked execution of all CICS commands. You probably remember from my warnings (and from your own experiences) that the number of commands to bypass before getting to the ones you want to track can be more than you want to handle. This is especially true when the transaction uses many XCTL or LINK commands to reach the program in which you are interested. That is where this option can be helpful.

If you have a multiple-program transaction (such as a menu structure), you can speed up debugging efforts by specifying NOEDF when compiling those programs that are rock-solid stable. Doing so causes CEDF to skip completely over them, not slowing down your debug efforts. Otherwise, I recommend always using EDF, as there is no performance trade-off.

[NO]FE You should never need to worry about this. NOFE is the usual default. Specifying FE causes the translator to list all generated CICS arguments in hexadecimal. Unless you're debugging the translator itself, you will never need such information.

FLAG(I|W|E|S) This specifies the minimum severity error messages that should be produced.

FLAG(I) produces all messages. This is my preference, as I don't want to miss any feedback on something I didn't code appropriately. I always want to receive a RETURN CODE of 0 from the translator. This helps me do that.

FLAG(W) produces all error messages, but no informational messages. W messages produce a RETURN CODE of 4 by the translator.

FLAG(E) produces critical and severe messages. Usually, E-level messages are those where you coded it incorrectly and the translator has made some assumptions. E-level messages produce a RETURN CODE of 8. I don't recommend this option, as you miss all W errors.

FLAG(S) produces only messages that indicate the program is beyond hope. I don't recommend this option, because you miss all W and E errors.

LANGLVL(1|2) This option is for VS/COBOL and may be ignored if you are using COBOL II or COBOL/370. LANGLVL(1) specifies that you are using ANSI 68 COBOL rules. LANGLVL(2) specifies that you are using ANSI 74 rules. If you work for a company that still uses LANGLVL(1), then you should follow that standard for compatibility, but I hope your company embarks on a conversion program soon. The ANSI 74 standard has been available for over 17 years and the ANSI 85 standard (via COBOL II and COBOL/370) has been available for several years. Besides, COBOL II has been around for more than eight years. Companies that stay behind this long are missing many opportunities of newer standards. *Reminder*: You must also specify the same option for the COBOL compile step.

LINECOUNT(n) This is only to specify how many lines should be printed on each page of the translator listing. LINECOUNT (60) is the default.

[NO]NUM If your company standardizes on sequence numbers in columns one to six for your COBOL programs, you may want to specify NUM, telling the translator to use your numbers for diagnostic and cross-reference listings. My recommendation is NONUM, allowing the translator to generate its own numbers. NUM may have been useful when programs were on punched-cards, but that was eons ago.

[NO]OPT This applies only to VS/COBOL and is ignored if COBOL2 or ANSI85 is specified. This specifies whether optimized object code is to be generated by the COBOL compiler, in which case the translator generates SERVICE RELOAD statements for the EIB and DFHCOMMAREA. The same option must also be specified for the COBOL compile step. If you are using VS/COBOL, I recommend OPT.

If you use COBOL/370 or COBOL II, you may be a little confused, since COBOL II also has an OPT option for generating optimized code. The difference is that the translator must do something for VS/COBOL programs and need do nothing for COBOL/370 and COBOL II programs for the optimize/nooptimize issue.

[NO]OPTIONS This specifies whether the translator should include a list of the options used for the translation. I recommend OPTIONS.

QUOTE|APOST This corresponds to the identical COBOL compile option, identifying whether literals are separated by quotes (") or apostrophes ('). The COPYbooks supplied by IBM use APOST. Although the ANSI standard specifies QUOTE, the norm at almost every company is APOST. Use whatever your company uses, which is probably APOST.

[NO]SEQ Ignored if ANSI85 is specified (assumes NOSEQ), this indicates whether the translator is to check the sequence of your source statements. This option dates (as does NUM) from the days of punched-cards when there was the chance of dropping the cards and getting them out of sequence. I'll wager your source program is on DASD, so specify NOSEQ.

[NO]SOURCE This specifies whether the COBOL program source statements should appear on the listing. Normally, this should be SOURCE. If you're compiling clean programs and will produce the COBOL compiler listings on paper, you can save a tree by specifying NOSOURCE. This is because the CICS listing isn't usually needed for productional documentation and is used only until the CICS commands themselves are error free.

SP (not available prior to CICS/ESA) This specifies that the program contains special commands normally used by systems programmers. Such commands include INQUIRE, SET, PERFORM, and COLLECT. Those commands are not explained in this book for that reason. This change in CICS/ESA is to help a company impose some controls on what technical features should/should not be available from application programs. I support this move, as some CICS applications have used such commands when other facilities are available for the same functions. You may find that the SP option has been disabled, preventing any program from being translated that contains such statements.

SPACE(1|2|3) This specifies line spacing for the printed translator listing. Your company probably has the default at SPACE(1).

[NO]SPIE This option specifies whether or not the translator should intercept any possible abends during translation. This can be confusing, as some programmers think it relates to intercepting application program execution. It doesn't. Always leave this at SPIE (I'm sure it's your company default). NOSPIE is sometimes used by systems programmers if the translator has an IBM-related bug. I've never heard of this being used, but I recognize that IBM needed to provide the facility just in case of a technical problem.

[NO]VBREF This specifies that the translator is to include a cross-reference listing of CICS commands on the output listing. I find it useful when learning about a program written by someone else, as this is an easy way to assess whether there are some CICS commands used that aren't familiar to you. XREF and NOXREF are acceptable for compatibility because they were used in previous versions of CICS (prior to CICS/VS 1.7).

I summarized the options in Figure 10.2, using four categories. My intent is to help you quickly determine which of the following options might affect your program or your documentation.

- *Debug options:* These are options that help you debug your application at run time.

- *CICS options:* These are options that affect the commands that the translator will process and the generated code that is prepared for the COBOL compiler.

- *Document options:* These options affect the printed output listing. They have no affect on generated code.

- *COBOL options:* These options specify what version of COBOL is being used and variations on COBOL coding options.

	Debug Options	CICS Options	Document Options	COBOL Options
ANSI85		X		X
APOST/QUOTE				X
CICS		X		
COBOL2		X		X
DEBUG	X			
DLI		X		
EDF	X			
FE			X	
FLAG			X	
LANGLVL				X
LINECOUNT			X	
NUM			X	
OPT		X		
OPTIONS			X	
SEQ			X	
SOURCE			X	
SP		X		
SPACE			X	
SPIE				
VBREF			X	

Figure 10.2. Summary of CICS options.

CICS options can be specified either on the JCL EXEC statement on or a CBL statement within the COBOL program. See the information on specifying options following the next topic.

10.3. COBOL OPTIONS

In my *COBOL II Power Programming* books, I use almost 20 pages to describe the many options and how they can affect your application. In this book, I will focus only on the options that are important for the generation of CICS applications. Several of the others that you will see on your COBOL listings are similar (or identical) to those for the translator (e.g., SOURCE, SPACE, LINECOUNT).

VS/COBOL

If you use VS/COBOL, here are the options that are of most significance for your CICS transactions. There aren't many, since VS/COBOL isn't sensitive to the CICS environment.

BATCH — This option allows you to use the CBL statement, explained later. The CBL statement allows you to retain desired compile options with the specific program.

LIB — This is *required*, as all CICS programs use the COPY statement to include appropriate CICS facilities.

OPT — This generates more efficient code. Using it requires that the same option be used for the CICS translator.

RES — This allows the application to use a system resident copy of the COBOL subroutines, thereby reducing main memory requirements for the application.

These are VS/COBOL options that you *cannot use*. They invoke system services that corrupt the CICS environment.

```
COUNT, ENDJOB, FLOW,DYNAM, STATE, SYMDMP, TEST
```

COBOL II and COBOL/370

Since COBOL II and COBOL/370 are sensitive to the CICS environment, they offer a rich array of options that affect application performance. Some of the benefits of COBOL/370 and COBOL II over VS/COBOL are in the section in this book comparing the three compilers. Here are the options that are most important for your applications:

DATA(value) — (irrelevant to VSE) This option specifies where your WORKING STORAGE area is allocated. DATA(24) allocates it below the 16 megabyte line, and DATA(31) allocates it above that line. DATA(31) is the preferred choice unless your program CALLs a program that runs in 24-bit mode.

LIB — Required, because all CICS applications use the COPY statement.

NOCMPR2 — Required to ensure no incompatibilities exist from an earlier version of COBOL II (COBOL II, version 2 had some incompatibilities with COBOL II, version 3).

NODYNAM — Required to ensure no system services are invoked.

OPT — As with VS/COBOL, this generates efficient code.

RENT — Required, allowing CICS programs to access memory above the 16-megabyte line in MVS (or SVA in VSE).

RES — Required, allowing applications to share a common COBOL subprogram library. (Note: This does not apply to COBOL/370, as all COBOL/370-compiled programs use this feature.)

TRUNC — IBM recommends TRUNC(BIN) for full support of any possible binary (COMP) value. Since this is the more inefficient option, I suggest you experiment with TRUNC(OPT) if your application used COMP variables for efficiency. This can burn you if your program passes memory addresses in COMP fields, since addresses above the 16-megabyte line can exceed PIC S9(9).

Whereas VS/COBOL did not allow any of its debugging options to be specified for CICS programs, that is not true for COBOL II. The debugging options, TEST, FDUMP, and SSRANGE, may be used for CICS programs. (See the chapter on debugging for more information.)

10.4.   SPECIFYING OPTIONS

More than likely, you will often want to override the default options at your company. That can be done either from outside the program with JCL, or from within the program with CBL statements. Let's review each for its merits.

10.4.1. Using JCL to Specify Options

To override any options, you may include them on the EXEC statement, being sure to override them by step in the order in which the steps occur (e.g., override COBOL options before overriding Linkage Editor options). Here is an example, using the PROC in Figure 10.1:

```
//COMPILE   EXEC DFHEITCL,MEMBER=SAMPLE,
//      PARM.TRN='NOSEQ,COBOL2',
//      PARM.COB=NOXREF
//SYSIN     DD  DSN=DAVES.TEST.COBOL(SAMPLE),DISP=SHR
```

Notice in the example that I repeated the COBOL2 option. This is because the PARM option completely replaces that which appeared in the PROC. In this example, the COBOL step uses your shop's installed default options.

10.4.2. Using CBL or PROCESS Statements

In addition to using JCL to specify options, you can also imbed the desired options directly at the beginning of the program. This is done with the CBL statement (may also be called PROCESS in COBOL II). I find this exciting because it allows me the ability to affix permanently desired translator and COBOL options to a COBOL program. The technique varies slightly between VS/COBOL and COBOL II, but the statement is coded the same for both.

The CBL statement (again, may be written as PROCESS for COBOL II) appears before the IDENTIFICATION DIVISION statement. There may be more than one of them, if desired. All options specified on CBL statement take precedence over any statements specified via JCL. The CBL statement is always allowed for COBOL II, but requires a specific COBOL compile option for VS/COBOL. (*Note*: Refer back to Figure 2.4, where you will see that the CICS translator uses a CBL statement to force certain COBOL compile options for a COBOL II program.)

The following is the statement syntax:

* CBL must appear somewhere in columns 1–66 (again, PROCESS may be substituted, if desired, with COBOL II).

* Each option must be separated by a comma.

- If CICS options are also specified, they must be in parentheses, proceeded by XOPTS, such as

  CBL XOPTS(ANSI85,NOEDF),TRUNC(BIN).

- No embedded blanks are allowed.

For example, a program that uses lower-case text, does not want EDF processing, and wants optimized binary arithmetic might have this statement within the program:

```
CBL  XOPTS(ANSI85,NOEDF),TRUNC(OPT)
IDENTIFICATION DIVISION.
    .
    .
    .
```

If the CBL statement is to be used with VS/COBOL, be sure to include the BATCH option on the COBOL compiler step. This option, BATCH, tells the VS/COBOL compiler to acknowledge the CBL statement. Otherwise, you will receive an error message, stating that the CBL statement is unknown. *Note*: Specifying BATCH does *not* allow batch compilation with CICS for VS/COBOL programs. The ability to do batch compiles is inherent within COBOL II and COBOL/370.

10.5. LINKAGE EDITOR OPTIONS

There are very few Linkage Editor options that specifically affect a CICS program. Still, they do make a difference.

> **RENT**   (applies only to COBOL/370 and VS/COBOL II) This option is often confused with the COBOL II option of the same name. While both relate to the same concept, the meaning is different. In COBOL II compiles, RENT instructs the compiler to generate reentrant code. Specifying RENT to the Linkage Editor only causes the Linkage Editor to mark the load module as reentrant. *Note*: Specifying a module as RENT when the module is not reentrant (e.g., any VS/COBOL program or a COBOL II module not compiled with RENT) can cause unpredictable results.
>
> Even for COBOL/370 and COBOL II, RENT is only meaningful if the program will be in a shared system area, such

as a Link Pack Area (LPA) for MVS or the SVA for VSE. Otherwise, it generates no benefits. *Note: Reentrant* means that a single copy of a program can be assigned simultaneously to multiple terminals, thereby reducing overall memory requirements.

REUS (irrelevant to COBOL/370, VS COBOL II, and VSE) This option specifies that a program is serially-reuseable, in other words, after one transaction is through with it, the same program may be redispatched to another transaction. This improves performance for OS/VS COBOL applications.

AMODE/RMODE (irrelevant to VSE) These two options are generated automatically by COBOL/370 and COBOL II and should be avoided for OS/VS COBOL programs. If your shop's JCL includes these in the JCL PARM statement, they should be removed. These two options specify where a load module may reside in memory and what memory it can access, and, while they can be overridden for specific needs, you can easily create some unusual abends this way. You should normally see on the Linkage Editor listing that an OS/VS COBOL load module's AMODE and RMODE is 24, and a COBOL II or COBOL/370 load module's AMODE is 31 and RMODE is ANY.

Never attempt to link edit two COBOL CICS programs together unless they were produced by the same compiler. The Linkage Editor will not flag the act as an error, but the load module will not execute properly.

For an example of a Linkage Editor listing, see Figure 10.3. This is an example of a COBOL II program.

In Figure 10.3, notice that the first module is DFHECI, at location 0. This is the CICS interface module that is included by the INCLUDE statement that is inserted into your JCL link edit step (see prior example of compile/link JCL). The DFHECI module must appear first within the loadmodule, even though the logical beginning (the ENTRY address) is at location 48. This ruling applies to both MVS and VSE.

```
MVS/DFP VERSION 3 RELEASE 2 LINKAGE EDITOR
INVOCATION PARAMETERS - SIZE=(2000K,900K),XREF,LIST,RENT
ACTUAL SIZE=(1972224,905216)
OUTPUT DATA SET CICS.TEST.LOAD IS ON VOLUME CICS03
IEW0000  INCLUDE SYSLIB(DFHECI)

                            CROSS REFERENCE TABLE

CONTROL SECTION           ENTRY
NAME  ORIGIN  LENGTH  NAME LOCATION  NAME  LOCATION  NAME LOCATION NAME  LOCATION
DFHECI   00      48
                       DFHEI1    8    DLZEI01    8    DLZEI02    8   DLZEI03     8
                       DLZEI04   8    DFHCBLI   26
SAMPPROG48       8EA
IGZEBST *938     1A8
                       IGZEBS2   A3C

 LOCATION   REFERS TO SYMBOL   IN CONTROL SECTION   LOCATION   REFERS TO SYMBOL IN CONTROL SECTION
   B4          IGZEBST            IGZEBST             E8          DFHEI1           DFHECI
   AD0         GZETUN           $UNRESOLVED(W)        AD4         IGZEOPT        $UNRESOLVED(W)

ENTRY ADDRESS     48
TOTAL LENGTH      AE0
** SAMPPROG DID NOT PREVIOUSLY EXIST BUT WAS ADDED AND HAS AMODE 31
** LOAD MODULE HAS RMODE ANY
** AUTHORIZATION CODE IS        0.
**MODULE HAS BEEN MARKED REENTERABLE, AND REUSABLE.
```

Figure 10.3. Sample Linkage Editor listing for MVS.

SUMMARY

There were several options in this chapter that do not affect your programming. In fact, most of these options are probably set adequately at your shop for any programs you develop early in your CICS experiences. Their usefulness will become more aware to you as you learn more about CICS. This information is useful to you today, but it will be even more useful in the future.

Appendix A:
Using CICS

A.1. LISTINGS OF COMMON CICS AREAS USED IN COBOL PROGRAMS

A.1.1. DFHEIBLK (EIB)

The Executive Interface Block (EIB) is placed in your LINKAGE SEC-
TION *automatically* by the CICS translator program. It must always be
the first entry in the LINKAGE SECTION. This is where CICS places
values prior to giving control to your program and is where you can find
almost any information about your transaction. An example of the EIB
is in Figure A.1. *Tip*: When you want to know the maximum size that
a field may be (e.g., the COMM area), the EIB usually contains such
information simply by examining the size of the field. For example,
EIBCALEN contains the length of the COMM area. In Figure A.1, you
see that it is PIC S9(4) COMP. Since the maximum value is 32K, you
know that a COMM area cannot exceed 32K.

```
  01 EIBLK.
*          EIBTIME      Time  In  0hhmmss  Format
       02  EIBTIME      PIC  S9(7)         COMP-3.
*          EIBDATE      Date  In  00yyddd  Format
       02  EIBDATE      PIC  S9(7)         COMP-3.
*          EIBTRNID     Transaction  Identifier
```

```
      02  EIBTRNID    PIC  X(4).
*         EIBTASKN    Task  Number
      02  EIBTASKN    PIC  S9(7)        COMP-3.
*         EIBTRMID    Terminal  Identifier
      02  EIBTRMID    PIC  X(4).
*         DFHEIGDI    Reserved
      02  DFHEIGDI    PIC  S9(4)        COMP.
*         EIBCPOSN    Cursor  Position
      02  EIBCPOSN    PIC  S9(4)        COMP.
*         EIBCALEN    Commarea  Length
      02  EIBCALEN    PIC  S9(4)        COMP.
*         EIBAID      Attention  Identifier
      02  EIBAID      PIC  X(1).
*         EIBFN       Function  Code
      02  EIBFN       PIC  X(2).
*         EIBRCODE    Response  Code
      02  EIBRCODE    PIC  X(6).
*         EIBDS       Dataset  Name
      02  EIBDS       PIC  X(8).
*         EIBREQID    Request  Identifier
      02  EIBREQID    PIC  X(8).
*         EIBRSRCE    Resource  Name
      02  EIBRSRCE    PIC  X(8).
*         EIBSYNC     X'FF'  -  Syncpoint  Requested
      02  EIBSYNC     PIC  X.
*         EIBFREE     X'FF'  -  Free  Requested
      02  EIBFREE     PIC  X.
*         EIBRECV     X'FF'  -  Receive  Required
      02  EIBRECV     PIC  X.
*         EIBSEND     Reserved
      02  EIBSEND     PIC  X.
*         EIBATT      X'FF'  -  Attach  Data  Received
      02  EIBATT      PIC  X.
*         EIBEOC      X'FF'  -  Eoc  Received
      02  EIBEOC      PIC  X.
*         EIBFMH      X'FF'  -  Fmhs  Received
      02  EIBFMH      PIC  X.
*         EIBCOMPL    X'FF'  -  Data  Complete
      02  EIBCOMPL    PIC  X(1).
*         EIBSIG      X'FF'  -  Signal  Received
```

```
       02  EIBSIG       PIC  X(1).
  *         EIBCONF      X'FF'  -  Confirm  Requested
       02  EIBCONF      PIC  X(1).
  *         EIBERR       X'FF'  -  Error  Received
       02  EIBERR       PIC  X(1).
  *         EIBERRCD     Error  Code  Received
       02  EIBERRCD     PIC  X(4).
  *         EIBSYNRB     X'FF'  -  Sync  Rollback  Requested
       02  EIBSYNRB     PIC  X.
  *         EIBNODAT     X'FF'  -  No  Appl  Data  Received
       02  EIBNODAT     PIC  X.
  *         EIBRESP      Internal  Condition  Number
       02  EIBRESP      PIC  S9(8)        COMP.
  *         EIBRESP2     More  Details  On  Some  Responses
       02  EIBRESP2     PIC  S9(8)        COMP.
  *         EIBRLDBK     Rolled  Back
       02  EIBRLDBK     PIC  X(1).
```

A.1.2. DFHAID

If you plan to control use of AID keys within your program instead of letting CICS do it, or instead of using the HANDLE AID command, then you need to COPY the DFHAID COPYbook member into your WORKING STORAGE section. Since I recommend this technique and use it for examples in the book, I hope that you agree with me that it is a preferable approach. Since you may not know all the possible values to use, a listing of DFHAID entries is in Figure A.2. The test is normally done by comparing the EIB entry containing the value of the AID key (EIBAID) with an entry in DFHAID. For example, to test for use of the PF1 key, the COBOL statement might be

```
IF  EIBAID  =  DFHPF1  ...
```

```
01       DFHAID.
    02   DFHNULL   PIC  X  VALUE  IS  ' '.
    02   DFHENTER  PIC  X  VALUE  IS  QUOTE.
    02   DFHCLEAR  PIC  X  VALUE  IS  '_'.
    02   DFHCLRP   PIC  X  VALUE  IS  '|'.
```

```
02   DFHPEN     PIC   X   VALUE IS '='.
02   DFHOPID    PIC   X   VALUE IS 'W'.
02   DFHMSRE    PIC   X   VALUE IS 'X'.
02   DFHSTRF    PIC   X   VALUE IS 'h'.
02   DFHTRIG    PIC   X   VALUE IS '"'.
02   DFHPA1     PIC   X   VALUE IS '%'.
02   DFHPA2     PIC   X   VALUE IS '>'.
02   DFHPA3     PIC   X   VALUE IS ','.
02   DFHPF1     PIC   X   VALUE IS '1'.
02   DFHPF2     PIC   X   VALUE IS '2'.
02   DFHPF3     PIC   X   VALUE IS '3'.
                 .
                 .
                 .
                 .
02   DFHPF19    PIC   X   VALUE IS 'G'.
02   DFHPF20    PIC   X   VALUE IS 'H'.
02   DFHPF21    PIC   X   VALUE IS 'I'.
02   DFHPF22    PIC   X   VALUE IS '['.
02   DFHPF23    PIC   X   VALUE IS '.'.
02   DFHPF24    PIC   X   VALUE IS '<'.
```

A.1.3.   DFHBMSCA

While I recommend that your shop develop its own COPYbook for
screen attribute characters because you can make the names more
meaningful and can include the attributes that your company uses, I
include here the IBM COPYbook member, DFHBMSCA. Instead of
showing the VALUE clauses (which would be in hex, anyway), I show
the definition of each. Many of them will be unrecognizable to you,
and few will be useful. That is why I recommend (elsewhere in the
book) that you make your own COPYbook.

```
01   DFHBMSCA.
  02   DFHBMPEM   PICTURE X   Printer  end-of-message
  02   DFHBMPNL   PICTURE X   Printer  new-line
  02   DFHBMASK   PICTURE X   Autoskip
```

```
02   DFHBMUNP   PICTURE X   Unprotected
02   DFHBMUNN   PICTURE X   Unprotected, numeric
02   DFHBMPRO   PICTURE X   Protected
02   DFHBMBRY   PICTURE X   Bright
02   DFHBMDAR   PICTURE X   Dark
02   DFHBMFSE   PICTURE X   MDT Set
02   DFHBMPRF   PICTURE X   Protected, MDT set
02   DFHBMASF   PICTURE X   Autoskip, MDT set
02   DFHBMASB   PICTURE X   Autoskip, bright
02   DFHBMPSO   PICTURE X   Shift out X'0E'.
02   DFHBMPSI   PICTURE X   Shift in X'0F'
02   DFHBMEOF   PICTURE X   Field erased
02   DFHBMCUR   PICTURE X   Cursor        (CICS/ESA only)
02   DFHBMFLG   PICTURE X   Flags         (CICS/ESA only)
     88  DFHERASE  VALUES ARE X'80', X'82'.
     88  DFHCURSR  VALUES ARE X'02', X'82'.
02   DFHBMDET   PICTURE X   Field detected
02   DFHSA      PICTURE X   Set attribute
02   DFHCOLOR   PICTURE X   Color
02   DFHPS      PICTURE X   Pogrammed symbols
02   DFHHLT     PICTURE X   Highlight
02   DFH3270    PICTURE X   Base 3270attrribute
02   DFHVAL     PICTURE X   Validation
02   DFHOUTLN   PICTURE X   Field outlining
02   DFHBKTRN   PICTURE X   Background transparency
02   DFHALL     PICTURE X   Reset to defaults
02   DFHERROR   PICTURE X   Error code
02   DFHDFT     PICTURE X   Default
02   DFHDFCOL   PICTURE X   Default color
02   DFHBLUE    PICTURE X   Blue
02   DFHRED     PICTURE X   Red
02   DFHPINK    PICTURE X   Pink
02   DFHGREEN   PICTURE X   Green
02   DFHTURQ    PICTURE X   Turquoise
02   DFHYELLO   PICTURE X   Yellow
02   DFHNEUTR   PICTURE X   Neutral
02   DFHBASE    PICTURE X   Base symbols
02   DFHDFHI    PICTURE X   Normal
02   DFHBLINK   PICTURE X   Blink
```

```
02  DFHREVRS  PICTURE X  Reverse
02  DFHUNDLN  PICTURE X  Underscore
02  DFHMFIL   PICTURE X  Mandatory  fill
02  DFHMENT   PICTURE X  Mandatory  enter
02  DFHMFE    PICTURE X  Mandatory  enter  and  fill
02  DFHUNNOD  PICTURE X  Unprot,  dark,  nonprint,  MDT
02  DFHUNIMD  PICTURE X  Unprot,  intense,  light pen,  MDT
02  DFHUNNUM  PICTURE X  Unprot,  numeric,  MDT
02  DFHUNINT  PICTURE X  Unprot,  num,  intens,  lightP,MDT
02  DFHUNNON  PICTURE X  Unprot,num,dark,nonprint,MDT
02  DFHPROTI  PICTURE X  Prot,lightpen,intense
02  DFHPROTN  PICTURE X  Prot,dark,nonprint
02  DFHMT     PICTURE X  Trigger
02  DFHMFT    PICTURE X  Mandatory  fill  and  trigger
02  DFHMET    PICTURE X  Mandatory  enter  and  trigger
02  DFHMFET   PICTURE X  Mandatory  fill,enter,trigger
02  DFHDFFR   PICTURE X  Default  outline
02  DFHLEFT   PICTURE X  Left  vertical  line
02  DFHOVER   PICTURE X  Overline
02  DFHRIGHT  PICTURE X  Right  vertical  line
02  DFHUNDER  PICTURE X  Underline
02  DFHBOX    PICTURE X  Underline,right/left vert,over
02  DFHSOSI   PICTURE X  SOSI=yes
02  DFHTRANS  PICTURE X  Background  transparency
02  DFHOPAQ   PICTURE X  No  background  transparency
```

A.1.4. DLIUIB

If your program interacts with DL/I, you will need the DLIUIB COPYbook member for the scheduling call. This feature is covered elsewhere in the book. For COBOL II, I recommend that the member be changed to reflect COBOL II's POINTER capability (explained more fully in the *COBOL II Power Programming* book. As with other COPYbook members that use hex values, such as DFHBMSCA, the VALUE clauses are often nonprintable and should *not* be modified.

```
  01  DLIUIB
*     DLIUIB       EXTENDED CALL USER INTERFACE BLOCK
      02 UIBPCBAL PICTURE S9(8) USAGE IS COMPUTATIONAL.
*        UIBPCBAL      PCB ADDRESS LIST
      02 UIBRCODE.
*        UIBRCODE      DL/I RETURN CODES
         03  UIBFCTR PICTURE X.
*             UIBFCTR      RETURN CODES
             88  FCNORESP     VALUE ''.
             88  FCNOTOPEN    VALUE ' '.
             88  FCINVREQ     VALUE ' '.
             88  FCINVPCB     VALUE ' '
         03  UIBDLTR PICTURE X.
*             UIBDLTR      ADDITIONAL INFORMATION
             88  DLPSBNF      VALUE ' '.
             88  DLTASKNA     VALUE ' '.
             88  DLPSBSCH     VALUE ' '.
             88  DLLANGCON    VALUE ' '.
             88  DLPSBFAIL    VALUE ' '.
             88  DLPSBNA      VALUE ' '.
             88  DLTERMNS     VALUE ' '.
             88  DLFUNCNS     VALUE ' '.
             88  DLINA        VALUE '~'.
```

A.2.   CICS TABLES

Regrettably, CICS tables seem to retain an aura of mystique, partially because most of them are now administered by systems programmers. That perception is unfortunate, as you and I rarely need to know anything about the actual tables. I have always found that a supportive technical services group can alleviate all such concerns. Yes, there was a time when programmers updated these tables themselves, but that doesn't mean it was a productive time. While we may moan and groan when procedures are instituted that regulate changes to the CICS tables, most of us do better in such an environment.

I never really wanted accountability for everything; I just wanted to know what was going on. The best technical services groups keep that in mind and actively seek your feedback. The worst ones (yes, they're still there) become annoyed or angry whenever a programmer questions anything. If you ever feel that your technical services personnel are giving you short shrift, I encourage you to get closer to them. Too often, our technical personnel receive so many bruises that they develop a hard attitude toward our needs. If we focus on personalities alone, we will fail in the pursuit of our goal. I have always found that I could easily assemble supporters towards any reasonable goal if I only remembered to view each person as an individual, and not as a cog in a wheel.

I know, you may be thinking that programmers shouldn't care about such "politics," and there are many senior personnel (possibly in your shop) who encourage such an attitude towards the technical support staff. Well, dear reader, that's just not productive. We're all in this together, and, as a beginning CICS programmer, I do encourage you to get to know those persons who make CICS function at your shop. Who knows? You may find out some special features that aren't known to the rest of us. You will also be rewarded to find that many members of your technical support staff do not know the application-oriented functions of CICS, allowing you to contribute to their knowledge while learning from them. This two-way dialogue can only benefit both of you.

The following information is primarily a recap of information presented elsewhere in this book. Your main concern should be to ensure the right information is stored there, rather than to be concerned on how the data is entered into these tables or how it is stored. (No, these are not all of the CICS tables. If you ever change your career goals and become a systems programmer, you will then need such information. Otherwise, it's a waste of your valuable time.)

A.2.1. FCT

The FCT (File Control Table) is necessary for the transparent interface for I/O from CICS. You will recall that CICS only uses an eight-byte name for all files. That simplifies the programming considerations, but anything that simplifies a process usually requires more planning efforts. So it is with the FCT. The FCT provides a means for CICS to tie the eight-byte name in the CICS commands to the real dataset name as defined in the particular operating environment (such as MVS or VSE). This allows a high degree of portability of programs between two environments that are not 100 percent compatible otherwise.

The FCT also provides a degree (but only a degree) of security. For example, the FCT contains information on what types of accesses to a file are allowed, such as READ, BROWSE, WRITE. If a file is intended for read-only processing, the FCT can be an effective enforcement tool. CICS commands that are otherwise correctly coded will receive INVREQ as a condition code if an attempt is made to access the file in an unauthorized fashion.

A.2.2. PCT

We've covered this pretty well, I think. The Program Control Table (PCT) ties the four-byte transaction code to the program that should be invoked. The only programs that need a transaction ID are those programs that are invoked directly by a terminal user or by CICS (via RETURN TRANSID command). All other programs should not be listed here. The PCT was once a prime means to enforce system security, but that is disappearing with ESA, relying instead on other products (such as IBM's RACF) for this important function.

A.2.3. PPT

The Processing Program Table (PPT) must contain an entry for every program that will be invoked from CICS commands (e.g., LINK, XCTL) or from a PCT entry. Programs that are invoked directly from operating systems services (e.g. a dynamic CALL statement), and that do not contain any CICS commands, do not need to be identified here. In addition to programs, all MAPSETs are stored in the PPT (each individual MAP is not identified).

A.2.4. TCT

The TCT (Terminal Control Table) is beyond our concerns in this book. This is where information on all terminals is stored so CICS knows what type of terminal it is interacting with. The TCT informs CICS about such concerns as screen size, color options, and other terminal attributes that could affect the CICS commands that may be issued to it. Maintaining the TCT is obviously a responsibility of a central technical group. Unfortunately, we usually take this service for granted.

A.3. CICS CONTROL BLOCKS

CICS has several internal control blocks that, once upon a time, were considered important by application programmers. That was in a time when it was common to access and modify these control areas. Today, fortunately, CICS has reached a level of performance and integrity where such casual access is discouraged. As such, I envision many of these control areas will recede into inaccessible areas of the system or otherwise disappear from the application programmer's view. For that reason, I avoid using these areas in this book and encourage you, if you are maintaining a program that accesses them, to plan new ways to accomplish the same goal.

There was a time, not so long ago, when teaching the control areas was part of any CICS training course. In most cases, it was a tendency to keep bowing at the temples of former gods. (I can also recall when, as a young instructor, I insisted on teaching students how to write programs in machine language. It served no purpose other than to annoy the students, but I thought it was important at the time. Thank goodness I was able to learn from the experience!)

This information is presented primarily so you can relate to the terms, not so you can use the data areas directly.

A.3.1. CSA

You should never need to access the CSA (Common System Area) for application programs. This is a control block for central control of the CICS environment.

A.3.2. TCA

This is a dynamic area, containing information from the TCT (the affected terminal) and the transaction that is interacting with it (from the PCT). This ties physical terminals to the appropriate transaction. To me, the TCA is sort of a "traffic cop." Remember, a task is a single invocation of a program for an interaction with a terminal. A dialogue will consist of multiple tasks.

A.3.3. TIOA

Similar to the dynamic structure of the TCA, the TIOA contains data that is to be directed to/from a given terminal. As you might envision, the TIOA and TCA are interconnected.

A.4.   CICS COMMAND SYNTAX

This section lists most CICS commands but without explanation. Those that are covered in this book can be identified by entries in the table of contents or in the index. Other commands that are listed may require that you collect additional information prior to using them. As you progress in your career, their use will become more apparent.

ABEND

```
EXEC CICS  ABEND
     [ ABCODE() ]
     [ CANCEL ]
     [ NODUMP ]
END-EXEC
```

ADDRESS

```
EXEC CICS  ADDRESS SET()
     USING()
     [ HANDLE | NOHANDLE [ RESP() ] ]
END-EXEC
```

ALLOCATE

```
EXEC CICS  ALLOCATE
     SESSION() | SYSID()
     [ PROFILE() ]
     [ NOQUEUE | NOSUSPEND ]
     [ HANDLE | NOHANDLE [ RESP() ] ]
END-EXEC
```

ASKTIME

```
EXEC CICS  ASKTIME
     [ ABSTIME() ]
END-EXEC
```

ASSIGN

```
EXEC CICS  ASSIGN
     [ ABCODE() ]
     [ APPLID() ]
     [ BTRANS() ]
     [ COLOR() ]
```

[CWALENG()]
[DELIMITER()]
[DESTCOUNT()]
[DESTID()]
[DESTIDLENG()]
[EXTDS()]
[FACILITY()]
[FCI()]
[GCHARS()]
[GCODES()]
[HILIGHT()]
[INPARTN()]
[KATAKANA()]
[LDCMNEM()]
[LDCNUM()]
[MAPCOLUMN()]
[MAPHEIGHT()]
[MAPLINE()]
[MAPWIDTH()]
[MSRCONTROL()]
[NETNAME()]
[NUMTAB()]
[OPCLASS()]
[OPERKEYS()]
[OPID()]
[OPSECURITY()]
[OUTLINE()]
[PAGENUM()]
[PARTNPAGE()]
[PARTNSET()]
[PARTNS()]
[PRINSYSID()]
[PS()]
[QNAME()]
[RESTART()]
[SCRNHT()]
[SCRNWD()]
[SIGDATA()]
[SOSI()]
[STARTCODE()]
[STATIONID()]
[SYSID()]

```
            [ TCTUALENG() ]
            [ TELLERID() ]
            [ TERMCODE() ]
            [ TWALENG() ]
            [ UNATTEND() ]
            [ USERID() ]
            [ VALIDATION() ]
    END-EXEC
```

BIF

```
    EXEC CICS  BIF DEEDIT
            FIELD()
            [ LENGTH() ]
    END-EXEC
```

BUILD

```
    EXEC CICS  BUILD ATTACH
            ATTACHID()
            [ IUTYPE() ]
            [ DATASTR() ]
            [ RECFM() ]
            [ PROCESS() ]
            [ RESOURCE() ]
            [ RPROCESS() ]
            [ RRESOURCE() ]
            [ QUEUE() ]
            [ HANDLE | NOHANDLE [ RESP() ] ]
    END-EXEC
```

CANCEL

```
    EXEC CICS  CANCEL
            [ REQID() [ TRANSID() ] [ SYSID() ] ]
            [ HANDLE | NOHANDLE [ RESP() ] ]
    END-EXEC
```

CONNECT

```
    EXEC CICS  CONNECT PROCESS
            SESSION() | CONVID()
            PROCNAME()
            [ PROCLENGTH() ]
            SYNCLEVEL()
```

```
            [ PIPLIST() [ PIPLENGTH() ] ]
            [ HANDLE | NOHANDLE [ RESP() ] ]
      END-EXEC
```

CONVERSE

```
      EXEC CICS  CONVERSE
            [ FROM() [ FROMLENGTH() | FROMFLENGTH() ]
            [ FMH ] ]
            [ LDC() ]
            [ SET() | INTO() ]
            [ TOLENGTH() | TOFLENGTH() ]
            [ MAXLENGTH() | MAXFLENGTH() ]
            [ NOTRUNCATE ]
            [ DEST() ]
            [ LINEADDR() ]
            [ SESSION() | CONVID() ]
            [ ATTACHID() ]
            [ STRFIELD | [ ERASE ] [ CTLCHAR() ] ]
            [ ASIS ]
            [ LEAVEKB ]
            [ DEFRESP ]
            [ PSEUDOBIN ]
            [ HANDLE | NOHANDLE [ RESP() ] ]
      END-EXEC
```

DELAY

```
      EXEC CICS  DELAY
            [ INTERVAL() | TIME() ]
            [ REQID() ]
            [ HANDLE | NOHANDLE [ RESP() ] ]
      END-EXEC
```

DELETE

```
      EXEC CICS  DELETE
            FILE()
            [ SYSID() ]
            [ RIDFLD() [ KEYLENGTH() [ GENERIC [
            NUMREC() ] ] ]
            [ RBA | RRN ]
            [ HANDLE | NOHANDLE [ RESP() ] ]
      END-EXEC
```

```
EXEC CICS  DELETEQ TD
     QUEUE()
     [ SYSID() ]
     [ HANDLE | NOHANDLE [ RESP() ] ]
END-EXEC

EXEC CICS  DELETEQ TS
     QUEUE()
     [ SYSID() ]
     [ HANDLE | NOHANDLE [ RESP() ] ]
END-EXEC
```

DEQ

```
EXEC CICS  DEQ
     RESOURCE()
     [ LENGTH() ]
     [ HANDLE | NOHANDLE [ RESP() ] ]
END-EXEC
```

DISABLE

```
EXEC CICS  DISABLE
     PROGRAM()
     [ ENTRYNAME() ]
     [ EXIT() | EXITALL ]
     [ STOP ]
     [ TASKSTART ]
     [ HANDLE | NOHANDLE [ RESP() ] ]
END-EXEC
```

DUMP

```
EXEC CICS  DUMP
     DUMPCODE()
     [ FROM() LENGTH() | FLENGTH() ]
     [ TASK ]
     [ STORAGE ]
     [ PROGRAM ]
     [ TERMINAL ]
     [ TABLES ]
     [ COMPLETE ]
     [ PCT ]
     [ PPT ]
```

```
                    [ SIT ]
                    [ TCT ]
                    [ FCT ]
                    [ DCT ]
                    [ HANDLE | NOHANDLE [ RESP() ] ]
            END-EXEC
```

ENABLE

```
      EXEC CICS  ENABLE
            PROGRAM()
            [ EXIT() ]
            [ ENTRY() ]
            [ GALENGTH() | GAENTRYNAME() ]
            [ ENTRYNAME() ]
            [ TALENGTH() ]
            [ START ]
            [ TASKSTART ]
            [ HANDLE | NOHANDLE [ RESP() ] ]
      END-EXEC
```

ENDBR

```
      EXEC CICS  ENDBR
            FILE()
            [ SYSID() ]
            [ REQID( ) ]
            [ HANDLE | NOHANDLE [ RESP() ] ]
      END-EXEC
```

ENQ

```
      EXEC CICS  ENQ
            RESOURCE()
            [ LENGTH() ]
            [ NOSUSPEND ]
            [ HANDLE | NOHANDLE [ RESP() ] ]
      END-EXEC
```

ENTER

```
      EXEC CICS  ENTER
            TRACEID()
            [ FROM() ]
            [ RESOURCE() ]
```

```
        [ ENTRYNAME() ]
        [ ACCOUNT ]
        [ MONITOR ]
        [ PERFORM ]
        [ HANDLE | NOHANDLE [ RESP() ] ]
  END-EXEC
```

EXTRACT

```
  EXEC CICS  EXTRACT ATTACH
        [ SESSION() | CONVID() ]
        [ ATTACHID() ]
        [ IUTYPE() ]
        [ DATASTR() ]
        [ RECFM() ]
        [ PROCESS() ]
        [ RESOURCE() ]
        [ RPROCESS() ]
        [ RRESOURCE() ]
        [ QUEUE() ]
        [ HANDLE | NOHANDLE [ RESP() ] ]
  END-EXEC

  EXEC CICS  EXTRACT EXIT
        PROGRAM()
        GASET()
        GALENGTH()
        [ ENTRYNAME() ]
        [ HANDLE | NOHANDLE [ RESP() ] ]
  END-EXEC

  EXEC CICS  EXTRACT LOGONMSG
        SET() | INTO()
        LENGTH()
        [ HANDLE | NOHANDLE [ RESP() ] ]
  END-EXEC

  EXEC CICS  EXTRACT PROCESS
        [ SESSION() | CONVID() ]
        [ PROCNAME() PROCLENGTH() ]
        [ SYNCLEVEL() ]
        [ PIPLIST() PIPLENGTH() ]
        [ HANDLE | NOHANDLE [ RESP() ] ]
  END-EXEC
```

330 CICS: A HOW-TO FOR COBOL PROGRAMMERS

```
EXEC CICS  EXTRACT TCT
     NETNAME()
     [ TERMID() | SYSID() ]
     [ HANDLE | NOHANDLE [ RESP() ] ]
END-EXEC
```

FORMATTIME

```
EXEC CICS  FORMATTIME
     ABSTIME()
     [ YYDDD() ]
     [ YYMMDD() ]
     [ YYDDMM() ]
     [ DDMMYY() ]
     [ MMDDYY() ]
     [ DATE() [ DATEFORM() ] ]
     [ DATESEP() ]
     [ DAYCOUNT() ]
     [ DAYOFWEEK() ]
     [ DAYOFMONTH() ]
     [ MONTHOFYEAR() ]
     [ YEAR() ]
     [ TIME() [ TIMESEP() ] ]
     [ HANDLE | NOHANDLE [ RESP() ] ]
END-EXEC
```

FREE

```
EXEC CICS  FREE
     [ SESSION() | CONVID() ]
     [ HANDLE | NOHANDLE [ RESP() ] ]
END-EXEC
```

FREEMAIN

```
EXEC CICS  FREEMAIN
     DATA()
END-EXEC
```

GETMAIN

```
EXEC CICS  GETMAIN
     SET()
     LENGTH() | FLENGTH()
     [ INITIMG() ]
```

```
        [ SHARED ]
        [ NOSUSPEND ]
        [ HANDLE | NOHANDLE [ RESP() ] ]
   END-EXEC
```

HANDLE

```
   EXEC CICS  HANDLE ABEND
        [ LABEL() | PROGRAM() | CANCEL | RESET ]
        [ HANDLE | NOHANDLE [ RESP() ] ]
   END-EXEC

   EXEC CICS  HANDLE AID
        [ ANYKEY() ]
        [ OPERID() ]
        [ PA1() ]
        [ PA2() ]
        [ CLEAR() ]
        [ PA3() ]
        [ PF1() ]
        [ PF2() ]
        [ PF3() ]
        [ PF4() ]
        [ PF5() ]
        [ PF6() ]
        [ PF7() ]
        [ PF8() ]
        [ PF9() ]
        [ PF10() ]
        [ PF11() ]
        [ PF12() ]
        [ ENTER() ]
        [ LIGHTPEN() ]
        [ PF13() ]
        [ PF14() ]
        [ PF15() ]
        [ PF16() ]
        [ PF17() ]
        [ PF18() ]
        [ PF19() ]
        [ PF20() ]
        [ PF21() ]
        [ PF22() ]
```

```
      [ PF23() ]
      [ PF24() ]
      [ CLRPARTN() ]
      [ TRIGGER() ]
      [ HANDLE | NOHANDLE [ RESP() ] ]
END-EXEC

EXEC CICS  HANDLE CONDITION
      [ ERROR() ]
      [ RDATT() ]
      [ WRBRK() ]
      [ EOF() ]
      [ EODS() ]
      [ EOC() ]
      [ ENDINPT() ]
      [ NONVAL() ]
      [ NOSTART() ]
      [ TERMIDERR() ]
      [ DUPREC() ]
      [ DUPKEY() ]
      [ INVREQ() ]
      [ IOERR() ]
      [ NOSPACE() ]
      [ NOTOPEN() ]
      [ ENDFILE() ]
      [ ILLOGIC() ]
      [ LENGERR() ]
      [ QZERO() ]
      [ SIGNAL() ]
      [ QBUSY() ]
      [ ITEMERR() ]
      [ PGMIDERR() ]
      [ TRANSIDERR() ]
      [ ENDDATA() ]
      [ INVTSREQ() ]
      [ EXPIRED() ]
      [ RETPAGE() ]
      [ RTEFAIL() ]
      [ RTESOME() ]
      [ TSIOERR() ]
      [ INVERRTERM() ]
      [ INVMPSZ() ]
```

[IGREQID()]
[OVERFLOW()]
[INVLDC()]
[NOSTG()]
[JIDERR()]
[QIDERR()]
[NOJBUFSP()]
[DSSTAT()]
[SELNERR()]
[FUNCERR()]
[UNEXPIN()]
[NOPASSBKRD()]
[NOPASSBKWR()]
[SYSIDERR()]
[ISCINVREQ()]
[ENQBUSY()]
[ENVDEFERR()]
[IGREQCD()]
[SESSIONERR()]
[SYSBUSY()]
[SESSBUSY()]
[NOTALLOC()]
[CBIDERR()]
[INVEXITREQ()]
[MAPFAIL()]
[INBFMH()]
[NOTFND()]
[INVPARTNSET()]
[INVPARTN()]
[PARTNFAIL()]
[TERMERR()]
[ROLLEDBACK()]
[END()]
[DISABLED()]
[ALLOCERR()]
[STRELERR()]
[OPENERR()]
[SPOLBUSY()]
[SPOLERR()]
[NODEIDERR()]
[NOSPOOL()]
[NOTAUTH()]

```
        [ FILENOTFOUND() ]
        [ SUPPRESSED() ]
        [ LOADING() ]
        [ OUTDESCRERR() ]
        [ HANDLE | NOHANDLE [ RESP() ] ]
    END-EXEC
```

IGNORE

```
    EXEC CICS  IGNORE CONDITION
        [ ERROR ]
        [ RDATT ]
        [ WRBRK ]
        [ EOF ]
        [ EODS ]
        [ EOC ]
        [ ENDINPT ]
        [ NONVAL ]
        [ NOSTART ]
        [ TERMIDERR ]
        [ DUPREC ]
        [ DUPKEY ]
        [ INVREQ ]
        [ IOERR ]
        [ NOSPACE ]
        [ NOTOPEN ]
        [ ENDFILE ]
        [ ILLOGIC ]
        [ LENGERR ]
        [ QZERO ]
        [ SIGNAL ]
        [ QBUSY ]
        [ ITEMERR ]
        [ PGMIDERR ]
        [ TRANSIDERR ]
        [ ENDDATA ]
        [ INVTSREQ ]
        [ EXPIRED ]
        [ RETPAGE ]
        [ RTEFAIL ]
        [ RTESOME ]
        [ TSIOERR ]
```

[INVERRTERM]
[INVMPSZ]
[IGREQID]
[OVERFLOW]
[INVLDC]
[NOSTG]
[JIDERR]
[QIDERR]
[NOJBUFSP]
[DSSTAT]
[SELNERR]
[FUNCERR]
[UNEXPIN]
[NOPASSBKRD]
[NOPASSBKWR]
[SYSIDERR]
[ISCINVREQ]
[ENQBUSY]
[ENVDEFERR]
[IGREQCD]
[SESSIONERR]
[SYSBUSY]
[SESSBUSY]
[NOTALLOC]
[CBIDERR]
[INVEXITREQ]
[MAPFAIL]
[INBFMH]
[NOTFND]
[INVPARTNSET]
[INVPARTN]
[PARTNFAIL]
[TERMERR]
[ROLLEDBACK]
[END]
[DISABLED]
[ALLOCERR]
[STRELERR]
[OPENERR]
[SPOLBUSY]
[SPOLRR]
[NODEIDERR]

```
            [ NOSPOOL ]
            [ NOTAUTH ]
            [ FILENOTFOUND ]
            [ SUPPRESSED ]
            [ LOADING ]
            [ OUTDESCRERR ]
            [ HANDLE | NOHANDLE [ RESP() ] ]
    END-EXEC
```

INQUIRE

```
    EXEC CICS  INQUIRE CONNECTION()
            [ START | END | NEXT ]
            [ NETNAME() ]
            [ ACCESSMETHOD() ]
            [ PROTOCOL() ]
            [ ACQSTATUS() ]
            [ CONNSTATUS() ]
            [ SERVSTATUS() ]
            [ PENDSTATUS() ]
            [ XLNSTATUS() ]
            [ HANDLE | NOHANDLE [ RESP() ] ]
    END-EXEC

    EXEC CICS  INQUIRE FILE()
            [ ACCESSMETHOD() ]
            [ TYPE() ]
            [ DSNAME() ]
            [ OBJECT() ]
            [ REMOTESYSTEM() ]
            [ REMOTENAME() ]
            [ BASEDSNAME() ]
            [ RECORDFORMAT() ]
            [ BLOCKFORMAT() ]
            [ KEYLENGTH() ]
            [ KEYPOSITION() ]
            [ RECORDSIZE() ]
            [ BLOCKSIZE() ]
            [ DISPOSITION() ]
            [ LSRPOOLID() ]
            [ STRINGS() ]
            [ OPENSTATUS() ]
            [ ENABLESTATUS() ]
```

```
        [ RECOVSTATUS() ]
        [ EMPTYSTATUS() ]
        [ READ() ]
        [ UPDATE() ]
        [ BROWSE() ]
        [ DELETE() ]
        [ ADD() ]
        [ RELTYPE() ]
        [ EXCLUSIVE() ]
        [ BLOCKKEYLEN() ]
        [ HANDLE | NOHANDLE [ RESP() ] ]
END-EXEC

EXEC CICS  INQUIRE MODENAME()
        [ START | END | CONNECTION() [ NEXT ]
        [ MAXIMUM() ]
        [ AVAILABLE() ] [ ACTIVE() ] ]
        [ HANDLE | NOHANDLE [ RESP() ] ]
END-EXEC

EXEC CICS  INQUIRE NETNAME()
        [ TERMINAL() ]
        [ REMOTESYSTEM() ]
        [ MODENAME() ]
        [ TRANSACTION() ]
        [ TERMPRIORITY() ]
        [ USERAREA() ]
        [ USERAREALEN() ]
        [ OPERID() ]
        [ USERID() ]
        [ DEVICE() ]
        [ TERMMODEL() ]
        [ ACCESSMETHOD() ]
        [ CREATESESS() ]
        [ ACQSTATUS() ]
        [ SERVSTATUS() ]
        [ ATISTATUS() ]
        [ TTISTATUS() ]
        [ PAGESTATUS() ]
        [ SCREENHEIGHT() ]
        [ SCREENWIDTH() ]
        [ GCHARS() ]
```

```
            [ GCODES() ]
            [ HANDLE | NOHANDLE [ RESP() ] ]
      END-EXEC

      EXEC CICS  INQUIRE PROGRAM()
            [ START | END | NEXT ]
            [ LANGUAGE() ]
            [ PROGTYPE() ]
            [ STATUS() ]
            [ LENGTH() ]
            [ RESCOUNT() ]
            [ USECOUNT() ]
            [ HANDLE | NOHANDLE [ RESP() ] ]
      END-EXEC

      EXEC CICS  INQUIRE SYSTEM
            [ RELEASE() ]
            [ OPSYS() ]
            [ OPREL() ]
            [ MAXTASKS() ]
            [ AMAXTASKS() ]
            [ AKP() ]
            [ CUSHION() ]
            [ TIME() ]
            [ RUNAWAY() ]
            [ STALL() ]
            [ HANDLE | NOHANDLE [ RESP() ] ]
      END-EXEC

      EXEC CICS  INQUIRE TERMINAL()
            [ NETNAME() ]
            [ START | END | NEXT ]
            [ REMOTESYSTEM() ]
            [ MODENAME() ]
            [ TRANSACTION() ]
            [ TERMPRIORITY() ]
            [ USERAREA() ]
            [ USERAREALEN() ]
            [ OPERID() ]
            [ USERID() ]
            [ DEVICE() ]
            [ TERMMODEL() ]
            [ ACCESSMETHOD() ]
```

```
        [ CREATESESS() ]
        [ ACQSTATUS() ]
        [ SERVSTATUS() ]
        [ ATISTATUS() ]
        [ TTISTATUS() ]
        [ PAGESTATUS() ]
        [ SCREENHEIGHT() ]
        [ SCREENWIDTH() ]
        [ GCHARS() ]
        [ GCODES() ]
        [ HANDLE | NOHANDLE [ RESP() ] ]
  END-EXEC

EXEC CICS  INQUIRE TRANSACTION()
        [ START | END | NEXT ]
        [ REMOTESYSTEM() ]
        [ PROGRAM() ]
        [ STATUS() ]
        [ PRIORITY() ]
        [ HANDLE | NOHANDLE [ RESP() ] ]
  END-EXEC
```

ISSUE

```
EXEC CICS  ISSUE ABEND
        [ SESSION() | CONVID() ]
        [ HANDLE | NOHANDLE [ RESP() ] ]
  END-EXEC

EXEC CICS  ISSUE ABORT
        [ DESTID() [ DESTIDLENG() ] ] | [ SUBADDR()]
        [ CONSOLE | PRINT | CARD |
        WPMEDIA1 | WPMEDIA2 | WPMEDIA3 |
        WPMEDIA4 ] ]
        [ DFTPROF ]
        [ VOLUME() [ VOLUMELENG() ] ]
        [ HANDLE | NOHANDLE [ RESP() ] ]
  END-EXEC

EXEC CICS  ISSUE ADD
        DESTID()
        [ DESTIDLENG() ]
        [ VOLUME() [ VOLUMELENG() ] ]
```

```
            FROM()
            [ LENGTH() ]
            [ NUMREC() ]
            [ DEFRESP ]
            [ NOWAIT ]
            [ RIDFLD() RRN ]
            [ HANDLE | NOHANDLE [ RESP() ] ]
     END-EXEC

     EXEC CICS  ISSUE CONFIRMATION
            [ SESSION() | CONVID() ]
            [ HANDLE | NOHANDLE [ RESP() ] ]
     END-EXEC

     EXEC CICS  ISSUE COPY
            TERMID()
            [ CTLCHAR() ]
            [ WAIT ]
            [ HANDLE | NOHANDLE [ RESP() ] ]
     END-EXEC

     EXEC CICS  ISSUE DISCONNECT
            [ SESSION() ]
            [ HANDLE | NOHANDLE [ RESP() ] ]
     END-EXEC

     EXEC CICS  ISSUE END
            [ DESTID() [ DESTIDLENG() ] |
            [ SUBADDR() ]
            [ CONSOLE | PRINT | CARD |
            WPMEDIA1 | WPMEDIA2 | WPMEDIA3 |
            WPMEDIA4 ] ]
            [ DFTPROF ]
            [ VOLUME() [ VOLUMELENG() ] ]
            [ HANDLE | NOHANDLE [ RESP() ] ]
     END-EXEC

     EXEC CICS  ISSUE ENDOUTPUT
            [ ENDFILE ]
            [ HANDLE | NOHANDLE [ RESP() ] ]
     END-EXEC

     EXEC CICS  ISSUE EODS
            [ HANDLE | NOHANDLE [ RESP() ] ]
```

```
END-EXEC

EXEC CICS  ISSUE ERASE
     DESTID()
     [ DESTIDLENG() ]
     [ VOLUME() [ VOLUMELENG() ] ]
     RIDFLD()
          [[ KEYLENGTH() ] [ KEYNUMBER() ] | RRN ]
     [ NUMREC() ]
     [ DEFRESP ]
     [ NOWAIT ]
     [ HANDLE | NOHANDLE [ RESP() ] ]
END-EXEC

EXEC CICS  ISSUE ERASEAUP
     [ WAIT ]
     [ HANDLE | NOHANDLE [ RESP() ] ]
END-EXEC

EXEC CICS  ISSUE ERROR
     [ SESSION() | CONVID() ]
     [ HANDLE | NOHANDLE [ RESP() ] ]
END-EXEC

EXEC CICS  ISSUE LOAD
     PROGRAM()
     [ CONVERSE ]
     [ HANDLE | NOHANDLE [ RESP() ] ]
END-EXEC

EXEC CICS  ISSUE NOTE
     DESTID()
     [ DESTIDLENG() ]
     [ VOLUME() [ VOLUMELENG() ] ]
     RIDFLD()
     RRN
     [ HANDLE | NOHANDLE [ RESP() ] ]
END-EXEC

EXEC CICS  ISSUE PASS
     LUNAME()
     [ FROM() LENGTH() ]
     [ HANDLE | NOHANDLE [ RESP() ] ]
END-EXEC
```

```
EXEC CICS  ISSUE PREPARE
     [ SESSION() | CONVID() ]
     [ HANDLE | NOHANDLE [ RESP() ] ]
END-EXEC

EXEC CICS  ISSUE PRINT
     [ HANDLE | NOHANDLE [ RESP() ] ]
END-EXEC

EXEC CICS  ISSUE QUERY
     DESTID()
     [ DESTIDLENG() ]
     [ VOLUME() [ VOLUMELENG() ] ]
     [ HANDLE | NOHANDLE [ RESP() ] ]
END-EXEC

EXEC CICS  ISSUE RECEIVE
     SET() | INTO()
     [ LENGTH() ]
     [ HANDLE | NOHANDLE [ RESP() ] ]
END-EXEC

EXEC CICS  ISSUE REPLACE
     DESTID()
     [ DESTIDLENG() ]
     [ VOLUME() [ VOLUMELENG() ] ]
     FROM()
     [ LENGTH() ]
     RIDFLD()
          [[ KEYLENGTH() ] [ KEYNUMBER() ] | RRN ]
     [ NUMREC() ]
     [ DEFRESP ]
     [ NOWAIT ]
     [ HANDLE | NOHANDLE [ RESP() ] ]
END-EXEC

EXEC CICS  ISSUE RESET
     [ HANDLE | NOHANDLE [ RESP() ] ]
END-EXEC

EXEC CICS  ISSUE SEND
     FROM()
     [ LENGTH() ]
     [ DESTID() [ DESTIDLENG() ] ] |
```

```
        [ SUBADDR() ] [ CONSOLE | PRINT | CARD |
        WPMEDIA1 | WPMEDIA2 | WPMEDIA3 |
        WPMEDIA4 ] ]
        [ DFTPROF ]
        [ VOLUME() [ VOLUMELENG() ] ]
        [ NOWAIT ]
        [ DEFRESP ]
        [ HANDLE | NOHANDLE [ RESP() ] ]
END-EXEC

EXEC CICS  ISSUE SIGNAL
        [ SESSION() | CONVID() ]
        [ HANDLE | NOHANDLE [ RESP() ] ]
END-EXEC

EXEC CICS  ISSUE WAIT
        [ DESTID() [ DESTIDLENG() ] ] |
        [ SUBADDR() ] [ CONSOLE | PRINT | CARD |
        WPMEDIA1 | WPMEDIA2 | WPMEDIA3 |
        WPMEDIA4 ] ]
        [ DFTPROF ]
        [ VOLUME() [ VOLUMELENG() ] ]
        [ HANDLE | NOHANDLE [ RESP() ] ]
END-EXEC
```

JOURNAL

```
EXEC CICS  JOURNAL
        JFILEID()
        JTYPEID()
        FROM()
        [ LENGTH() ]
        [ REQID() ]
        [ PREFIX() [ PFXLENG() ] ]
        [ NOSUSPEND ]
        [ STARTIO ]
        [ WAIT ]
        [ HANDLE | NOHANDLE [ RESP() ] ]
END-EXEC
```

LINK

```
EXEC CICS  LINK
        PROGRAM()
```

```
          [ COMMAREA() [ LENGTH() ] ]
          [ HANDLE | NOHANDLE [ RESP() ] ]
     END-EXEC
```

LOAD

```
     EXEC CICS  LOAD
          PROGRAM()
          [ SET() ]
          [ LENGTH() | FLENGTH() ]
          [ ENTRY() ]
          [ HOLD ]
          [ HANDLE | NOHANDLE [ RESP() ] ]
     END-EXEC
```

POINT

```
     EXEC CICS  POINT
          [ SESSION() | CONVID() ]
          [ HANDLE | NOHANDLE [ RESP() ] ]
     END-EXEC
```

POP

```
     EXEC CICS  POP
          HANDLE
          [ HANDLE | NOHANDLE [ RESP() ] ]
     END-EXEC
```

POST

```
     EXEC CICS  POST
          [ INTERVAL() | TIME() ]
          [ REQID() ]
          SET()
          [ HANDLE | NOHANDLE [ RESP() ] ]
     END-EXEC
```

PURGE

```
     EXEC CICS PURGE  MESSAGE
          [ HANDLE | NOHANDLE [ RESP() ] ]
     END-EXEC
```

PUSH

```
     EXEC CICS  PUSH
```

```
        HANDLE
        [ HANDLE | NOHANDLE [ RESP() ] ]
    END-EXEC
```

READ

```
    EXEC CICS  READ
        FILE()
        [ SYSID() ]
        SET() | INTO()
        [ LENGTH() ]
        RIDFLD()
        [ KEYLENGTH() [ GENERIC ] ]
        [ RBA | RRN | DEBREC | DEBKEY ]
        [ GTEQ | EQUAL ]
        [ UPDATE ]
        [ HANDLE | NOHANDLE [ RESP() ] ]
    END-EXEC

    EXEC CICS  READNEXT
        FILE()
        [ SYSID() ]
        SET() | INTO()
        [ LENGTH() ]
        RIDFLD()
        [ KEYLENGTH() ]
        [ REQID() ]
        [ RBA | RRN ]
        [ HANDLE | NOHANDLE [ RESP() ] ]
    END-EXEC

    EXEC CICS  READPREV
        FILE()
        [ SYSID() ]
        SET() | INTO()
        [ LENGTH() ]
        RIDFLD()
        [ KEYLENGTH() ]
        [ REQID() ]
        [ RBA | RRN ]
        [ HANDLE | NOHANDLE [ RESP() ] ]
    END-EXEC
```

```
EXEC CICS  READQ TS
     QUEUE()
     [ SYSID() ]
     SET() | INTO()
     [ LENGTH() ]
     [ ITEM() | NEXT ]
     [ NUMITEMS() ]
     [ HANDLE | NOHANDLE [ RESP() ] ]
END-EXEC

EXEC CICS  READQ TD
     QUEUE()
     [ SYSID() ]
     SET() | INTO()
     [ LENGTH() ]
     [ NOSUSPEND ]
     [ HANDLE | NOHANDLE [ RESP() ] ]
END-EXEC
```

RECEIVE

```
EXEC CICS  RECEIVE
     [ SET() | INTO() ]
     [ LENGTH() | FLENGTH() ]
     [ MAXLENGTH() | MAXFLENGTH() ]
     [ NOTRUNCATE ]
     [ SESSION() | CONVID() ]
     [ PASSBK | [ PSEUDOBIN ] [ ASIS ] ]
     [ BUFFER ] [ LEAVEKB ] ]
     [ HANDLE | NOHANDLE [ RESP() ] ]
END-EXEC

EXEC CICS  RECEIVE MAP()
     [ SET() | INTO() ]
     [ MAPSET() ]
     [ FROM() [ LENGTH() ] | TERMINAL
     [ ASIS ] [ INPARTN() ] ]
     [ HANDLE | NOHANDLE [ RESP() ] ]
END-EXEC

EXEC CICS  RECEIVE PARTN()
     SET() | INTO()
     LENGTH()
     [ ASIS ]
```

```
        [ HANDLE | NOHANDLE [ RESP() ] ]
    END-EXEC
```

RELEASE

```
    EXEC CICS  RELEASE
        PROGRAM()
        [ HANDLE | NOHANDLE [ RESP() ] ]
    END-EXEC
```

RESETBR

```
    EXEC CICS  RESETBR
        FILE()
        [ SYSID() ]
        RIDFLD()
        [ KEYLENGTH() [ GENERIC ] ]
        [ REQID() ]
        [ RBA | RRN ]
        [ GTEQ | EQUAL ]
        [ HANDLE | NOHANDLE [ RESP() ] ]
    END-EXEC
```

RESYNC

```
    EXEC CICS  RESYNC
        ENTRYNAME()
        [ IDLIST() [ IDLISTLENGTH() ] ]
        [ HANDLE | NOHANDLE [ RESP() ] ]
    END-EXEC
```

RETRIEVE

```
    EXEC CICS  RETRIEVE
        [ SET() | INTO() ]
        [ LENGTH() ]
        [ RTRANSID() ]
        [ RTERMID() ]
        [ QUEUE() ]
        [ WAIT ]
        [ HANDLE | NOHANDLE [ RESP() ] ]
    END-EXEC
```

RETURN

```
    EXEC CICS  RETURN
```

```
        [ TRANSID() [ COMMAREA() [ LENGTH() ] ] ]
        [ HANDLE | NOHANDLE [ RESP() ] ]
    END-EXEC
```

REWRITE

```
    EXEC CICS  REWRITE
        FILE()
        [ SYSID() ]
        FROM()
        [ LENGTH() ]
        [ HANDLE | NOHANDLE [ RESP() ] ]
    END-EXEC
```

ROUTE

```
    EXEC CICS  ROUTE
        [ INTERVAL() | TIME() ]
        [ ERRTERM() ]
        [ TITLE() ]
        [ LIST() ]
        [ OPCLASS() ]
        [ REQID() ]
        [ LDC() ]
        [ NLEOM ]
        [ HANDLE | NOHANDLE [ RESP() ] ]
    END-EXEC
```

SEND

```
    EXEC CICS  SEND
        [ FROM() [ LENGTH() | FLENGTH() ] [ FMH] ]
        [ LDC() ]
        [ DEST() ]
        [ LINEADDR() ]
        [ SESSION() | CONVID() ]
        [ ATTACHID() ]
        [ CTLCHAR() | STRFIELD ]
        [ WAIT | CONFIRM ]      E
        [ LAST | INVITE ]
        [ PASSBK | CBUFF | [ ERASE ]
        [ PSEUDOBIN ] [ ASIS ] [ LEAVEKB ]
        [ CNOTCOMPL | DEFRESP ] ]
        [ HANDLE | NOHANDLE [ RESP() ] ]
    END-EXEC
```

```
EXEC CICS  SEND MAP()
      [[ FROM() ] [ DATAONLY ] | MAPONLY ]
      [ LENGTH() ]
      [ MAPSET() ]
      [ FMHPARM() ]
      [ REQID() ]
      [ LDC() | [ ACTPARTN() ] [ OUTPARTN() ] ]
      [ MSR() ]
      [ CURSOR() ]
      [ SET() | PAGING | TERMINAL
      [ WAIT ] [ LAST ] ]
      [ PRINT ]
      [ FREEKB ]
      [ ALARM ]
      [ L40 | L64 | L80 | HONEOM ]
      [ NLEOM ]
      [ ERASE | ERASEAUP ]
      [ ACCUM ]
      [ FRSET ]
      [ FORMFEED ]
      [ HANDLE | NOHANDLE [ RESP() ] ]
END-EXEC

EXEC CICS  SEND CONTROL
      [ LDC() | [ ACTPARTN() ] [ OUTPARTN() ] ]
      [ MSR() ]
      [ CURSOR() ]
      [ SET() | PAGING | TERMINAL
      [ WAIT ] [ LAST ] ]
      [ PRINT ]
      [ FREEKB ]
      [ ALARM ]
      [ L40 | L64 | L80 | HONEOM ]
      [ ERASE | ERASEAUP ]
      [ ACCUM ]
      [ FRSET ]
      [ FORMFEED ]
      [ REQID() ]
      [ HANDLE | NOHANDLE [ RESP() ] ]
END-EXEC

EXEC CICS  SEND PAGE
         [[ TRANSID() ] RELEASE | RETAIN ]
```

```
            [ TRAILER() ]
            [ FMHPARM() ]
            [ SET() ]
            [ NOAUTOPAGE | AUTOPAGE [ CURRENT | ALL ]]
            [ OPERPURGE ]
            [ LAST ]
            [ HANDLE | NOHANDLE [ RESP() ] ]
      END-EXEC

      EXEC CICS  SEND TEXT
            FROM()
            [ LENGTH() ]
            [ FMHPARM() ]
            [ REQID() ]
            [ CURSOR() ]
            [ LDC() | [ ACTPARTN() ] [ OUTPARTN() ] ]
            [ MSR() ]
            [ SET() | PAGING | TERMINAL
            [ WAIT ] [ LAST ] ]
            [ PRINT ]
            [ FREEKB ]
            [ ALARM ]
            [ L40 | L64 | L80 | HONEOM ]
            [ ERASE ]
            [ NLEOM ]
            [ NOEDIT [ MAPPED ] | ACCUM [[ JUSFIRST |
            JUSLAST | JUSTIFY() ]
            [ HEADER() ] [ TRAILER() ] ] ]
            [ FORMFEED ]
            [ HANDLE | NOHANDLE [ RESP() ] ]
      END-EXEC

      EXEC CICS  SEND PARTNSET()
            [ HANDLE | NOHANDLE [ RESP() ] ]
      END-EXEC
```

SET

```
      EXEC CICS  SET CONNECTION()
            [ SERVSTATUS() | INSERVICE | OUTSERVICE ]
            [ ACQSTATUS() | ACQUIRED | RELEASED ]
            [ CONNSTATUS() | ACQUIRED | RELEASED ]
            [ NOTPENDING ]
```

```
        [ PURGE [ FORCE ] ]
        [ HANDLE | NOHANDLE [ RESP() ] ]
END-EXEC

EXEC CICS  SET FILE()
        [ OPEN | CLOSED [ EMPTY ] ]
        [ ENABLED | DISABLED ]
        [ WAIT | NOWAIT | FORCE ]
        [ DSNAME() ]
        [ STRINGS() ]
        [ LSRPOOLID() ]
        [ READ() | READABLE | NOTREADABLE ]
        [ UPDATE() | UPDATABLE | NOTUPDATABLE ]
        [ BROWSE() | BROWSABLE | NOTBROWSABLE ]
        [ ADD() | ADDABLE | NOTADDABLE ]
        [ DELETE() | DELETABLE | NOTDELETABLE ]
        [ DISPOSITION() | OLD | SHARE ]
        [ EMPTYSTATUS() | EMPTYREQ | NOEMPTYREQ ]
        [ HANDLE | NOHANDLE [ RESP() ] ]
END-EXEC

EXEC CICS  SET MODENAME()
        CONNECTION()
        [ AVAILABLE() ]
        [ ACQUIRED ]
        [ HANDLE | NOHANDLE [ RESP() ] ]
END-EXEC

EXEC CICS  SET PROGRAM()
        [ STATUS() | ENABLED | DISABLED ]
        [ NEWCOPY ]
        [ HANDLE | NOHANDLE [ RESP() ] ]
END-EXEC

EXEC CICS  SET SYSTEM
        MAXTASKS() | AMAXTASKS() | AKP() |
        CUSHION() | TIME() | RUNAWAY() | STALL()
        [ HANDLE | NOHANDLE [ RESP() ] ]
END-EXEC

EXEC CICS  SET TERMINAL()
        [ SERVSTATUS() | INSERVICE | OUTSERVICE ]
        [ ACQSTATUS() | ACQUIRED | RELEASED |
```

```
          COLDACQ ]
          [ CREATESESS() | CREATE | NOCREATE ]
          [ ATISTATUS() | ATI | NOATI ]
          [ TTISTATUS() | TTI | NOTTI ]
          [ PAGESTATUS() | PAGEABLE | AUTOPAGEABLE ]
          [ TERMPRIORITY() ]
          [ PURGE [ FORCE ] ]
          [ HANDLE | NOHANDLE [ RESP() ] ]
    END-EXEC

    EXEC CICS  SET TRANSACTION()
          [ STATUS() | ENABLED | DISABLED ]
          [ PURGEABILITY() | PURGEABLE |
          NOTPURGEABLE ]
          [ PRIORITY() ]
          [ HANDLE | NOHANDLE [ RESP() ] ]
    END-EXEC
```

SPOOL

```
    EXEC CICS  SPOOLCLOSE
          TOKEN()
          [ KEEP | DELETE ]
          [ HANDLE | NOHANDLE [ RESP() ] ]
    END-EXEC

    EXEC CICS  SPOOLOPEN INPUT
          TOKEN()
          USERID()
          [ CLASS() ]
          [ PRINT | PUNCH ]
          [ HANDLE | NOHANDLE [ RESP() ] ]
    END-EXEC

    EXEC CICS  SPOOLOPEN OUTPUT
          TOKEN()
          USERID()
          NODE()
          [ CLASS() ]
          [ OUTDESCR() ]
          [ NOCC | ASA | MCC ]
          [ PRINT | PUNCH ]
          [ HANDLE | NOHANDLE [ RESP() ] ]
    END-EXEC
```

```
EXEC CICS  SPOOLREAD
     TOKEN()
     INTO()
     MAXFLENGTH()
     [ TOFLENGTH() ]
     [ HANDLE | NOHANDLE [ RESP() ] ]
END-EXEC

EXEC CICS  SPOOLWRITE
     TOKEN()
     FROM()
     [ FLENGTH() ]
     [ LINE | PAGE ]
     [ HANDLE | NOHANDLE [ RESP() ] ]
END-EXEC
```

START

```
EXEC CICS  START
     TRANSID()
     [ INTERVAL() | TIME() ]
     [ REQID() ]
     [ FROM() [ LENGTH() [ FMH ] ] ]
     [ TERMID() ]
     [ SYSID() ]
     [ RTRANSID() ]
     [ RTERMID() ]
     [ QUEUE() ]
     [ NOCHECK ]
     [ PROTECT ]
     [ HANDLE | NOHANDLE [ RESP() ] ]
END-EXEC
```

STARTBR

```
EXEC CICS  STARTBR
     FILE()
     [ SYSID() ]
     RIDFLD()
     [ KEYLENGTH() [ GENERIC ] ]
     [ REQID( +00000 ) ]
     [ RBA | RRN | DEBREC | DEBKEY ]
     [ GTEQ | EQUAL ]
     [ HANDLE | NOHANDLE [ RESP() ] ]
END-EXEC
```

SUSPEND

```
EXEC CICS  SUSPEND
     [ HANDLE | NOHANDLE [ RESP() ] ]
END-EXEC
```

SYNCPOINT

```
EXEC CICS  SYNCPOINT
     [ ROLLBACK ]
     [ HANDLE | NOHANDLE [ RESP() ] ]
END-EXEC
```

TRACE

```
EXEC CICS  TRACE
     ON | OFF
     [ SINGLE ]
     [ SYSTEM ]
     [ USER ]
     [ ALL ]
     [ KC ]
     [ SC ]
     [ PC ]
     [ IC ]
     [ DC ]
     [ FC ]
     [ TD ]
     [ TS ]
     [ EI ]
     [ DI ]
     [ SP ]
     [ TC ]
     [ BF ]
     [ BM ]
     [ JC ]
     [ IS ]
     [ UE ]
     [ PS ]
     [ HANDLE | NOHANDLE [ RESP() ] ]
END-EXEC
```

UNLOCK

```
EXEC CICS  UNLOCK
     FILE()
```

        [SYSID()]
        [HANDLE | NOHANDLE [RESP()]]
    END-EXEC

WAIT

    EXEC CICS WAIT CONVID()
        [HANDLE | NOHANDLE [RESP()]]
    END-EXEC

    EXEC CICS WAIT EVENT
        ECADDR()
        [HANDLE | NOHANDLE [RESP()]]
    END-EXEC

    EXEC CICS WAIT JOURNAL
        JFILEID()
        [REQID()]
        [STARTIO]
        [HANDLE | NOHANDLE [RESP()]]
    END-EXEC

    EXEC CICS WAIT SIGNAL
        [HANDLE | NOHANDLE [RESP()]]
    END-EXEC

    EXEC CICS WAIT TERMINAL
        [SESSION() | CONVID()]
        [HANDLE | NOHANDLE [RESP()]]
    END-EXEC

WRITE

    EXEC CICS WRITE
        FILE()
        [SYSID()]
        FROM()
        [LENGTH()]
        RIDFLD()
        [KEYLENGTH()]
        [RBA | RRN]
        [MASSINSERT]
        [HANDLE | NOHANDLE [RESP()]]
    END-EXEC

```
EXEC CICS  WRITEQ TS
     QUEUE()
     [ SYSID() ]
     FROM()
     [ LENGTH() ]
     [ ITEM() [ REWRITE ] ]
     [ MAIN  I  AUXILIARY ]
     [ NOSUSPEND ]
     [ HANDLE  I  NOHANDLE [ RESP() ] ]
END-EXEC

EXEC CICS  WRITEQ TD
     QUEUE()
     [ SYSID() ]
     FROM()
     [ LENGTH() ]
     [ HANDLE  I  NOHANDLE [ RESP() ] ]
END-EXEC
```

XCTL

```
EXEC CICS  XCTL
     PROGRAM()
     [ COMMAREA() [ LENGTH() ] ]
     [ HANDLE  I  NOHANDLE [ RESP() ] ]
END-EXEC
```

A.5.   CICS CONDITION CODES AND ABEND CODES

This is a list of many of the CICS condition codes and abend codes that might be raised by a CICS command. The abend codes, of course, occur only when an error was detected in the execution of a CICS command that did not contain the NOHANDLE option. Many of the condition codes are defined in the CICSRESP COPYbook mentioned elsewhere in this book. Your program can test for these conditions by doing the following

1. Specifying NOHANDLE on the CICS command

2. Specifying RESP (dataname) on the CICS command, where dataname is the name of a data area defined as PIC S9(8) COMP

3. If your program uses the CICSRESP COPYbook, code

    `IF CICS-conditioncodename` e.g. `IF CICS-DUPREC`
    If your program does not contain the COPYbook, specify

    `IF dataname = DFHRESP(conditioncodename)`
    where dataname is the dataname specified in RESP.

    Here are two examples:

```
EXEC CICS DELETEQ TS QUEUE(queuename)
    NOHANDLE
    RESP (CICS-RESP-CODE)
END-EXEC
IF CICS-QIDERR
        .
        .

            or

EXEC CICS DELETEQ TS QUEUE(queuename)
    NOHANDLE
    RESP (RESP-FIELD)
END-EXEC
IF RESP-FIELD = DFHRESP(QIDERR)
        .
        .
```

Few of these conditions apply to all CICS commands. In fact, several CICS commands return no condition codes. If you are having difficulty determining what conditions are being raised for your application, see Chapter 7 for information on using the CEDF transaction to assist you. If no abend code is listed, that means that CICS does not abend for this condition, but takes some default action. For more information on debugging, see Chapter 8.

Abend code	Condition code	Description
AEIA	ERROR	General error condition - not specific
	RDATT	ATTN key pressed during RECEIVE
	WRBRK	ATTN key pressed during SEND
	EOF	End of file reached
AEIE	EODS	No data received from 3770 terminal
AEID	EOC	End-of-chain condition, normally occurs when end of buffer reached
AEIH	ENDINPT	End of input indicator received
AEII	NONVAL	3650 program name is invalid
AEIJ	NOSTART	3651 cannot initiate 3650 program
AEIK	TERMIDERR	Specified terminal not in TCT
AEIL	DSIDERR	File not in FCT
AEIN	DUPREC	Duplicate record condition
AEIO	DUPKEY	Duplicate key with alternate index
AEIP	INVREQ	Invalid request
AEIQ	IOERR	I/O error occurred
AEIR	NOSPACE	No space available to complete I/O
AEIS	NOTOPEN	File not open
AEIT	ENDFILE	End-of-file during BROWSE
AEIU	ILLOGIC	Generic VSAM error
AEIV	LENGERR	Length error, record size exceeds that specified in LENGTH field
AEIW	QZERO	Queue empty or READQ TD
	SIGNAL	SIGNAL control received
	QBUSY	Queue conflict for READQ TD
AEIZ	ITEMERR	Item number for READQ TS OR WRITEQ TS is invalid
AEIO	PGMIDERR	Program not found in PPT or is disabled

AEI1	TRANSIDERR	Trans id specified in START is not in PCT
AEI2	ENDDATA	End of data for RETRIEVE command
AEI3	INVTSREQ	Temporary storage RECEIVE not supported
	EXPIRED	Time delay for DELAY or POST has expired
	RETPAGE	SET specified when pages ready for return
	RTEFAIL	ROUTE specifies that originating terminal is only receiver
	RTESOME	Terminal on ROUTE will not receive message
AEI8	TSIOERR	Unrecoverable temporary storage error
AEYA	INVERRTERM	Invalid term ID on ROUTE command
AEYB	INVMPSZ	Invalid MAP size for terminal
AEYC	IGREQID	Conflict in REQID option on SEND
	OVERFLOW	Mapped data does not fit current page
AEYE	INVLDC	Incorrect LDC mnemonic
	NOSTG	Requested storage is not available
AEYG	JIDERR	Journal ID not in JCT
AEYH	QIDERR	Queue not found
	NOJBUFSP	Insufficient journal buffer space
AEYJ	DSSTAT	Data stream suspended or aborted
AEYK	SELNERR	Error in destination selection
AEYL	FUNCERR	Error in batch data interchange command
AEYM	UNEXPIN	Unexpected data from batch data interchange terminal
AEYN	NOPASSBKRD	No passbook in input operation
AEYO	NOPASSBKWR	No passbook on output operation

AEYQ	SYSIDERR	Error in SYSID option
AEYR	ISCINVREQ	Error in remote system
	ENQBUSY	ENQ specifies unavailable resource
AEYT	ENVDEFERR	RETRIEVE specifies option not in START command
AEYU	IGREQCD	SEND command follows SIGNAL command
AEYV	SESSIONERR	SESSION in ALLOCATE command cannot be allocated
	SYSBUSY	Request for a session cannot be serviced
	SESSBUSY	Request for a session cannot be serviced
AEYY	NOTALLOC	Facility specified not owned by application
AEYZ	CBIDERR	Terminal control options not found
AEY0	INVEXITREQ	Invalid Exit request
AEI9	MAPFAIL	MAP from 3270 contains no data
AEIG	INBFMH	Function management header present
AEIM	NOTFND	Record not found
AEY1	INVPARTNSET	Invalid partition set specified
AEY2	INVPARTN	Partition not defined in partition set
AEY3	PARTNFAIL	User enters data into incorrect partition
	TERMERR	Terminal-related error
	ROLLEDBACK	Remote system unable to commit on SYNCPOINT
AEXL	DISABLED	Resource is disabled
AEY7	NOTAUTH	Resource security check failed
AEIL	FILENOTFOUND	File not found in FCT

Appendix B: Related Publications

One of the goals of all professional programmers is to have an adequate reference library, not full of "concepts" books or other books for novices, but those that contribute to building applications. It was with that view that I developed this list. Where books are shown in brackets, the books are mutually exclusive.

FROM QED

These books from QED were selected by me for inclusion here because they share in the goal of helping the professional programmer develop better CICS applications. (There are many other books from QED that may assist you in learning other environments.) Each book listed here complements the material in this book by providing in-depth additional information.

MVS COBOL II Power Programmer's Desk Reference

VSE COBOL II Power Programmer's Desk Reference

> The COBOL II books provide complete coverage of COBOL II techniques plus information on converting older CICS applications to COBOL II.

DB2: Maximizing Performance of Online Production Systems If you are involved in designing and programming CICS/DB2 applications, there is much here about the DB2 aspects of online applications.

VSAM: The Complete Guide to Optimization & Design If your shop uses VSAM datasets, this can help you improve application performance. Covers MVS and DOS/VSE.

CICS/VS: A Guide to Application Debugging Although the emphasis here is on CICS/OS/VS 1.7 and VS/COBOL, there is a wealth of information on CICS tables, internal program logic, and how to read CICS dumps. Covers MVS and VSE.

FROM IBM

Your shop may already have a library of IBM manuals but all too often they are out of date. This listing may help you confirm whether appropriate IBM reference material is available to you. Most of these books contain information you may need only occasionally, if at all. These books were selected by me because they provide more in-depth information about CICS. You should check with your technical staff to confirm what IBM publications are appropriate for your environment, as this list may be incomplete or list the incorrect IBM manual for your shop.

When using IBM manuals, you should check that the release level of the book corresponds with the level of software you are using. For example, if your shop is using CICS/MVS, and your CICS manuals are for CICS/ESA, there will be features in the manual that won't function. When in doubt, check with your technical staff. Finally, if your company is serious about improving screen design, the text on Common User Access is excellent.

FOR PROGRAMMING WITH COBOL

GC26-4047, *VS COBOL II Language Reference* This is a definition of the COBOL II language for MVS and VSE.

SC26-4769, *COBOL/370 Language Reference*

GC26-3857, *VS COBOL for OS/VS*

SC26-4045, *VS COBOL II Application Programming Guide* for MVS

SC26-4697, *VS COBOL II Application Programming Guide for VSE*

SC26-47647, *COBOL/370 Programming Guide*

SC28-6483, *OS/VS COBOL Compiler and Library Programmer's Guide* Needed if your shop still uses VS/COBOL (MVS only).

SC28-6478, *DOS/VS COBOL Compiler and Library Programmer's Guide*

FOR CICS

SC33-0241, *CICS/OS/VS Application Programmer's Reference*

SC33-0512, *CICS/MVS Application Programmer's Reference*

SC33-0676, *CICS/ESA Application Programmer's Reference*

SC33-0713, *CICS/VSE Application Programmer's Reference*

SC33-0675, *CICS/ESA Application Programmer's Guide*

SC33-0712, *CICS/VSE Application Programmer's Guide*

SC33-0226, *CICS/OS/VS Rel 1.7 Messages and Codes*

SC33-0514, *CICS/MVS Messages and Codes*

SC33-0672, *CICS/ESA Messages and Codes*

SC33-6507, *CICS/VSE Messages and Codes*

MISCELLANEOUS TITLES

SC26-4818, *LE/370 Programming Guide*

SC26-4177, *IMS/VS Version 2 Application Programming for CICS Users*

SC26-4080, *IBM DATABASE 2 Application Programming Guide for CICS Users*

SC33-0232, *CICS/OS/VS 3270 Data Stream Device Guide*

SC33-0096, *CICS/DOS/VS 3270 Data Stream Device Guide*

SC26-4351, *SAA Common User Access Panel Design and User Interaction*

SC33-0736, *Communicating with CICS/OS2*

SC33-0616, *CICS OS/2 System and Application Guide*

Application —————
MAPSET —————

Copybook name —————
MAP name —————

RESPONSE FORM

Book: *CICS: A How-To for COBOL Programmers.*

I want to hear from you. You may have questions, you may find errors, or you may have comments that will help me develop the next edition of the book. The purpose of this book is to help you, the professional programmer. Thank you.

David Shelby Kirk

Dear Dave,

If a reply is desired, please fill in your address:

Name: _____

Address: _____

Index

3270 terminal, 91

A

ABEND, 175, 323
    CODES, 356
ACCEPT, 188
ADDRESS, 323
AID keys, 16, 139
ALLOCATE, 323
AMODE, 41
ANSI 85, 187, 300
ASKTIME, 230, 323
ASRA, 283
ASSIGN, 231, 323
Attribute byte, 93

B

Basic Mapping Support, 49
BIF, 325
BIF DEEDIT, 231
BLL, 210
BMS, 7, 49
Browsing files, 201
BUILD, 325

C

CALL, 228
CANCEL, 325
CBL, 40, 308
CEBR, 236, 278, 286
CECI, 236, 268
CECS, 236, 278
CEDA, 236, 240
CEDB, 236
CEDC, 236, 240
CEDF, 236, 256, 286
CEMT, 192, 236, 248, 286
CESN, 237, 279
CICS/OS2, 4
COBOL II, 185
COBOL/370, xix, 185
COBOL2, 301
Command syntax, 19
COMMAREA, 68
CONNECT, 325
Conversational transaction, 13
CONVERSE, 326
COUNT, 188
CSA, 322
CSSF, 237, 280
CSSN, 237, 279
CUA, 47
CURSLOC, 145, 149
Cursor, 142

MASSINSERT, 197
MDT, 168
Modified data tag, 93
Move-mode, 210

N
NEWCOPY, 254
NOHANDLE, 80
Nonconversational transaction, 12

P
PCT, 16, 48, 321
PGMIDERR, 164
POINT, 344
POP, 344
POST, 344
PPT, 16, 48, 321
PRINT NOGEN, 103
PROCESS, 40, 308
PSB, 219
Pseudoconversational transaction, 13
PURGE, 344
PUSH, 344

R
READ, 193, 344
READNEXT, 205
READPREV, 206
READQ TS, 223
RECEIVE, 56
    MAP, 136
Reference Modification, 77, 300
RELEASE, 347
RESETBR, 207, 347
RESP, 80
RESYNC, 347
RETRIEVE, 347
RETURN, 20, 69, 347
REWRITE, 198, 348
RMODE, 41
ROUTE, 348

S
SAA, 47
SEND, 348
    MAP, 131

TEXT, 58
SERVICE RELOAD, 34, 214
SET, 213, 350
SNA, 92
SORT, 188
SPOOL, 352
SQL, 148
SSRANGE, 285
START, 160, 162, 353
STARTBR, 202, 353
STATE, 188
STOP RUN, 188, 189
STRING, 156, 188
SUSPEND, 354
Symbolic MAP, 98
SYNCPOINT, 354
SYMDMP, 188

T
Task, 160
TCA, 322
TCT, 321
Temporary storage queues, 222
TEST, 188, 285
TIOA, 322
TITLE, 77, 103
TRACE, 354
TRANSFORM, 188
TRANSID, 67

U
UNLOCK, 200, 354
UNSTRING, 188

V
VSAM, 7
VTAM, 6

W
WAIT, 355
WHEN-COMPILED, 154
WRITE, 197, 355
WRITEQ TS, 225

X
XCTL, 162, 228, 356